*Haydn's
Ingenious Jesting
with Art*

Haydn's Ingenious Jesting with Art

Contexts of Musical Wit and Humor

GRETCHEN A. WHEELOCK

SCHIRMER BOOKS
An Imprint of Macmillan Publishing Company
NEW YORK

Maxwell Macmillan Canada
TORONTO

Maxwell Macmillan International
NEW YORK   OXFORD   SINGAPORE   SYDNEY

Schirmer Books
An Imprint of Macmillan Publishing Company
866 Third Avenue
New York, NY 10022

Maxwell Macmillan Canada, Inc.
1200 Eglinton Avenue East, Suite 200
Don Mills, Ontario M3C 3N1

Macmillan Publishing Company is part of the Maxwell Communication Group of Companies

Library of Congress Catalog Card Number: 91-46730

Printed in the United States of America

printing number

1 2 3 4 5 6 7 8 9 10

LIBRARY OF CONGRESS CATALOGING-IN-PUBLICATION DATA

Wheelock, Gretchen A.
    Haydn's ingenious jesting with art : contexts of musical wit and
humor / Gretchen A. Wheelock.
        p.   cm.
    Includes bibliographical references and index.
    ISBN 0-02-872855-6
    1. Haydn, Joseph, 1732–1809—Humor.   2. Haydn, Joseph, 1732–1809
Instrumental music.   3. Instrumental music—History and criticism.
4. Wit and humor, Musical—History and criticism.   I. Title.
    ML410.H4W47   1992
784'.092—dc20   91-46730
                                                           CIP
                                                           MN

The paper used in this publication meets the minimum requirements of American National Standard for Information Sciences—Permanence of Paper for Printed Library Materials. ANSI Z39.48–1984. ♾™

for Ingrid, Sarah, and Ben

Contents

Preface

Few accounts of Haydn's music, from his own day to ours, fail to mention wit and humor in connection with his instrumental works. Modern writers tend to use these words interchangeably and uncritically, most often to invoke a seemingly self-evident species of the comic in music that elicits a knowing smile, chuckle, or hearty laugh. Yet the broad hermeneutical implications of music that moves listeners in this way, without the aid of words, are rarely addressed. Curious, too, is the lack of attention to understandings of wit and humor in Haydn's day. Even if eighteenth-century writers themselves attest the changeable meanings of each term, they do not generally confuse them as meaning the same thing; nor do they assume that either invariably, or even primarily, invites laughter. In view of Haydn's enormous success with critical and popular audiences, it is of interest to know how his contemporaries used these words and what they may have been responding to when they applied them to his instrumental music. Estimating the shifting values of *wit* and *humor* as critical terms in eighteenth-century literary essays can provide needed grounding, then, for evaluating the reactions, both favorable and unfavorable, to Haydn's instrumental works by listeners of his day. I address the terms of such an evaluation in Part I of this study.

The significance of artful jesting is of more than local, historical interest, however, and here a range of contemporary theories can help to clarify the challenge, recognition, and value of musical wit and humor for listeners of Haydn's day and our own. In the belief that this aspect of Haydn's style is best approached from the works themselves, in the various contexts of their use, I offer in Part II a number of models for musical analysis that is responsive to a process of engagement in which the role of the listener is salient. The means and ends of such a process are as various as the works and audiences they animate, and in seeking to describe them in Haydn's music, I do not aspire to a systematic taxonomy of the comic. Nor is mine a chronological

account of Haydn's development as musical humorist. Rather, I have sought
to locate the strategies of musical jests, along with the aesthetic and kinesthetic paradoxes they introduce, in those genres and procedures noted as
humorous by Haydn's contemporaries. Chapter 4 investigates Haydn's symphonic minuet movements in view of overlapping traditions of functional
dance, didactic model, and social marker. In the context of these associations,
the artful minuet presents an especially salient opportunity for kinesthetic
recognition of incongruous humors. I focus in Chapter 5 on the Op. 33 string
quartets and on provocative gestures in the chamber that engage players and
listeners in discovering the wit of compositional ingenuity. Haydn's procedures in these works invite comparison with dysfunctional conversations, in
which seeming impediments to lucid and continuous discourse signal a jesting mode of address, alerting listeners to the playing out of syntactic anomalies. Taking *scherzando* finales as a point of departure in Chapter 6, I examine the wit of Haydn's play with formal design in symphonic closing
movements and with the signals that dramatize their structure for the listener. In displaying trespasses against the decorum of style and genre as more
than simply eccentric, Haydn demonstrates that the persuasion of jesting en-
hances formal coherence even as it challenges stylistic norms. Haydn's Symphony No. 60 is a model case in Chapter 7 for investigating comic intention
in instrumental music and its recognition by contemporary listeners. I discuss
the humor of seeming distraction in this and other works and locate the paradox of its artful function in the larger context of music's role as public and
private diversion. As an epilogue, Chapter 8 recaptures the ingenuity of
Haydn's artfully playful persuasions against the background of early essays
on musical wit and humor, and considers the role of the listener in light of
more recent theories.

In limiting my discussion to Haydn's instrumental music, I do not mean to
imply that there is no wit and humor to be found in his vocal works. It cannot
be supposed that the composer of numerous comic operas—to mention only
the most obvious genre—reserved his humor for music without words. My
particular interest, however, is in the capacity for jesting of music unassisted
by words, and in the responses of listeners to procedures that challenge and
delight both sense and sensibilities. Although I have avoided technical language when possible, I do assume readers who are conversant in the basic
harmonic vocabulary and conventions of the music we have come to call
Classical in style. In recent years, the term *classical* has lost its innocence,
whether in reference to a period or a style, as writers have rightly questioned
its lexical, historiographic, and ideological integrity.[1] Without entering those
lists, I readily acknowledge the limitations of a term that, as Samuel Johnson
noted of comedy, is "unpropitious to definers." My references to Classical
(music, style, and era) follow an admittedly compromised but expedient path
to term recognition by readers today, despite the absence of such terminology
from the critical vocabulary of eighteenth-century writers.

Ideally, the many musical examples reproduced throughout the book
would be accompanied by a sound recording, the immediacy of which can

make a far more compelling point than words and a score can do. In any case, I have provided as many excerpts as the discussion warrants, and trust that readers will want to consult the full context of each example. In referring to Haydn's works, I follow the standard Hoboken numbers, except in the case of his string quartets, which are more familiar to most readers by opus numbers. Some will no doubt wish for a more rigorous theoretical approach to the pieces I discuss, and others will miss attention to their favorite works. Perhaps the discussions started here will move readers to listen to unfamiliar works and to familiar works anew. I hope that this beginning ultimately will motivate broader exploration of Haydn's music and that of his contemporaries.

This book has grown out of work begun in a dissertation I completed in 1979, and as a project long in process it owes much to the help and encouragement of many. The brief mention made here of individuals and institutions can partially acknowledge that debt, but can in no way express adequately my gratitude to those named. From the beginning, Leon Plantinga has been an unfailingly generous mentor, whose enthusiasm for Haydn's music nurtured my own. His encouragement was a determining factor in my undertaking a thesis rather off the beaten track, and his continuing interest has sustained my efforts ever since. A postdoctoral fellowship at the Mary Ingraham Bunting Institute of Radcliffe College gave me the gift of time to explore new approaches to my subject in various disciplines, and the company of astute listeners for whom Haydn was not a household word. Among these, Blair Tate and Eve Kosofsky Sedgwick were especially helpful in offering fresh perspectives and insights. Of many longtime friends and colleagues at Smith College, Monica Jakuc, Philipp Naegele, and Donald Wheelock helped to focus my ideas on performance and compositional issues in Haydn's music. In addition to his astute advice as a Haydn scholar, Vernon Gotwals shared valuable materials on Haydn's early biographer, Carpani. Special thanks are also due to Ruth Solie, who was an abundantly patient reader and valued critic of early drafts of material that has made its slow way into final chapters of this book.

More recent work owes much to my students and colleagues at the Eastman School of Music and the University of Rochester. Conversations in and out of class with my seminar students, along with live music making in coaching sessions and performances, have helped me to think more critically about the roles of performers and listeners in Haydn's music. And material assistance provided by a Junior Faculty Fellowship was timely in supporting a semester's leave for writing. My colleagues Kerala Snyder and Ralph Locke were more than generous of their time, reading extended portions of the manuscript with attentive eyes and ears and offering valuable advice; Matthew Brown, Gerald Bond, Douglas Dempster, Patrick Macey, Robert Morris, and Jurgen Thym also made helpful comments on specific chapters. I am particularly indebted to Jonathan Baldo for his comments on the full draft, for suggestions of relevant readings in literary criticism, and for stimulating talk about them in many sessions over coffee. At various stages of writing, conversations and correspondence with Wye J. Allanbrook, Robert Dawidoff, Janet Levy, Elaine Sisman, Jane Stevens, and James Webster spurred fresh views, and often headed off wrongheaded ones; I have only myself to thank, of course, for any of the latter that remain.

My research has been assisted by kind and attentive librarians of the music and rare book collections at Yale University, Harvard University, the British Library, the Library of Congress, Smith College, the Eastman School of Music, and the University of Rochester. Special thanks are due to Susan Chodorow and Dillon Parmer for their assistance in eleventh-hour checking of bibliographic items and to Mary Frandsen for her helpful advice and stamina in reading proofs. In the final blizzard of index cards, David Abbott was an astute helper and a calming influence. For permission to use copyrighted editions of Haydn's music, I am grateful to G. Henle Verlag; Doblinger, U.S.A.; and European American Music Distributors Corporation.

Of many others who assisted in bringing this book to print, I am especially grateful to Maribeth Payne, Editor-in-Chief of Schirmer Books, whose enthusiasm for the project encouraged me through its various stages of preparation. Larry Hamberlin's editing of the completed manuscript extended well beyond flags of inconsistencies and helped to improve many sentences gone awry. And Garrett Schure was remarkably patient in assisting final stages of production.

If the last shall be first, I thank my children, Ingrid, Sarah, and Ben, for their forbearance and encouragement. In dedicating this book to them, I also salute their abundant wit and good humor.

Haydn's
Ingenious Jesting
with Art

I

Coming to Terms

1

The Musical Joke: A Laughing Matter?

The size of a man's understanding might always be justly measured by his mirth.[1]

Coming from one whose critical judgment and lexical authority set a high standard for English letters during Haydn's lifetime, the words of Samuel Johnson make an appealing epigraph for this study. His pronouncement seems fitting in its metaphoric "measure" of reason's share in mirth's pleasures. Some latter-day investigators of the relationship between *homo sapiens* and *homo ridens* have taken up the matter of measurement quite literally, seeking to define and quantify the physiology, mechanisms, conditions, and utility of laughter and humor from a variety of perspectives. If, in the words of a recent commentator, "the struggle to make visible the structure of the risible"[2] has met with only qualified success, there is nonetheless ample evidence to support Dr. Johnson's confidence in mirth as signifying an achievement of the mind.

Among terms of general agreement about jokes, for example, is the view that their challenge involves some verbal trick or conceptual incongruity; laughter signals the listener's surprise and delight in recognizing the trick, and it effectively rewards the teller in turn. In characterizing the effect of a successful joke, D. H. Monro linked these cognitive and affective aspects in terms that Johnson might approve. Asking what a good joke *"feels"* like, Monro proposes "an exhilarating sense of enlarged mental horizons."[3] Even though both question and answer are attractive, one wants to question Monro further: What determines the "horizons" of a good joke? *Whose* horizons and in what sense expanded? (Why not simply reinforced—as might be the case in ethnic and sexist jokes, for example?) In short, one wants to know about the context of the joke and its audience. If, as Shakespeare insists, "A jest's prosperity lies in the ear / Of him that hears it,"[4] the success of a joke

3

is conditional, qualified by various factors governing the receptive "ear"—
common ground in language and experience, appropriate time and place,
tastes and dispositions of listeners. Whether amiable or aggressive, gratuitous
or tendentious, jokes require ready listeners who understand the terms of the
jester.

To investigate these terms in Haydn's instrumental music is to circum-
scribe listening readiness in particular ways: by cognitive and affective "horizons" that are independent of a verbal text, and by general expectations of
accountability within the aesthetic of music we describe as Classical in style.
Few who write about Haydn's instrumental music fail to note some aspect of
artful jesting as characteristic of his style; such words as *witty, humorous,
comic, jocular,* and the like are frequently met with in commentaries from his
own day to ours. Yet the broader implications of these terms rarely come
under serious critical scrutiny, least of all in historical contexts of music
making.

Taking musical jokes as a point of departure, I want to suggest some basic
issues that seem to me critical to the study of this aspect of Haydn's music,
most especially in relation to the listeners of his day. In order to state these
most simply, I will ignore for now the distinctions between jokes, wit, humor,
and the comic, taking jokes as a stand-in for all: How is a joke different from
a non-joke? Why make a joke? Why does the joke succeed? What does the
joke accomplish? The first of these touches on the structure of the joke itself,
the second on the motivation for a joke, the third on conditions that favor
its recognition and appreciation, and the last on its function and value. In
the chapters that follow, musical and historical contexts frame and focus the
relevance of these questions in specific terms. They serve here as preface to
the chief sticking points in discussions of musical wit and humor, and to
suggest some of their implications for this study.

How is a joke different from a non-joke? At a considerable disadvantage
in comparison to studies of verbal and pictorial humor, analysis of jokes in
instrumental music has understandably focused on their local syntactic and
formal aspects. As in discussions of jokes in general, critics have cited surprise, incongruity, exaggeration, understatement, economy, and the like as
characteristic of the comic in music.[5] Any of these may well be components
of musical jesting; that they are not defining properties, however, is clear
enough in musical examples in which such features promote quite different
impressions. Are the surprise and economy of the opening chords of Beethoven's *Eroica* Symphony comic, for example? the exaggeration of the closing
ones of his Fifth, witty? The conflicting metric patterns in the minuet of
Mozart's Symphony in G Minor, K. 550, sound incongruous, but is this humorous?

While the overall context of a given movement may provide some basis for
making such a judgment, the more specific framing of a musical joke will
presumably be set up by more explicit means, by something akin to the devices that frame a verbal joke—where the cues may range from a special tone

of voice, to particular gestures and facial expressions, to "Have you heard the one about . . . ?" These signals of intent rely in turn on patterns of style and genre, and on attendant habits of listening, that are governed by the norms of "non-jokes." As in verbal jokes, departures from conventions of language and local usage are the measure of salience in musical jokes—some may be too subtle for all but the most receptive ears, while others can be assured of a hearty laugh. But if a musical jest is perceived as simply incongruous, bizarre, or irregular, one might suspect that its terms *as a jest* have been mistaken and its artful effect underestimated.

Why make a joke? Comprehensive theories of the comic in music beg this question in taking laughter to be its own reward, in assuming, that is, that any music that makes you laugh is essentially comic music. At its extremes, this position embraces incongruity at the expense of musical context, listener readiness, and compositional accountability: an unusual scoring, an unfamiliar style and syntax, for example, become comic in prompting laughter as funny-strange.[6] Foregoing the "found comic" and the attempt to be comprehensive, I mean to focus on musical jests as compositionally motivated choices that serve various ends specific to the composer, audience, and work at hand.

Thus, questions of a joke's utility address not only the relation of a composer to his audience, but also the local (intra-opus) provocation of a musical jest—how it plays in the work—and the implications of jesting as an interactive process that engages listeners, players, and works in progress. The question behind the question, then, is not simply its reverse (Why *not* make a joke?), but rather, Why make a joke instead of something else? To the extent that a musical jest reminds listeners of the "something else" they might have expected, even as it subverts that expectation, we might infer that part of a joke's work is to promote the liberating awareness of alternatives.

Why does the joke succeed? For a musical jest, as for any joke, conditions favorable to recognition do not guarantee appreciation. When a joke "works," the audience not only understands its terms but also enjoys its point. Given the vast range of humor and the specificity of its appeals, the question of why a musical jest succeeds necessarily includes others: Why does this joke succeed with this audience, at this time and place, and in this work?[7] These are questions that have been scarcely addressed in studies of musical humor, and that of historical context least of all. Perhaps because the question of audience is rarely considered, eighteenth-century distinctions between wit, humor, and comic all but disappear in more recent discussions.[8]

The extent to which historical contexts condition the making and interpretations of jests has bearing, I believe, not only on their success with listeners in Haydn's day but also on the terms of the jest itself and explanations of its effect. Relevant to the means and effects of musical jesting, then, are such factors as performance setting, medium, genre, and style in the middle to late eighteenth century—factors that are related in turn to music's changing functions among diverse communities of listeners.

What does the joke accomplish? This goes to the heart of the matter, of course, and entails all of the preceding questions. Even the simplest joke can be seen to accomplish something beyond the laughter it provokes, whether in benefits to the teller or the listener or both. A jest in music challenges the listener not simply as a local event but also in its influence on subsequent events and on the interpretation of prior events. In this respect, though, a jest is not different from some other surprising disturbance that commands the listener's attention. The difference emerges, I will argue, in a self-consciousness of play with alternatives—with ambiguities, seeming contradictions, discontinuities, delays, and the like—that a jest invites in rehearsing the composer's own play with the materials of his art. In this process of engagement, the dividend of laughter is neither a frivolous nor an irrelevant accomplishment. Ultimately, though, the "prosperity" of musical jests lies not only in the ear of the listener but also in the "enlarged horizons" they provoke in the work in progress and in the elasticity of stylistic and interpretive procedures that accrues to the making and experience of subsequent works.

Having advanced some preliminary questions (and some broad claims), I want to examine their particulars more closely in the discussion that follows.

Two Musical Jokes: Jesting with Intent?

Part of the business of a musical jest, I have suggested, is to heighten consciousness of play, to signal this intent for the listener. As an illustration of the delicate balance of the ludicrous and the fitting, the playful and the serious, in this interactive process, I want to compare two musical jokes that suggest the range of a jest's challenge and accomplishment. Both are works that rely for their full effect upon listeners familiar with conventions of late eighteenth-century style and on surprising the expectations associated with those conventions. And both provoke laughter, though to rather different ends.

From start to finish, Mozart's *Ein musikalischer Spaß* (A Musical Joke), K. 522, takes pretension as comic subject and object. Completed in Vienna in 1787, the work is scored for two violins, viola, bass, and two horns—a combination typical in divertimenti and serenades of the day.[9] Commenting on Mozart's assumed persona of a bumbling and overambitious *Kleinmeister,* Hermann Abert observed that "this *maestro* has no desire to write a Divertimento—that is much too trifling for him—but rather a genuine Symphony in four movements," and that the putative composer found "interpreters" worthy of his efforts.[10] But the fact that this work was dubbed *Dorfmusikanten,* or "Village Musicians"—perhaps encouraged by a caricature of the players on the title page of early printed editions[11]—has blunted the point of Mozart's joke somewhat. For the ultimate target of this travesty is not simply inept playing, but bad musicianship on all levels of competence and taste—most especially bad composing. The title page of a French edition of 1804 called the work "Raillerie musicale," and carried the following notice above the caricature: "This satire, originally directed against the students of Prague, is no less applicable to every bad composer and musician."[12] While the reference to student players in Prague is probably gratuitous, this notice is evidence that Mozart's broader intent was recognized.

Fair notice is given at the outset in the failure of the opening movement to get started (Ex. 1–1). This self-important call to order makes no headway, as

EXAMPLE 1–1.   Mozart, *Ein musikalischer Spaß*/i, mm. 1–7

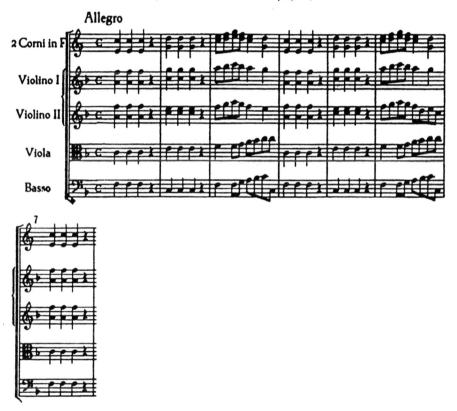

the opening seven bars founder in an elision of opening and closing gestures, neither of which can fulfill its proper function. The effect is somewhat analogous to "Once upon a time there / was a story that began / Once upon a time there / was . . ."[13] Doomed to continue by starting again, the opening measures must be simply cut off (although they will return to plague the development section, as well as the elaborately contrapuntal variation that brings the movement to an end). The continuation confirms that Mozart's composer has a passing acquaintance with the syntactic conventions and rhetorical gestures of an opening movement, but has no talent for making a coherent and pleasing piece of music. Decidedly square and graceless phrases, piling up as antecedents without consequents, fail to prepare or achieve logical goals; modulation is awkwardly attempted, and change of key accomplished by fiat. Formulaic melodic materials, relentlessly repeated, are treated to variation that does nothing to enhance them. And textural interest, when it is attempted, produces all manner of voice-leading problems.

While each movement proposes its own catalog of misadventures, the work is perhaps most widely known for its excruciating final cadence—or cadences—in which the six players close in five different "keys." This is only the most audible blunder, perhaps attributed by the listener to the collective ineptitude of composer, copyist, and players. For, overall, the finale is a compendium of abused conventions for which the composer deserves full credit: beset by horizontal and vertical thirds, it is ruled by sequences that modulate inadvertently and often in impossibly remote directions; each attempt at "learned" techniques of counterpoint succeeds in violating at least one rule in the student's book. The list is endless, as is the movement.

There can be little doubt that Mozart's *Musikalischer Spaß* does succeed gloriously on one count: it unfailingly provokes laughter. Here the ludicrous has two faces, however, as the work of two composers: the impersonated and the impersonating. The laughter of ridicule would be sufficient response to the object of Mozart's scorn, but recognition of travesty admits as intentional the joke of a controlling, assumed voice. Drawn into complicit laughter with the "real" composer at the putative composer, competent listeners can admire the artful play that unmasks pretentious composition and displays it as ludicrous.

Freud viewed parody, travesty, and unmasking as providing comic façades for the deeper "admonitions" of jokes. All are, for him, examples of the hostile purpose—long associated with theories of laughter—that is served in making other people comic by degradation.[14] Something of this tradition is suggested in the distinction that Heinrich Koch made between a jest and a joke in his *Kurzgefaßtes Handwörterbuch der Musik* (1807). "The jest [*Scherz*]," Koch notes, "is a kind of game, which has as its intention the awakening and maintaining of a gay mood." Whereas with a jest "one seeks to please," a joke [*Spaß*] is meant to "disturb."[15]

Hans Robert Jauss notes an additional dimension of admonition in what he terms "the comic of the counterimage." Travesty and parody can take as their target "the authority of a norm handed down from the past. But when this classical object of the parody is itself taken as medium or pretext, the target can also be the validity of norms that have currency in the social life and conduct of the contemporary public."[16] Perhaps Mozart intends in his joke a lesson not only to incompetent composers and players but also to uncritical listeners who allow pretentious ineptitude to flourish. In any case, the tendentious aspect of travesty charges the work with critical intent, and its success as a joke depends on recognition of that function.

Recognition of comic intent puts a particular twist on the question that sounds the theme of Edward T. Cone's *The Composer's Voice*: "If music is a language, then who is speaking?"[17] In exploring the implications of this question, particularly for the analysis of "voice" in song, Cone sustains a view of music as inherently dramatic. Starting from the premise that "every composition is an utterance depending on an act of impersonation," he addresses himself primarily to the performer, whose responsibility it is to become "a living personification of . . . the mind that experiences the music."[18] While this would seem to open inquiry about those "spoken" to, and how the terms of the "message" are constituted in the experiences of various listeners, Cone's analysis turns on the "complete musical persona" as resident in (emanating from) the mind of the composer: "it is a projection of his musical intelligence, constituting the mind, so to speak, of the composition in question."[19] And he argues that "to listen to music is to yield our inner voice to the composer's domination. Or better: it is to make the composer's voice our own."[20]

Cone's emphasis on impersonation as inherent in dramatistic conceptions of music making and interpretation does not, of course, leave listeners unaccounted for. It can be assumed that every performer is at once a listener, and one whose active engagement in interpretation enables that of other listeners. In Cone's view, it is presumably the performer—as ideal listener, perhaps—who mediates in questions of interpretation (and impersonation) for other listeners. Still, one can reasonably ask if the "complete musical persona" is a stable and authoritative entity—if it is indeed "complete"—without reference to the interpretive responsibilities of those listeners addressed in performance.

Mozart's *Ein musikalischer Spaß* is a case in point. Ultimately it is up to the listener to identify a double voice, or split persona, in this work and to recognize it as an extended act of impersonation. Even the performers are implicated from the start in impersonating inept players; as "interpreters" they must act their parts as a projection of Mozart's "dummy" composer. The challenge of unmasking imposters calls upon listeners to resist the domination of sounding voices, to imagine tacit voices in taking the aesthetic measure of "who is speaking." Those who make the voice of the putative composer their own have obviously failed the taste discrimination test.

Even if recognized as intentional jesting, though, comic travesty requires that the imposter behave true to form: however "artful" in displaying bad art, Mozart must prove his composer incapable of generating an aesthetically pleasing work. Whether playful spoof or scornful indictment, the piece is self-enclosed, as incapable of escaping its own premises as are its opening seven measures. The larger dimension of accomplishment in Mozart's joke, then, lies in the listener's understanding of how convention and invention *should* interact in a work of art, and of what has gone wrong here. Implicit in the "comic of the counterimage," as Jauss notes, is a reception process of recognition in the listener's comparing of the parody with its model.[21] Indeed, one might imagine Mozart continuously testing that understanding in such a work—the ending of which should persuade any listener that something has gone very wrong. In this respect the "horizons" of the musical joke extend beyond an artful imitation of incompetence to affirm the ideals of art shared by able composers and cognizant listeners.

Like the finale of Mozart's *Musikalischer Spaß,* the last movement of Haydn's String Quartet in E-flat Major, Op. 33, No. 2 (Hob. III:38; 1781), nicknamed "The Joke," is endless—but in an entirely different sense. Whereas Mozart's composer tries the listener's patience for 454 bars with music that is forever cutting itself off with "inadvertent" and premature cadences, Haydn engages the listener in a game of second-guessing about when the piece will end and, in the event, whether in fact it has. His ploy is to delay the actual ending while offering progressively less stable conclusions— and in the end no conclusion at all. Recognition that this is both amusing and clever rather than embarrassing and incompetent assumes close attention to the set-up and unfolding of a joke in progress.

The movement's opening gesture will be the agent of subversion, but it does not announce itself as such. Indeed, everything about the theme of this

EXAMPLE 1–2. *Op. 33/2/iv, mm. 1–8*

Joseph Haydn Werke, XII/3: Streichquartette "Opus 20" und "Opus 33," eds. Georg Feder and Sonja Gerlach. Copyright 1974 G. Henle Verlag München. Used by permission of G. Henle.

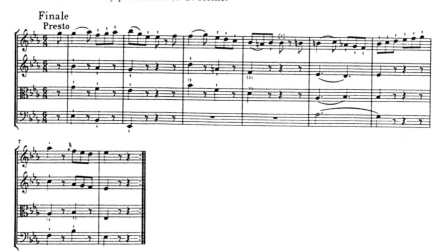

Presto finale seems straightforward (Ex. 1–2): it is a simple, dancelike tune, set in an uncomplicated homophonic texture and harmonized without fuss in the balanced phrases typical of a rondo melody. Repetitions within the

theme itself, together with the reiterations of a refrain scheme, ensure the listener's familiarity with the tune in the course of the movement. Although episodic passages offer intensive recasting of the theme, its regularity of pulse and pace remains undisturbed—at least until the preparatory moves for what seems its final, if abbreviated, statement in mm. 136–40 (Ex. 1–3).

EXAMPLE 1–3.   *Op. 33/2/iv, m. 136 to end*

Joseph Haydn Werke, XII/3: Streichquartette "Opus 20" und "Opus 33," eds. Georg Feder and Sonja Gerlach. Copyright 1974 G. Henle Verlag München. Used by permission of G. Henle.

The *adagio* passage that follows has the effect of a subversive addendum to a familiar phrase, as in "Remembrance of Things Past Due." Abrupt changes in meter, tempo, and dynamics account in part for the incongruity of such a close for this rondo. Perhaps more disorienting, though, is the con-

tradiction inherent in the material itself: the overrefinement of rhythmic gesture and articulation, attenuated harmonic rhythm, and thicker texture of
the cadence formula strike an affected pose. But the manner disguises the
matter, for—as shown in Example 1–3—this close presents an altered version
of the last four measures of the theme. Sufficiently subtle, this correspondence is likely to pass unnoticed by most listeners; the *adagio* "conclusion"
remains, in any case, a somber intrusion, clearly at variance with the prevailing climate of the movement. And its mock-serioso imposture is confirmed
by the *presto* return of the theme.

The previous intrusion of the unfamiliar is a mild upset compared with
this peculiar alteration of the familiar. Replacing the straightforward eight-
bar tune, a strangely fragmented sixteen-bar version introduces a new pattern
of two measures of silence regularly followed by two-measure fragments of
the theme. Even its original four-bar balancing phrase (Ex. 1–2, mm. 5–8) is
broken up into two, with adjustments made to produce identical rhythms in
each "phraselet." With the emergence of a discernible pattern of two-bar
phrases expanded to include two-bar silences, the listener adjusts expectations of continuation accordingly. Whether in hearing an internal echo of
each fragment in the silence that precisely accommodates it, or an echo in
the music played of the fragment anticipated, listeners are likely to become
increasingly aware of a participatory role in playing out the ending of this
finale.

Despite the three-measure grand pause, a careful listener might again sus-
pect that the piece is not over. Whereas a strong $\hat{4}$–$\hat{3}$–$\hat{2}$–$\hat{1}$ descent is heard in
the theme's closing bars (see Ex. 1–2, mm. 7–8), the effect of closure in mea-
sures 164–65 is subtly undermined: in retaining the rhythmic and melodic
shape of the upbeat–downbeat–escape tone gesture of the theme in each
two-measure fragment, Haydn has rearranged the accompanying voices in
this "conclusion." Indeed, this close collapses two prior endings: that of the
original theme and its elaborated version in measures 150–51.

That the tune should now continue in a *pianissimo* version with *four*-bar
silences between phrases is unthinkable, though. Or is it? Haydn's use of
opening-as-closing in this surprise ending again discloses a subtle ambiguity:
the melodic progression, so clearly identified throughout the movement as
an opening move, is nonetheless supported by a I–V–I cadential formula.
Technically speaking, the close is made in the accompaniment, while the melody and the phrase remain incomplete. The joke of Haydn's departing gesture is thus not simply that the opening phrase contradicts presumed closure,
but that this beginning implies a continuation of even more outrageous manipulation than those heard previously.

This manifestly playful strategy calls attention not only to artful subversions of the conventional in music—in which stylistic conventions are stock
in trade—but also to distinct roles of listeners and performers in the play of
that music. Seen simply as a practical joke in performance, Haydn's ending
becomes a mild rebuke to the unsuspecting by those in the know. But the
composer casts a wider net that includes performers in their initial encounter

with a new work. In a first reading of the finale in 1782, four string players in private chambers might have been confounded before they were amused by the extended rests in their individual parts. (Perhaps they first blame an inattentive copyist, then question the attention of the other players.) Still, it is in playing the work before others that the joke finds its point. The standard notational convention of a final double bar confirms the end for the performers, but, "in play," seeming denial of closure assumes auditors catching themselves in the act of listening.

Seen thus, Haydn's is a strategy of inclusion, one that engages his listeners as highly self-conscious participants in a process of completing the jest. Signals of intent are abundantly clear in prolonged and repeated manipulation of the simplest and most basic elements of music: endings and beginnings, repetition and variation, sound and silence. The interruptions that surprise, contradict, and finally transform the straightforward continuity of the theme provoke a series of what might be called "kinesthetic double takes"—a somatic effect of musical humor that we will note in several specific contexts in this study. The instability of Haydn's ending also leaves an aesthetically provocative question hanging in the balance: if prolonged silence can be absorbed into what has been a decidedly continuous theme, and made an integral part of a new continuity, then how prolonged must the silence be in order to confirm that the movement is over, even as it seems to begin again? At this uncertain juncture between musical time and "real time,"[22] the definitive closure that is a fundamental expectation of late eighteenth-century music is suspended "indefinitely."

If we take the lexical measure of Haydn's "Joke" from Dr. Johnson's *Dictionary of the English Language,* a fitting analogue is found under his entry for *amuse:* "to draw on from time to time, to keep in expectation; to divert in order to gain, or waste time; to entertain with expectations not to be fulfilled." Even if this sounds rather more sinister than what we would take our amusement to be, "disconfirming" of expectation is common to both of the musical jokes we have examined—albeit with different results. Expectations betrayed in Mozart's *Musikalischer Spaß* are those most basic to his art, and listeners who know the "right" way conventions are supposed to function laugh at the "wrong" ways in which the composer enslaves his music to them. The means of raising and betraying expectation in Haydn's "Joke," though similarly anchored in normative practice of the period, are specific to the materials and ongoing procedures of the movement. Johnson's definition of amusement calls attention to this temporal aspect of process in the experience of active expectations.

Dramatizing closure as an interactive process, Haydn also invents new possibilities for the conventions on which his art must rely, as he engages listeners in ingenious reinterpretations of stylistic and formal conventions. Steven Paul has suggested that in transgressing practices normative in the Classical era, Haydn's humorous deviations represent a "mockery of convention."[23] I would argue that it is not convention but the *conventional*—the

simply routine, unthinking, and mechanical approach to stylistic conventions—that Haydn's transgressions challenge. Play with the unconventional
does not mock stylistic conventions as such; indeed, in calling attention to
departures from accepted patterns, jokes confirm that conventions are indis-
pensable to the musical proceedings. As Hans Teuber puts it, jokes "point
simultaneously at the value and at the limitations of all schemata. They force
us to realize that the communication process ... cannot do without the
schemata."[24] Similarly, musical jokes exploit mixed messages of immediate
and underlying patterns that govern coherence and comprehension in a given
style and work, patterns that Leonard Meyer has called music's "constraints."[25] Viewed in this light, musical jests provide an opportunity for conventions to comment on the conventional.

Characterizing a joke as a "play upon form," Mary Douglas provides a useful model for analyzing a musical joke in its various environments—not only
its function within a specific work and style, but also in relation to its audience. For Douglas, a joke "brings into relation disparate elements in such a
way that one accepted pattern is challenged by the appearance of another
which in some way was hidden in the first."[26] In this formulation, Haydn's
"Joke" finale, which can be seen as a series of disguised or distorted patterns
based on the movement's theme, is itself a pattern embedded within others.
The last of its seeming closes, present from the start, challenges conventions
of style that distinguish opening from closing functions in a movement or
work. Entailed in turn is the relationship of listeners and players in realizing
the work in a given performance setting. "Play upon form" in a broader
sense, then, is play upon patterns of decorum and the social structures that
frame them.

It is to this larger dimension of a joke's accomplishment that Douglas's
study directs our attention. As a cultural anthropologist, she seeks to relate
the structure and function of jokes to the social structures within which they
have meaning and value. A telling insight of her analysis is that the maker of
a joke serves an essential function in creating for others "an opportunity for
realizing that an accepted pattern has no necessity." While Douglas focuses
on the joke as a symbolic "attack on control" within the context of ritual, she
recognizes its achievement in reinforcing "community," for "the joke works
only when it mirrors social forms." Thus, even if a joke has subversive potential in challenging the status quo, "the strength of its attack is entirely restricted by the consensus on which it depends for recognition."[27] This seeming paradox is a useful reminder of the "peculiar" relationship of the comic
to the serious, the playful to the aesthetic. Appreciation of Haydn's joke, as
of Mozart's, confirms a decorum of style in recognition of departures from
it. Consensus is a matter of agreement not so much that the joke is a good
one as simply that a joke has been made, that the intention to joke has been
recognized.

Aside from consideration of the conditions under which jokes are recognized and allowed, Douglas's view urges attention to their cultural "work." It
is not insignificant, for example, that Haydn's six Op. 33 string quartets were

the first that he published under new contractual arrangements with his patron, arrangements that freed him to sell his music to publishers and accept
commissions without the express permission of Prince Nicolaus Eszterházy.
Addressing his new quartets to a broad and anonymous audience, Haydn
courts the listener in ways that depart significantly from his earlier efforts in
this genre. And his success was noted in contemporary reviews that applaud
his "most original humor" and "most lively, most agreeable wit," as well as
his ease and confident manner in the "careful handling of special musical
effects."[28] The contexts of Haydn's jest, then, extend beyond the movement
or work in question to include medium and genre, audience and performance
setting—all of which condition cognitive and affective "senses" of humor
and the success of a joke.

On Surprise and Jokes Twice-Told

Focusing on the cultural function of joking as ritual in tribal societies, Douglas does not address the fact that in the history of its retelling, a joke's success
may be reconditioned, so to speak, by new audiences and in changing times.
Even in a second hearing by the same listener, the novelty and surprise of a
joke will have a different effect than on first hearing. This point is of particular interest in considering music's capacity to reengage active listening despite a work's familiarity.[29] Following F. L. Lukas, Edward T. Cone has noted
that in repeated hearings a listener's initial surprise changes to a state of
heightened anticipation, or suspense, "not wondering what will happen, but
waiting for what we know must happen."[30] Such anticipation may enhance
not only one's own engagement in the second playing out of a musical jest—
where more particulars of its ingenuity may be appreciated—but awareness
of other listeners' responses as well. On rehearing the finale of Haydn's
"Joke" Quartet, for example, listeners can enjoy the composer's skillful game
of deception as insiders, anticipating the sudden stops and starts of its protracted ending; they might also take a certain delight in these set-ups that
ambush unwary, first-time listeners—replaying, perhaps, their own initial encounter with the work.

   That most famous of all Haydn's surprises, the Andante of Symphony No.
94, may be taken as a litmus test of this altered experience in repeated hearings. With this work we also have an exemplary case of the ways in which a
surprise takes on new meanings in the history of its reception among various
and changing audiences. Known in its own time as "The Surprise" in London and as the *Paukenschlag* ("drum stroke") among German-speaking audiences, the symphony is heard frequently in concert halls today. The tune of
its Andante is reproduced as well in children's piano primers, even with words
("Papa Haydn's dead and gone . . ."), and has acquired nearly universal recognition as a joke—for some, perhaps, a rather stale one.

On first hearing, however, the surprise of the slow movement may impress its auditors most forcibly as an assault on the nervous system. The *fortissimo* chord *cum* timpani that earned the work its title comes without warning, but not without the composer's careful preparation for maximum effect. Upon repetition, the first eight measures of the simple theme are played even more softly than in the initial statement, the tune by first violins only, with pizzicato chords articulating the downbeat of each measure. Despite these changes in dynamic level and scoring, no clues arouse suspicion that the repetition will differ significantly from the opening statement; attention is strained primarily in one's efforts to hear the music. In this context of lulled expectation and strained attention, the volume and placement of the tutti chord (on the second beat of the measure) make it especially startling. If there is a betrayal of expectation in what follows, it is that the theme continues unruffled by this astonishing intrusion. Kant's often-quoted definition of laughter's source as "the sudden transformation of a strained expectation into nothing" is given a strange turn here. On a first hearing of the Andante, listeners may laugh not only in the aftershock of surprise but also in a state of uneasiness that it will happen again. In either case, Haydn has effectively engaged the listener in aroused and lingering suspense.

A favorite interpretation of this surprise, circulated from Haydn's day to ours, is that it was meant to startle the listener out of a doze induced by the quiet beginning of the movement. Giuseppe Carpani, an early biographer of Haydn who could claim personal acquaintance with the composer in his last years, records with obvious relish his version of the surprise as a joke at the expense of the London audience:

> The English were well content with *Haydn's* instrumental compositions so long as the tempo was cheerful and lively, but they went to sleep quite easily when an *Andante* or *Adagio* came along, no matter how beautiful or well fashioned it might be. He composed a charming *Andante*—sweet, soft, and seductive—in which a huge crash, reinforced by a loud drumstroke, unexpectedly shatters a long *pianissimo* passage, and makes the audience leap from their seats. This alarum lends an air of novelty to that very simple melody, and makes it all the more pleasurable.[31]

The novelty of the "alarum" seems to please the Italian to the extent that it teaches the unsophisticated English audience a lesson.

At its debut, however, the "Surprise" might well have stunned more than it amused. A contemporary review of the symphony's first performance has some of the elements of Carpani's report, but none of his brand of humor about the surprise. A reporter for the *Oracle* writes on 24 March 1792:

> The Second Movement was equal to the happiest of this great Master's conceptions. The Surprise might not be unaptly likened to the situation of a beautiful Shepherdess who, lulled to slumber by the murmer of a distant Water-fall, starts alarmed by the unexpected firing of a fowling-piece.[32]

Georg August Griesinger, another of Haydn's early biographers and rather more reliable than Carpani, offers a different and allegedly firsthand report of the composer's intentions:

I asked him once in jest whether it was true that he had composed the Andante with the Drum Stroke to waken the English who fell asleep at his concert. "No," came the answer, "but I was interested in surprising the public with something new, and in making a brilliant debut, so that my student Pleyel, who was at that time engaged by an orchestra in London (1792) and whose concerts had opened a week before mine, should not outdo me."[33]

In view of the competitive musical scene in London in the 1790s, Haydn's response is credible as a candid admission of the value of novelty. Even so, such prodigious novelty may well have startled both inattentive and attentive listeners.

In this light, it should be noted that the *fortissimo* and its set-up were second thoughts on the composer's part: the autograph score shows that Haydn originally intended an exact repeat of the opening section.[34] This, together with Griesinger's account of the surprise, suggests that Haydn's dramatic alteration was calculated to please the tastes of the London audience rather than to chide them. As we shall see, such a technique would have been entirely compatible with eighteenth-century notions of the composer's humor.

There is no doubt, though, that the surprise of the *Paukenschlag* is dramatic. Depending on one's point of view, it might also be judged a practical joke, a stroke of comic exaggeration, a stunning novelty, even a shock to the nervous system. That a listener might laugh in response to any of these suggests that laughter itself is an insufficient index of what a jest accomplishes. The engagement of the listener in a first hearing of this work differs, surely, from the complicity in surprise proposed in the "Joke" Quartet finale— although in rehearing the Andante, the privilege of an insider's anticipation can enhance both appreciation of the set-up for surprise and awareness of the responses of others. In any case, the comments of Haydn's contemporaries about the "Surprise" Symphony remind us that perceptions of humor vary with the "ear" of the listener, and that eighteenth-century contexts can frame a range of interpretations of humor in music. Further, a composer's intentions do not preclude the possibility of a work's *becoming* humorous in its reception by later generations of listeners. While the nicknames of Haydn's works are suggestive of the reactions of listeners, the history of a work's performances and reception invests it with new meanings over time.

In taking jokes as the focus of this chapter, I have deliberately chosen emphatic models of the musical procedures and analytical issues I wish to investigate. The gerundive *jesting* in the title I have taken for this study is also deliberate in insisting upon an ongoing process of engagement rather than an isolated moment. The complete phrase, borrowed from the preface to Domenico Scarlatti's *Essercizi per gravicembalo* of 1738, captures the essence of this process as well as the aesthetic and historical contexts that frame it:

Reader

Whether you be Dilettante or Professor, in these Compositions do not expect any profound Learning, but rather an ingenious jesting with Art, to accommodate you to the mastery of the Harpsichord.[35]

Putting both expert and amateur on notice to expect challenges to traditions of solo keyboard composition, Scarlatti acknowledges that his "ingenious jesting" intends serious didactic ends. His modest disclaimer notwithstanding, both means and ends are indeed profound, for these are sonatas that make new demands on the expressive and technical capabilities of the player as well as the instrument itself, and that ultimately expand the dramatic potential of musical style and genre.

Inscribed in "ingenious jesting with Art" are key meanings of wit in the late eighteenth century—ingenuity and jest—as well as two senses, both of which are appropriate to wit and humor in music: the making of ingenious jests artfully, artistically, and ingeniously jesting (or jousting) with the art of music—challenging traditional attitudes toward music's expression and function. Implicit in this formulation are the players and listeners whose own ingenuity is tested by the challenges of "jousting." Suggestive as Scarlatti's phrase is, it remains to explore the relevance of such terms for Haydn's music. There are obvious perils in attempting to square meanings we take to be more or less self-evident with those of the eighteenth-century writer. Words are coined for local exchange and, like currency, have fluctuating values. Nonetheless, without some attempt to understand the perception of wit and humor in Haydn's music from a historical perspective, we run the risk of missing what was—and is still—more than a laughing matter.

2

The Decorum of Wit and the Nature of Humor in Eighteenth-Century Essays

*The music of Haydn obtains among its listeners that same
superiority that a man of good humor has in society.*[1]

The distinctions that eighteenth-century writers observe between wit and
humor are often more palpable in their attitudes than in their definitions. An
early example is Jonathan Swift's comparison of wit and humor in his "To
Mr. Delany" (1718). Here the exemplar of satiric wit betrays an obvious preference for humor:

> For, sure, by Wit is onely meant
> Applying what we first Invent:
> What Humour is, not all the Tribe
> Of Logick-mongers can describe;
> Here onely Nature acts her Part,
> Unhelpt by Practice, Books, or Art.
> For Wit and Humour differ quite,
> That gives Surprise, and this Delight:
> Humour is odd, grotesque, and wild,
> Onely by Affectation spoild,
> Tis never by Invention got,
> Men have it when they know it not.[2]

While Swift acknowledges the surprise of wit's invention, he appears to have
little confidence in its benign effects. It is humor, however indefinable, that
delights. Nature is its source and affectation its only enemy.

Toward the middle of the century, Corbyn Morris expresses similar sentiments in *An Essay towards Fixing the True Standards of Wit, Humour, Raillery,
Satire, and Ridicule* (1744). He favors humor for its unstrained naturalness,
its universality and durability, and its generosity. The exertions of wit fare
poorly by comparison:

> HUMOUR is *Nature*, or what really appears in the Subject, without any Embellish-
> ments; WIT is only a Stroke of *Art*, where the original Subject, being insufficient
> in itself, is garnished and deck'd with auxiliary Objects.

and:

> HUMOUR, in the Representation of the *Foibles* of *Persons* in *real Life*, frequently
> exhibits very *generous benevolent* Sentiments of Heart; And these, tho' exerted in
> a particular odd Manner, justly command our Fondness and Love.—Whereas in
> the Allusions of WIT, *Severity*, *Bitterness*, and *Satire*, are frequently exhibited.[3]

An association of humor with human nature and wit with artifice underlies
Morris's allegiance to the former as benevolent, heartfelt, and personal, even
if odd. Wit, on the other hand, is an intellectual ornament, "inanimate," and
often sharply pointed as criticism. Despite his obvious preference for humor
over wit, though, Morris grants the superiority of their combined effect in
something like the frosting on the cake: "where HUMOUR is the *Ground-work*
and chief Substance, and WIT happily spread *quickens* the whole with Embellishments."[4]

These associations of wit with the artful and humor with the natural are
abiding ones throughout the eighteenth century; the distinctions observed
by Swift are retained by William Hazlitt more than a century later: "Humour
is, as it were, the growth of nature and accident; Wit is the product of art
and fancy."[5] Attitudes toward wit and humor will, of course, reflect prevailing
views of what is judged "natural" and what "artful," judgments that inform
not only the changing fortunes of wit and humor but also critical estimates
of both the artist and his art.

In an effort to come to terms with wit and humor as eighteenth-century
writers seem to understand them, I quote liberally from critical essays of the
period. Aside from alerting us to complex and often ambiguous meanings of
the words themselves, these sources convey contemporary attitudes that help
us to understand critical responses to wit and humor in Haydn's music. It is
appropriate to begin with British sources, not simply because Haydn's music
achieved enormous popularity in England, but also because many German
writers of his day fashioned their aesthetic tastes and critical opinions after
the imported goods of English writers—a dependency that extended, as we
shall see, to notions of wit and humor. In Germany and England alike, critical
misgivings about wit's deceptions and humor's eccentricity would be dis-
armed by increasing admiration for the humorist as an original.

The Ambivalence of Wit

In his *Elements of the Philosophy of the Human Mind* (1792), Dugald Stewart likens the effect of wit to that of a magic trick: "[T]here is unquestionably a *smile* appropriated to the flashes of wit;—a smile of surprise and wonder;—not altogether unlike the effect produced on the mind and the countenance, by a feat of *legerdemain* when executed with uncommon success."[6] In Stewart's view, the display of wit is something of a performance. Despite the suggestion that wit's means are comparable to a sleight-of-hand deception, wit's charms are here implicitly benign: the "flashes" of wit stimulate a natural correspondence of physical and mental delight in a "smile of surprise and wonder."

The delights of surprise, of the unexpected and the novel, are commonly noted in eighteenth-century discussions of wit, though not always with complete assurance of benign intent.[7] In keeping with its origin in the Anglo-Saxon *witan,* to know, wit remained closely associated with the mind—its inventions and ingenuities—throughout the eighteenth century. So too, certain reservations about wit's facile manipulations persisted in echoes of John Locke's cautionary distinction between wit and judgment. As stated in his *Essay Concerning Human Understanding* (1690), wit was the work of *fancy* and consisted of the "assemblage of ideas, and putting those together with quickness and variety, wherein can be found any resemblance or congruity." *Judgment,* on the other hand, was the product of reason and required the careful "separation of ideas wherein can be found the least difference, thereby to avoid being misled by similitude, and by affinity to take one thing for another."[8] Perhaps it is this uncertainty, the possibility of being "misled by similitude," that informs Stewart's definition of wit as ingenious sleight of hand—a conception echoed by William Jackson: "Wit, then, is the dextrous performance of a legerdemain trick, by which one idea is *presented* and another *substituted.*"[9]

Locke's wariness of wit suggests that fancy's limitation lay in its partial and imperfect recall of associations resident in memory; hasty, dazzling, glancing fancies were at best incomplete or perhaps premature judgments, lacking the sober deliberation that carefully discriminated the particulars of things. The seduction of rational judgment by fanciful wit might well be suspect in an age that celebrated the powers of reason, for it could call into question the truth of ideas that relied upon stable identities of things in the world. With primary concern for stability of language in judging matters of knowledge and truth, Locke was obliged to suppress wit's artful fancies.[10]

Although the instability of meaning and intent that inhered in wit's surprise remained a hazard to be reckoned with, eighteenth-century critics would find a balance of reason and imagination in admitting judgment to wit's domain. The wide range of meanings assigned to wit at the turn of the century in the eleventh edition (1799) of Samuel Johnson's *Dictionary of the*

English Language is paralleled in German sources of the period.[11] "Wit" comprehends the general "powers of the mind," as well as the more particular
capacities of "imagination" and "quickness of fancy," "judgement" and
"sense." Wit may be those "sentiments produced by quickness of fancy, or
by genius," or it may be the "man of fancy," the "man of genius" himself.
Distrust of wit's powers lay in its ambivalence: its "invention" and "ingenuity" might be "contrivance; stratagem"; a witty person or expression might
be "judicious" and "full of imagination," but also "sarcastick; full of taunts."
As an invention of the mind, wit could only strive to appear natural and
spontaneous by artful means; and as an artful invention, its surprises might
strain naturalness of expression and clarity of meaning with excesses of artifice and cleverness. There was, then, a decorum of "true wit" to be preserved. In defining the limits of that decorum, literary critics approached the
subject of wit with a sense of purpose.

Wit: True and False

The specifically literary meanings attached to wit ranged from ingenious and
novel enhancement of language to the incongruous juxtaposition of "things
by nature most unneighbourly."[12] Mental agility pertained not only to the inventions of wit but also to appreciation of them. And although the effect
of surprise might shake the critical edifice with laughter, there is concern
throughout the century to uphold the standards of "true" wit in a just balance of the artful and the natural.

   Alexander Pope's famous definition in his *Essay on Criticism* (1711)
stressed the conjunction of art and nature in wit as the elegance of language
that elevates and transforms common expression: "True Wit is Nature to
advantage dress'd / What oft was thought but ne'er so well express'd." Echoing Pope's metaphor in an *Essay upon Wit* (1716), Sir Richard Blackmore locates a persuasive power in novelty that "raises and enlivens cold Sentiments
and cold Propositions by giving them an elegant and Surprizing Turn." For
wit

> always conveys the Thought of the Speaker or Writer cloath'd in a pleasing but
> foreign Dress, in which it never appeared to the Hearer before, who however had
> been long acquainted with it; this Appearance in the Habit of a Stranger must be
> admirable, since Surprize naturally arises from Novelty, as Delight and Wonder
> result from Surprize.[13]

Blackmore's conception of wit assumes that its novelty stimulates surprise,
which in turn arouses wonder and delight.

   In keeping with the Augustan poets' appreciation of wit, writers of the
early eighteenth century assume that it effects a natural succession from surprise to admiration. The chain reaction proposed by Blackmore is elaborated
by later writers, and his equation of surprise and wonder modified. Henry
Home, Lord Kames, notes in his *Elements of Criticism* (1762) that whereas

the unexpected occasions surprise, novelty causes wonder."[14] Adam Smith, for whom surprise was a "violent and sudden change produced upon the mind," and wonder, "uncertainty and anxious curiosity," described their succession in his *Essays on Philosophical Subjects* (1795):

> When one accustomed object appears after another, which it does not usually follow, it first excites, by its unexpectedness, the sentiment called surprise, and afterwards, by the singularity of the succession, or order of its appearance, the sentiment properly called wonder. We start and are surprised at seeing it there, and then wonder how it came to be there.[15]

By Smith's account, the experience of surprise assumes an interruption or reversal of customary succession. Wonder arises from uncertainty about what such a disturbance means in light of past events and curiosity about its implications for future ones.

In marking the temporal sequence of wit's surprise and delight, these writers point up a feature that distinguishes wit from humor, and one that has obvious relevance for music, namely the dependence upon succession. They also suggest basic conditions of that succession in the appreciation of wit's ingenuity: *stability* of conventions familiar in customary uses of language; *surprise* at unexpected uses of language in novel, even curious conjunctions of the familiar and the unfamiliar; and *insight* in the recognition that a seemingly incongruous combination disguises an unsuspected congruity of relationship. These conditions are examined in specifically musical terms in later chapters, but it might be noted here that an important element is missing in Stewart's comparison of wit's "smile of surprise and wonder" with the effect of a magic trick: in magic one is content to wonder at surprise without knowing "how it came to be." The listener's share in appreciation of wit depends upon both curiosity and recognition and, ultimately, the insight that surprise initiates.

While ingenuity of expression was admired as striking and novel, "in pure WIT," as Morris notes, "the Allusions are rather *surprizing*, than *mirthful*; and the *Agreements* or *Contrasts* which are started between Objects . . . are more fit to be *admired* for their *Happiness* and *Propriety*, than to excite our *Laughter*."[16] That forced "similitude" was a departure from true wit had been remarked by Francis Hutcheson in his essay "Reflections upon Laughter" (1725): "When we see, instead of the easy and natural resemblance which constitutes true wit, a forced straining of a likeness, our laughter is apt to rise."[17] The aim of true wit, then, was to engage the imagination without violating good sense. Delight in discovering an uncommonly apt turn of phrase or an unexpected allusion or metaphor, the originality of which was as remarkable as its truth, was consonant with that aim—a mere non sequitur would not qualify. Indeed, Morris stresses the capacity of wit to enlighten, to lend new clarity to an idea.

In this context, Samuel Johnson's criticism of the metaphysical poets reflects distaste for wit that is farfetched—for nature that is *overdressed*. Rather than "natural and just," these similes are "too laboured and factitious":

"[F]ascinated as we are by the ingenuity of these poets, our attention is distracted from their poems, and they consequently fail in their effect. Our minds, but not our feelings, are engaged."[18] Mental gymnastics in the "discovery of occult resemblances in things apparently unlike"—the result, perhaps, of a too lively and capricious fancy—put unreasonable strains of hyperbole and recondite allusions on true wit. "Quibbles," or puns, were similarly disdained, but as impoverished varieties of wit—mere wordplay lacking substance.[19] Thus, novel and surprising inventions were restrained by the decorum of truth, elegance, and ease of style: only when "strength of thought" is wed to "happiness of language" can wit move the mind and feelings to agreement.[20]

While Pope's appreciation of wit as rhetorical ingenuity persisted in the essays of later writers, increasing emphasis was placed on the surprise, the novelty, and the incongruity of the "dressing." Even Morris allowed that wit could enlighten "not by reasoning upon that Subject, but by a just and unexpected Introduction of another *similar* or *opposite* Subject."[21] In admitting the incongruous juxtaposition of *opposed* ideas, Morris departs from the strict separation of wit and judgment observed by Locke (although one might argue that Locke's own formulation of wit as something of a faulty comparison foreshadows its later association with incongruity and the ludicrous). Dr. Johnson notwithstanding, the "connection, invented or displayed unexpectedly, between incongruous and dissonant objects"[22] became for many a requirement of wit.

Emphasis on the effectiveness of sudden and surprising incongruity allowed the understanding of wit as lucid and ingenious elegance of expression to tilt toward an association with laughter. Lord Kames goes so far as to exclude the serious from the province of wit, dismissing as unnatural those "ludicrous combinations of things that have little or no relation."[23] The purveyors of wit had apparently fallen upon unsuitably remote, "ludicrous" comparisons.

While explanations of what provokes the "risible emotion," resemble those that expose the means of wit, the degree of incongruity might allow some distinction between the two. According to James Beattie, for example,

> Laughter often arises from the discovery of unexpected *likeness* between objects apparently *dissimilar*: and the greater the apparent dissimilitude, and new-discovered resemblance, the greater will be the surprise attending the discovery, the more striking the opposition of contrariety and relation, the more likely the risible emotion.[24]

Cautions such as Hutcheson's and Johnson's against strained likenesses in preposterous and simply novel comparisons suggest that true wit should not make sport of what Locke had esteemed the serious business of discriminating differences.

The impropriety of "sheer" wit is appreciated still in *British Synonymy* (1794), compiled by Johnson's friend Hester Thrale:

WIT, FERTILITY OF IMAGERY, POWERS OF COMBINATION, VIVACITY, HILARITY, PLEAS-
ANTRY, BRILLIANCY IN WRITING OR CONVERSATION ARE nearly, not strictly synonymous. The first word includes all the rest. . . . In these days, however, there needs
little caution against overdosing our compositions with sheer wit, or far-fetched
metaphors. Studied thoughts have given way to embellishments of expression.[25]

While the aim of wit, like that of comedy, changed in the course of the eighteenth century from the satirically pointed to the agreeably instructive,
Pope's appreciation of wit's pleasures lingers in Thrale's estimate of ingenuity as surprising but appropriate—and seemingly natural—"embellishments
of expression." Supporting the range of wit's amusements, a decorum of ease
and pleasantry attests here to abiding concerns for natural expression, now
tempered by social graces: wit agreeable in conversation should appear spontaneous, "unstudied." Most agreeable was the unmannered wit shared
among those of "good humor," that is, those most ready to be pleased.

Humor and the Humorist

Humor's earliest sense derived from theories of temperament, according to
which disproportions in the four basic bodily fluids, or humors, determined
the dominant temperament—the humor—of the man: choleric, phlegmatic,
sanguine, or melancholic. Thus manifestations of humor could range from
"morbid disposition; petulance; peevishness," to "caprice; whim; jocularity."
The humorous might be "pleasant; jocular, capricious," and "irregular," or
"full of grotesque or odd images." And even if the humorist is "one who has
odd conceits" or "violent and peculiar passions," in following his own bent
he "conducts himself by his own fancy," and "gratifies his own humour."[26]
The basis for a decorum appropriate to humor lay ultimately, then, in a social
code of manners and conduct:

> [T]here is a certain cast of mind, as well as turn of features, which distinguishes
> one man from another, and forms his particular character; according to which cast
> every sensible man will direct his actions, still managing the bias with a prudent
> regard to the ground he is to pass over. But should he . . . wilfully neglect the
> circumstance of place, or from too great an indulgence so increase the bias as to
> carry him out of the common road, he then commences Humorist; and, however
> contrary to reason, obstinately keeps his way.[27]

In deference to the rule of custom, "sensible" behavior presumed the constraints of reason and prudence on willful, antisocial humor.

Despite the seeming assurance that humor, in being natural, was preferable
to artful wit, definitions of what humor actually *was* remained elusive even
among the English, who were taken to be its true representatives. In an essay
on the subject, Henry Fielding remarked: "[In] truth there is nothing so unset-
tled and incertain, as our Notion of Humour in general. The most common
Opinion is, that whatever diverts or makes you laugh, is Humour."[28] For some

who observed a social code that discriminated between polite and vulgar laughter, the latter was more often allied with humor than with wit. In this connection, one commonly reads of the intellectual demands of wit as its distinguishing feature: "Humour is chiefly relished by the vulgar, whilst intellectual excellence is requisite to comprehend Wit."[29]

With the powerful assist of sentimental tastes, the measure of humor and laughter underwent significant changes in the context of the theater. In surveying eighteenth- and early nineteenth-century theories of comedy, Stuart Tave offers a nutshell description of the early and late stages of this development:

> In Restoration theory . . . it was a commonplace that the function of comedy is to copy the foolish and knavish originals of the age and to expose, ridicule, satirize them. By the middle of the nineteenth century, it was a commonplace that the best comic works present amiable originals, often models of good nature, whose little peculiarities are not satirically instructive, but objects of delight and love.[30]

Restoration authors had concerned themselves with two categories of humors: those deemed violent and sinister, and those of an unstable or merely silly sort. A temperament of the first type was governed by "violent and peculiar passions,"[31] of the second, by "a fainter, or weaker passion . . . without any rule but the present whim."[32] The attitude toward both sorts of temperament at the beginning of the eighteenth century was that they deserved censure, and comedy's means was satire—to the end of moral improvement. During the first half of the century "the word *humor* was rapidly assuming its modern meaning, and laughter grew mild and tender-hearted."[33] A man's humor came to be regarded as his human nature: an individual's unique characteristics, even if eccentric, were part of the natural man. The fitting target for comedy's ridicule (and correction) was, as Swift noted, affectation.

Growing indulgence of a man's eccentricities as evidence of his natural and unaffected humor extended beyond the characters of comedy to the artist himself. This attitude is unmistakable in Morris's *Essay*. Tave's summary of Morris's catalog of the humorist's virtues bears a striking resemblance, as we shall see, to idealized portraits of Joseph Haydn drawn more than fifty years later by his early biographers and contemporary admirers. Although "properly an older man, frequently very learned,"

> [t]he benevolent type of amiable humorist is 'simple,' in the sense of unaffected, spontaneous, without artifice, but he is not uncomplicated or easily comprehended. He is 'natural,' unstained by the corrupting influence of society, childlike and pure; he has idyllic, guileless Christian values; but he is not pastoral, not prelapsarian, not a noble savage, because he is necessarily the product of a rich civilization.[34]

As social constraints of manners increasingly rule the humors, "the state of society becomes more refined," notes Richard Cumberland in 1795, and "eccentricity of character wears away."[35] Whether it was the humorist who became less aberrant or the society that grew more tolerant, the fashion of sentimental comedy exerted a civilizing restraint on the humorous. Thus an advertisement for the first issue of *The Sentimental Magazine* of 1773 could firmly state: "Our Ancestors placed their Amusement in Laughter, we place our's in Chastity of Sentiment."[36] Oliver Goldsmith's plea in the same year for a return to the comedy of old, that should "excite our laughter by ridiculously exhibiting the follies of the lower part of mankind," no doubt fell on chastely sentimental ears.[37]

The reverence for genius and originality that becomes characteristic of criticism in the second half of the eighteenth century parallels indulgent attitudes toward the humorist. For some, the terms *genius, original,* and *humorist* were interchangeable. It is not surprising, then, that admiration for the humorist tempered theories of laughter and the satiric mode of comedy. Telling evidence of the change is Morris's devaluation of the comedies of Ben Jonson as compared to those of Shakespeare. Rather a far cry from Locke, Shakespeare's freedoms of fancy are tinged with the sublime:

> Johnson [sic] in his COMIC Scenes has expos'd and ridicul'd *Folly* and *Vice; Shakespear* [sic] has usher'd in *Joy, Frolic* and *Happiness.* . . . The one pointed his Satire with masterly Skill; the other was inimitable in touching the Strings of Delight. With *Johnson* you are confin'd and instructed, with *Shakespear* unbent and dissolv'd in Joy. . . . The first was cautious and strict, not daring to sally beyond the Bounds of Regularity. The other bold and impetuous, rejoicing like a Giant to run his Course, through all the Mountains and Wilds of Nature and Fancy.[38]

For Morris, the art of the satirist, however skillful, remains answerable to its didactic ends—unnatural impediments to the "wilds" of a bold imagination.

Liberated from the constraints of instructive satire, wit could exercise more playful freedoms; as an original, the humorist could claim such freedoms as a natural inclination. Latitude granted to the fancy of the natural humorist permitted not only the assimilation of wit in humor but also the identification of style with temperament. Johnson, in his classic preface to *The Plays of William Shakespeare* (1765), maintained that in comedy Shakespeare found "a mode of thinking congenial to his nature"; while tragedy revealed his skill, the comic was his by instinct.[39]

The high tribute that English reviewers of the 1790s paid to Haydn in comparing him to their own Shakespeare is a measure of the composer's success in London with critics and general audiences alike.[40] Such writers are more rhapsodic than specific, but a recurring theme in their perceptions of Haydn's musical humor is his matchless balance of the grand and the playful. The following concert review is typical: "Novelty of idea, agreeable caprice, and whim combined with all *Haydn's* sublime and wonten grandeur, gave additional consequence to the *soul* and feelings of every individual present."[41] With expressive powers that range from the sublime to the whimsical, his music delights professionals and amateurs alike. In features that will become fixed in the Haydn portrait, he is viewed above all as a *natural* genius, an original, whose bold flights of fancy are unfettered by conventional rules; and his natural inclination for cheerfulness and harmless teasing infects his music in turn, in gaiety, joy, and the humor of playful deception.[42]

To regard as inescapable the influence of a man's nature upon his art was to allow the alliance of wit and humor as both inevitable and estimable. If humor betrayed itself in the natural, in the personal style congruent with the artist's unique temperament, wit displayed itself in the artful, in the ingenuity of the artist who transformed the conventional with the strikingly original. The humorist, indisposed to conform to the quotidian, could offer art inventions "remote from all the common tracks and sheep-walks made in the mind ... removed from common apprehension, distant from the ordinary haunts of thought." And the ingenuity of his wit would challenge others to discover "things which are never brought together in the common events of life, and in which the mind has discovered relations by its own subtilty and quickness."[43] Aimed at recreation of the humors, the pleasures of "playsome, sportive, or jocular" wit superseded the corrective laughter of ridicule.

The German Connection

Given the wholesale importation and imitation of English literature in Germany during the eighteenth century, it is not surprising that parallels should exist in theories of comedy and the associated terms *wit* and *humor*.[44] In his encyclopedic *Allgemeine Theorie der schönen Künste* (1771–74), Johann Georg Sulzer echoes the sentiments of earlier English writers in recommending more useful ends for laughter (and music) than mere amusement. Comparing his own countrymen with the English, however, he finds "fewer comic originals to enjoy than [in] other lands where men live more freely." It would seem that political and social factors constrained both laughter and humorist: "The German is afraid of seeming awkward and hasn't enough courage to abandon himself entirely to his own proclivities; thus he is less original than many others."[45]

True to his word, Sulzer is eclectic in his approach to *Witz*. He begins with its original meaning of intellect, or good sense, and continues along Lockean lines:

> At present it has a somewhat narrower meaning, and wit is now reckoned, at least in educated parlance, as a particular gift of the mind which consists principally in the facility for quickly seeing and vividly feeling the various connections and relationships of one subject compared with another.[46]

The subterranean dangers of wit's deceptions are not explicit here, nor is the sharpness of its critical edge, but Locke's strict separation of wit and judgment lingers in Sulzer's assertion that a man of wit possesses "more of a lively fantasy than of judgment."

Georg Friedrich Meier, whose *Gedanken von Scherzen* (2d ed., 1754) appeared in London in English translation in 1764, put a twist on Locke's distinction. Defining *wit* as the discovery of similarities in things, and *jest* as "comparing, in an ingenious manner, objects which greatly differ," Meier notes: "It appears at first sight absurd that objects, differing greatly and palpably, should yet mutually coincide or agree in many particulars; and hence, by the discovery of such a variety of coincidences, we are agreeably surprised."[47] Meier appears to make a distinction here between wit in the Lockean sense and the wit of incongruity as Beattie later described it. Jests pose the absurdity of explicit incongruities, whose hidden similarities are more difficult to detect.

The influence of the humors on a man's behavior is also relatively benign in Sulzer's definition of *Laune* as

> a frame of mind in which a vague agreeable or disagreeable feeling [*Empfindung*] is so pervasive that all perceptions and utterances are infected by it. It is a passionate state in which the passion is not violent and has no definite object, but simply spreads pleasure or displeasure over the entire spirit. . . . Often the artist has no other muse than his humor [*Laune*] to support him.[48]

Here humor is comparable to dispositions of temperament or mood, the influence of which is felt in the creative impulse of the artist. Whereas some German writers—Gotthold Ephraim Lessing in particular—made an effort to distinguish the English *Humor* from the unpredictable changeableness of mood implicit in the German word derived from *luna*, others such as Sulzer used *Laune* as equivalent in meaning. In any case, as Sulzer noted, the humorous had generally positive connotations: "the ordinary and everyday has nothing that attracts one as remarkable; but every marked humor [*Laune*] has something in it that pleases us, such that we observe departures from calm reason with enjoyment."[49]

While Sulzer does not make explicit the connection noted in contemporary English sources between wit and humor, this association was apparently current, as seen in the definitions listed in a German-English dictionary of 1781:

> *Laune* is used with different meanings. *Der Mensch hat viel Laune*, means: he has, in his dealings with others, in his expression, in his writings, much wit, a very high-spirited manner. . . . *Launigt* is nearly the same as droll, witty, jocular.[50]

In a later formulation, Kant would distinguish between *launichter Witz*—favoring paradoxes and appropriate to the salon—and a more serious wit, "necessary to awaken insight into important matters," that "raises more admiration than amusement."[51] The use of such words as *humorous* and *laughable* to qualify *Witz* and *Laune* is a reminder of competing intentions associated with these terms.

It is in his articles on the laughable and jesting that Sulzer becomes more precise in defining means and ends. Basic to his conception of laughter is the paradox of ambivalence and resulting "uncertainty of our judgment" when "two contradictory things appear equally valid."[52] Such definitions emphasize the paradox of ambivalence as a kind of eccentric wit—here of apparent contradition. Laughter arises in the surprise of having to say "yes and no at the same time." One might laugh at the nonsense of such equivalence itself, or at the odd, fantastic connection that produces it. But "if persons of taste are to laugh at such incongruities, . . . the contradiction must not be immediately obvious, but must require a certain cleverness to discern it." Sulzer's conception seems close to incongruous wit, here of a rather subtle and urbane variety.

Ultimately, in Sulzer's view, laughter most appropriately serves the end of moral improvement, and "the laughable is different from jesting not in its essentials or material conditions but rather in the intention that brings it to light."[53] (Koch also stressed the intention of the jester, we recall, in distinguishing between the "disturbing" *Spaß* and the pleasing *Scherz*.) The uses of jesting are modest and direct: well-placed, "somewhat restrained drollery" can rouse the weary, cheer the melancholic, and promote efficiency in the performance of difficult tasks; simply arousing one's fellows to mirth, while not objectionable, appears to be a rather less worthy end.

Following English theories of comedy, Sulzer provides a hierarchic context for laughter in low, middle, and high varieties. The low comic, or farce, is hospitable to nonsense; the middle comic, urbane and refined, accommodates the humor of wit "so long as it passes among persons of good manners"; and the high comic "borders on tragedy, where strong and serious passions come into play."[54] The criteria for drama applied here have obvious implications in music for categories of opera, but we will find that they also figure in the criticism of Haydn's instrumental works.

In Germany as in England the association of wit and the humorous in refined comedy smoothes the rough edges of earlier meanings of each. Even Morris had allowed that humor was at its best when leavened by wit, and later writers, as we have seen, would regard this association as inevitable. An itinerant but telling document of the English-German connection appeared in London in 1789: "An Essay on Humour, Translated from the German." The anonymous German author, helping himself to a generous portion of Fielding's 1752 essay, recommends humor as an antidote to melancholy. He then offers some observations on humorous authors. "Humour in composition" requires "singularity and a certain air of seriousness." This air may be feigned, however, to best effect the comic: "An author possesses real humor when, with an air of gravity, he paints objects in such colors as promote mirth and excite laughter."[55] The contrast of an assumed seriousness in relating "ludicrous tales" is more estimable as humor than treating something truly serious in a burlesque style. The decorum of comedy would accommodate a mixture of manners, but not the mockery of genuinely serious matters. Notable here is the recognition of humor as an artful technique in assumed manners for comic effect. Mozart's *Ein musikalischer Spaß*, discussed in Chapter 1, comes to mind as an extreme and sustained example of such imposture.

Noteworthy as well is the author's observation concerning the relationship between artistic temperament and style: "Authors who possess humor in character, shew it also in their writings; strokes of it even escape involuntarily from them, when they wish to treat a subject in a grave and serious manner."[56] This view, which accords with Morris's definition of a humorist and Sulzer's of *Laune*, paralleled growing interest in the personality of the artist.[57] Sulzer's entry "Expression in Music," for example, notes the extent to which a composer's "personality" [*Gemut*] affects his music, and cites the contrast of Carl Heinrich Graun and Johann Adolf Hasse as evidence. The former, "to whom nature had granted a soul full of tenderness, gentleness, and agreeableness . . . was at home only in the gentle, the pleasant, and the charming emotions." Hasse, on the other hand, a man of "loftier courage, bolder emotions, and stronger desires . . . was most at home with the emotions that were consistent with his character." On this view, aesthetic categories of the pleasing and the sublime might seem genetically encoded in the humors. Sulzer concludes that even after intensive study of the emotions and the musical means by which they might be expressed, the artist must know himself well, and wherever possible should "undertake nothing that is inconsistent with his character."[58] In the 1790s, some twenty years later, the Reverend Robert Burrowes puts the case even more emphatically: "The digressions of an author are . . . indications of what is agreeable to his dispositions, for he cannot expatiate on what he dislikes."[59] Ernst Ludwig Gerber's evaluation of the inevitable relationship between Haydn's "character" and his "invention" is typical of the view around the turn of the century:

> The invention of a cheerful and delightful idea unfortunately does not always lie within the composer's power and free choice; often it stems from his individual character, often on the other hand from his situation and the influence of his environment, and perhaps only our jovial Haydn, despite his age, could make so many and such ever-new discoveries of this sort.[60]

It is not surprising that the inspirations of a "natural genius" occasioned more superlatives than interpretive comment. Indeed, a common premise in criticism of the late eighteenth century held with Immanuel Kant that the original artist "gave the rule to art" without himself knowing how he did so.[61] But even if the *hows* of Haydn's invention were often accepted as beyond critical understanding, his personality became a matter of interest to those seeking to explain the humorous, playful, "teasing strain" in his music. The retrospective view offered by Georg August Griesinger in his *Biographische Notizen* (1810) indicates an easy reconciliation of the humor of the man with that of his music. In such a portrait, one wonders if the style has become the man:

> A harmless roguery [*Schalkheit*], or what the British call *Humour*, was a dominant feature in Haydn's character. He easily and by preference discovered the comic side of a subject, and anyone who had spent even an hour with him must have noticed that the very spirit of Austrian cheerfulness breathed in him. In his compositions this mood [*Laune*] is most striking, and his allegros and rondeaux in particular are often planned to tease the audience by wanton shifts from the seemingly

serious to the highest degree of the comic, and to be tuned to an almost wild hilarity [*ausgelassenen Fröhlichkeit*].[62]

Griesinger's specific reference to the word *humor* as one of English extraction is brought in to elucidate Haydn's personal and Austrian nature, here intimately linked with that of his composition. (As we shall see, the stamp of a national humor is one that early critics viewed in a less favorable light.)

Albert Christoph Dies, whose *Biographische Nachrichten von Joseph Haydn* followed close on the heels of Griesinger's biography, also comments on Haydn's "teasing strain," both personal and musical:

> Woven into Haydn's character is a genial, witty, teasing strain, but always of a childlike innocence. His musical output attests to this (as several critics have already remarked), and now still in old age, his behavior in company often gives rise to the above observation. . . .
>
> In his character there was much cheerfulness, jest, and musical wit both popular and refined, but original to the highest degree. It has often been called *Humor*, from which is rightly derived Haydn's bent for musical teasing.[63]

The protective cover of naïve innocence, of everything being in good fun, renders teasing as harmless as "merry boys romping on the grass" from a sheer surplus of energy.[64]

If Dies and Griesinger adopted these character references whole and uncritically, it should be remembered that in such appreciations of Haydn's compositional humor as theirs, a composite view of the man had long since been shaped by the critical estimate of his music. Indeed, Haydn's "humorous" departures from various rules of style and decorum were not well received in the earliest reviews of his works. These earlier and less favorable critics will be more informative witnesses to the contexts in which Haydn's musical humor took root and in which stylistic deviance was salient.

3

"A Question of Taste"?
Early Views of Haydn
as Humorist

In questions of taste . . . every one must determine for himself; and what is humour is as much a question of taste as what is beauty.[1]

The prefaces of Charles Burney's A General History of Music and Sir John Hawkins's A General History of the Science and Practice of Music, both published in 1776, confronted their readers with two very different attitudes toward music—attitudes that signal prevailing tensions of the period regarding the claims of art and criteria for judging it. Implicit here are differences as well in communities of judges and "tasters." For Hawkins, music is a "science based on general and universal laws";[2] for Burney, it is an "innocent luxury, unnecessary, indeed, to our existence, but a great improvement and gratification of the sense of hearing."[3] Hawkins claims of music that "there is no science or faculty whatever that more improves the tempers of men, rendering them grave, discreet, mild and placid," and he takes it as his task to "reprobate the vulgar notion that [music's] ultimate end is merely to excite mirth." With faith in durable principles of composition, Hawkins means to submit the "capricious arbiter," Taste, to rational controls and "sober discussion." Such lofty concerns are nowhere in evidence in Burney's preface: music, "like other arts, pretends to no higher purpose than amusement," and "its history merits not, in reading, the labour of intense application, which should be reserved for more grave and important concerns."[4]

Hawkins's distrust of taste as a "capricious arbiter" and his concern for rational principles by which art should be judged are understandable in a period of widespread uncertainty about the possibility of a standard of taste.

In the spate of essays on taste that appeared in England and on the continent in the second half of the century, the claims of individual sensibility met head on the requirements of objective rules. Typical of the subjective approach is John Gilbert Cooper's endorsement of a spontaneously responsive heart in preference to the rule of reason. As he states in his *Letters Concerning Taste* (1757):

> The effect of a good Taste is that instantaneous Glow of Pleasure which thrills thro' our whole Frame, and seizes upon the Applause of the Heart, before the intellectual Power, Reason, can descend from the Throne of the Mind to ratify its Approbation.[5]

The privilege of intuitive judgment, of sensation preceding intellection, is again stressed by Alexander Gerard in his *Essay on Taste* (1759). For Gerard, "sense has a kind of instinctive infallibility," a

> noble *boldness* of genius, rising to the height of excellence, with a kind of supernatural ardor, which makes it negligent with regard to numberless *minutiae*; in fine, not to that *faultless* insipidity which escapes our blame, but to that daring *exaltation*, which however shaded by inaccuracies, or even debased by the mixture of gross transgressions, forces our admiration.[6]

Such pronouncements were bound to shake the faith in universal laws of composition and criticism. Moreover, they courted the idea that one person's taste is as good as another's—an aesthetic democracy that other writers sought to counteract by seeking standards of "correct" taste derived from "the joint verdict" of all just critics.[7] Jean-Jacques Rousseau asserted the primacy of a "general taste, about which all well-ordered people agree." Unlike individual preferences, "these are matters that are subject to rules, and the artist and connoisseur are generally agreed on them." (Individual preferences aside, Rousseau appeals to "a show of hands when there is disagreement on the taste of nature herself.")[8]

Tensions among theorists of conflicting critical orientations and national allegiances are well documented in the chronicle of Haydn's detractors and advocates, as are ambivalent attitudes regarding the so-called popular taste. The court of judgment in the late eighteenth century was such that critical response to instrumental music had to reckon with the appetites and fashions of a growing public audience. Indeed, Haydn's own career reflects this broad and fundamental transition from private to public patronage. Works written through the 1770s were composed in the main for functions and audiences at the Eszterházy court, although they also circulated widely in unauthorized manuscript and printed editions. Beginning in 1779, however, Haydn's contractual agreement with his patron permitted direct negotiations with publishers. As James Webster puts it, "Haydn's procedures in the main instrumental genres now underwent a sea change," and he rightly emphasizes that "the new contract actually symbolizes a profound alteration in the relations between composer and patron, related not only to changing patterns of the dissemination and consumption of music in the 1780s, but to Haydn's new 'public manner' in his instrumental music from those same years."[9]

Writing at the end of that decade, Burney could assure readers of the second volume of his *General History* (1789) that "the matchless HAYDN . . . is now as much respected by professors for his science as his invention." He also notes that "ideas so new and so varied were not at first so universally admired in Germany as at present," and he takes a backward look at Haydn's early detractors:

> The critics in the northern parts of the empire were up in arms. And a friend at Hamburg wrote me word in 1772, that "the genius, fine ideas, and fancy of Haydn, Ditters, and Filtz, were praised, but their mixture of serious and comic was disliked, particularly as there is more of the latter than the former in their works; and as for rules, they knew but little of them."[10]

References to the objections of "pedantic fidgets" and "strict theoreticians" appear routinely in writings about Haydn's reception by North German critics.[11] While some of these involved specific infractions of rules of part writing, more often it was the "debasement of music to comic fooling [*komischen Tändeleyen*]"[12] and the mixture of serious and comic styles that early critics deplored. In this respect, Johann Adam Hiller, for example, grouped Haydn with other Viennese composers charged with trifling disregard for serious matters: "We hear so many concertos, symphonies, etc., these days that impress us with music's dignity in serene and majestic tones; but before one suspects it, in comes Hans Wurst, who begs our indulgence with his low jokes."[13]

Early evidence of what H. C. Robbins Landon has called "a curious kind of Press battle between north and south" appeared in 1766 in an article, "On the Viennese Taste in Music," in which the author makes pointed reference to "prejudiced criticism" emanating from Berlin, Hamburg, and Leipzig.[14] Warming to his own biases, the writer inveighs against the "blunted feelings" and "dull wit" of northern critics, who "dare to write censorious opinions about our first composers, of which they understand not one single note," yet "live in the complete conviction that they have a monopoly on good taste." (The French—"still locked in the dullness of their Lully"—also come in for their share of criticism, and the Italians "more and more tend to the bizarre.") Defining taste as "a perception which differentiates with certainty between the good, the mediocre, and the bad," the author notes that "every nation, every province has its own dialect and taste, which are formed by the governing principle of its leaders." Among a number of composers noted for shaping the Viennese taste, Haydn is counted "the darling of our nation."

Resentment against an assumed "monopoly on good taste" in this heated response reflects a broader monopoly, namely the hegemony enjoyed by North German music critics, whose journals emanated almost exclusively from Leipzig, Hamburg, and Berlin. Thus critical reactions to Haydn's early works are as geographically bounded as they are aesthetically imbedded in often conservative views of instrumental composition. Promoting the virtues of contrapuntal art and elevated expression, North German reviewers put forward their own C. P. E. Bach, Graun, Hasse, and Quantz as models worthy of emulation. By comparison, "one need be only a half-connoisseur to remark the emptiness, the strange mixture of comic and serious, teasing and touching," in the new instrumental style of the Viennese—not to mention their "great ignorance of counterpoint."[15] Urging a more impartial view, one contributor explained the "bizarre" Viennese taste in terms that recall theories of the humours: "Bland food, thin air, and runny blood cause more cheerfulness than firm and salty foods and heavy air and drink, which make for thicker blood and phlegm."[16] Measured thus, the Berliner's taste is organically phlegmatic.

In consulting critical reactions of the 1770s to Haydn's early works, we find a number of perceived norms of musical decorum as well as disapproving attitudes toward deviations from them. It is useful, in evaluating such responses, to distinguish various meanings of the term *taste* that emerge in eighteenth-century writings, meanings that, although not mutually exclusive, are identifiable with different orientations and audiences. First, taste signified the capacity to make discriminating, educated judgments of the beautiful in art. The primary arbiters in matters of "good" taste were the *Kenner*—the connoisseurs who, by virtue of their training, possessed true knowledge of music. Second, taste was identified with style or manner, national and regional as well as individual. Thus we read of the French or the Italian taste, as distinct from that of the Germans or the English, in contexts that clearly indicate stylistic features perceived as peculiar to the music of each country. In partisan exchanges, critics often located differences in style as natural to the national and regional humors of composers and audiences, in turn promoting the excellences of their own local artists. Furthermore, the stylistic peculiarities of an individual artist are assigned to *personal taste*, as the "capricious taste" of C. P. E. Bach. The compositions of an individual might be judged on both idiosyncratic and more general grounds, then, as expressing a personal as well as a national temperament. Allied with both discriminating judgment and personal style is an additional sense of taste as judicious performance practice—taste in execution and expression appropriate to a given style and genre. Many of the pedagogical studies addressed to the amateur performer that appear in the second half of the eighteenth century are concerned with this meaning of taste. Finally, taste could also mean fashion: the "popular taste" or modish preferences of a public made up largely of *Liebhaber*, those who simply loved music without really knowing why. Predictably, this *Modegeschmack* was the subject of much handwringing among critics concerned with establishing more enduring principles of beauty in art.

These meanings of taste suggest three interacting spheres of influence: that of the theorists and critics, of the artists themselves, and of the various audiences that constituted a "consumer market" for instrumental music as entertainment in private and public settings. As music became increasingly accessible to a broader public, whether in concert halls or domestic music rooms, in publications of authorized editions or simplified arrangements, in private lessons or published tutors and how-to manuals, demand moved beyond the controlled sectors of court and church patronage: whoever could buy a concert ticket or purchase a published work was in a position to exercise his or her privilege of taste. While certainly not immune to changes of fashion, music theorists and critics were obliged to preserve traditional standards of "correct" taste and to improve the tastes of their readers. Indeed, the impact of fashion—and changes of style responsive to it—can often be estimated from the vigor (and rigor) of their disapproving pronouncements. It is not surprising that someone like Sir John Hawkins would perceive the function of his *General History of Music* to be a didactic and "scientific" one—nor that Charles Burney would be the more engaging chronicler of changing tastes of his day.

Objections to the unseemly mixture of styles in Haydn's instrumental works—most especially in his symphonies—reflect habitual premises of style and decorum of genre. The distinction between comic and serious styles had as its corollary the belief that certain genres of instrumental music (and venues of music making) were appropriate to one or the other of these styles; some observers felt that small solo ensembles for the chamber were more fitting vehicles for the humorous, or comic, style than the concerto or symphony.[17] A further distinction was made between "pure" and functional music, a decorum that was violated, in the opinion of some writers, by the inclusion of minuet movements in the symphony. As late as 1791, Johann Gottlieb Karl Spazier regretted the presence of minuets in symphonies as a twofold violation of decorum: they spoiled the affective symmetry of a three-movement cycle, and their functional association with dance was unseemly.[18] Underlying these premises was a lingering allegiance—more durable among North Germans—to traditional categories of affect and rules governing their expression. In addition, some critics of Haydn's early instrumental works betray a general distaste for the indecorous "popular" flavor of the new Viennese and South German style. Brief attention to the contexts of these critical premises will help to frame the view of deviant manners in early reviews of Haydn's music.

The Decorum of Style and Genre

The distinction between serious and comic styles was a durable one, even if more observed in theory than in practice, and it derived in part from the hierarchy of values accorded to music of the church, theater, and chamber.[19] In this ranking the attendant virtues of moral improvement were computed on a sliding scale in which vocal music enjoyed primacy; lacking the clarity provided by words, instrumental music could accomplish meaningful ends indirectly at best, preferably by taking vocal compositions as models for its borrowed "voices."[20] *Affekt*-associated characteristics of the serious style were derived from church polyphony and the sacred oratorio, opera seria, the ceremonial style of courtly functions, and the like; those of the comic style relied in large part on opera buffa, folk song, and lively dances.

Meter, texture, articulation, and tempo were among distinguishing markers of comic and serious styles in instrumental genres. In his *Versuch einer Anweisung die Flöte traversiere zu spielen* of 1752, Johann Joachim Quantz details some of these features in the concerto, assigning certain ritornelli to the gay and humorous style, others to the serious, high style. The latter required a more contrapuntal texture interspersed with unison passages, a full ensemble of instruments, and $\frac{4}{4}$ meter in a moderate tempo. He recommends for the gay, playful ritornello a small ensemble, simple and singing melodies that are "easy, so that quickness is not impeded," quick harmonic rhythm, and virtually any meter but common time, "since this would be too serious."[21] At the end of the century, Francesco Galeazzi reiterates the affective qualities of meters in his *Elementi teorico-practici de musica* (Rome, 1791–96): common time suits serious, solemn music; triple meter is appropriate for "familiar" and "ordinary" things; $\frac{2}{4}$ is "still lighter and more humble"; and $\frac{6}{8}$ "serves only for expressions of the comic and the humorous."[22] Heinrich Koch adds that the "jesting" manner is one that is staccato rather than legato, light and "rounded off" in articulation, and "mild rather than accented in the strength of tone" appropriate to serious expression.[23]

Despite considerable blurring of stylistic and affective categories in late eighteenth-century practice, theorists tended to reiterate traditional distinctions in manners of composition in the "strict," or "bound" style and the "free" manner—two different ways of "handling the materials of art" associated with genre, audience, and venue of music making. In his *Musikalisches Lexikon* (1802) Koch continues to maintain that church, chamber, and theater styles not only express different sorts of feelings but also reflect "contingent circumstances, such as time, place, and occasion."[24] In the learned, contrapuntal manner, intricate part writing and frequent use of suspensions produce complex harmonies in a tightly woven polyphonic texture; here contrast and ornament are subordinate to "continuance of the principal idea and the note figures that come from it." Because each voice shares equally in presenting the principal subject, a composition in this style "contains the unified expression of feeling of several persons," and thus is "supremely suited to church music." For the church style itself, Koch proscribes "sumptuous ornaments" and virtuosic display, since here "the ear should not be tickled, nor the imagination given opportunity for a whimsical play of ideas, but rather the heart should be moved."[25] Implicit in such descriptions is the notion of a homogeneous community in which the distracting idiosyncrasies of individual voices are suppressed.

In comparison with the strict style, the free, or "galant," manner featured more contrasts, more variety in melodic embellishments and rhythmic contour, simpler harmonies, and prevailingly homophonic textures. While Koch does not explicitly prescribe this manner for chamber pieces, he notes the

listener's role as a much more independent, "fanciful" one in this more intimate setting:

> If music aims to please individual persons or a whole group of them through the
> expression of a capricious sequence of gay, tender, sad, or sublime feelings, or to
> present such tone pictures as allow the imagination free play with the ideas created
> by them, then one uses for this purpose the *chamber style*; because pieces of this
> sort are meant chiefly for connoisseurs or exceptional amateurs of the art, [they]
> distinguish themselves especially in the fact that all parts of the whole are more
> finely drawn than in pieces that have another intention.[26]

By comparison, the theater style, which addressed a "larger and mixed public
audience," required "simplicity of expression." Koch goes on to note, however, that in 1802 it is "now difficult to draw a distinct boundary" between
chamber and theatrical styles.

   Theorists' attempts to maintain a separation of comic and serious styles
derived, then, from various traditional categories of affect, of function and
performance setting, and of compositional technique. If, as Koch reports,
boundary lines of style and function had blurred, so too had the ground of
critical authority become less firm in determining "correct" styles and tastes.
Along with the public appetite for novelty, the prevailing taste for comic opera was viewed with some alarm by certain theorists, especially the North
Germans. When features from the realm of comic opera invaded that of serious instrumental music, these critics judged it an unseemly breach of decorum; they appear to regard the symphony, emancipated from its functional
role as overture to serious opera, as an elevated and serious genre, the expressive dignity of which is severely compromised by stylistic features appropriate
to (and in) comic opera. The comic style is held responsible for the demise
of contrapuntal writing, as well as for the preference for fast, "wanton and
hopping" movements dismissed as plebeian in origin.[27]

   It is significant that his contemporaries generally admired Karl Ditters von
Dittersdorf for his comic operas but faulted him for the admixture of comic
and serious styles in his symphonies.[28] This accords with the premise of a
place for everything and everything in its place. But there is, in addition, a
largely unspoken assumption of a place for every*one* and everyone in his
place. Noteworthy in this connection are the comments of Dittersdorf himself about the audience for comic opera, where "the composer has more lee-
way and can allow his humor and fancy freer rein" than in opera seria:

> Just as the serious composer must seek to interest [his audience] chiefly through
> the newness of his ideas, so too—I dare say it flatly—so too will the comic com-
> poser succeed to the extent that he knows how to write pieces that are easy for
> the public to comprehend and easy to hum afterward. It is self-evident that if he
> truly possesses genius, he will find occasions in such pieces to offer something
> to the educated listener [as well], in the instrumental accompaniment, variations,
> etc.[29]

The association of simple tunefulness with the unsophisticated listener parallels that of comic theater with the popular taste.

Dittersdorf's comment recalls Mozart's famous remark to his father about the "happy medium between what is too easy and too difficult" sustained in his three piano concertos of 1782–83 (K. 413–415): "They are very brilliant, pleasing to the ear, and natural, without being vapid. There are passages here and there from which connoisseurs alone can derive satisfaction; . . . but written in such a way that the less learned cannot fail to be pleased, though without knowing why."[30] Both composers speak to the necessity of engaging listeners in venues that welcomed mixed audiences of *Kenner und Liebhaber*. And both attest to their efforts to accommodate mixed tastes in their compositions.

Leonard Ratner has remarked that the many distinctions in style observed in critical writings of the period were "geared to what was probably the most profound stylistic opposition—the high versus the low," reflecting in turn the careful observance of rank and station in eighteenth-century society.[31] Protests against the "vulgar" and "tasteless" comic style in South German and Viennese symphonic composition leave an impression of class distinctions in the high and low tastes that delineated courtly privilege on the one hand and public fashion on the other. While the avowed target of criticism was the "odd mixture of styles, of the serious and the comic, of the lofty and the vulgar," one suspects that the increasingly mixed audiences for music of all kinds was also the cause of some dismay to those seeking standards of "correct" taste.[32]

Incompatible Manners: The Musical Evidence Examined

The responses to Haydn's individual and Austrian humors cited thus far give a general picture of the reservations some writers had about unseemly mixtures of the comic and serious styles, popular and regional tastes, and indecorous trifling. A review from Leipzig in Johann Adam Hiller's *Musikalische Nachrichten und Anmerkungen auf das Jahr 1770* is the earliest to address specific works, thus affording an opportunity to examine more closely the early pieces of Haydn that provoked critical objections.[33]

A mixture of comic and serious styles is only one of the improprieties that offends the reviewer of Haydn's *Six sinfonies à huit parties* published as *oeuvre* VII by Bailleux in Paris in 1766–67.[34] Of this set, five—Symphonies Nos. 17, 29, 28, 9, and 3—are authentic works by Haydn, composed between roughly 1760 and 1765. Our writer is correct in suspecting the second of the collection (Hob. I:Es1) as spurious. But he doubts the authenticity of Symphonies Nos. 28 and 29 as well, claiming that they lack the "personal and

original manner of Herr Hayden [*sic*]."[35] His criticisms of these two works are
thus of special interest.

Symphony No. 29 is praised for its "thoroughly charming little Allegro
movement at the beginning," but faulted for its Andante and finale. Com-
plaining of the "laughable manner" in which the melody is split up between
first and second violins in the Andante, the reviewer cites a passage (Ex.
3–1a) that is not in fact from this movement—nor, indeed from any in this

EXAMPLE 3–1.

a. Citation in *Musikalische Nachrichten und Anmerkungen
auf das Jahr 1770*, p. 37

b. *Symphony* 29/ii, mm. 1–4

collection.[36] The technique that he illustrates is very much in evidence, however, in Haydn's considerably more elegant version (Ex. 3–1b). Implicit in
criticisms of such scoring is an allegiance to melody as song: fragmentation
of a tune in motivic play violates its vocal integrity, and thus, by North German lights, its expressive coherence. Although the later presentation of the
tune by the violins in octaves does not provoke comment, this was a sound
that others found objectionable.[37]

The two symphonies singled out for criticism do, however, exhibit the
kinds of peculiarities that might well have counted as trespasses against this
reviewer's code of correct stylistic manners. Of Symphony No. 28 he remarks:
"A local composer has recently put the fourth symphony into a more bear-
able form and eliminated its abuses; the last movement, in ⅜ meter, is left out
entirely in the print; would that instead he had suppressed the silly trio, together with the minuet."[38] The trio so emphatically dismissed (Ex. 3–2) is an
almost eerily simple affair, the inconclusive little tune of which H. C. Robbins
Landon likens to a "half-remembered Gypsy melody."[39] W. H. Hadow
claimed to find here a Slavonic melody;[40] perhaps it was indeed the exotic
folk flavor that was not to the Leipziger's taste. In any case, the persistent

EXAMPLE 3–2. *Symphony 28/iii, trio*

hovering of antecedent phrases that find no satisfactory closing balance results in an elusive and open-ended structure, especially in the second section. The rocking harmonic and melodic patterning, together with the fast tempo, produces in the trio a feeling of $\frac{6}{8}$ meter—noted earlier as a feature associated with the "comic style." Heard thus, the overlapping of phrases (at mm. 46–47) that displaces tonic arrival (to m. 49) creates the mildly upsetting asymmetry of a concluding three-bar phrase. (The reviewer might have found objectionable irregularities in the trio of Symphony No. 29 as well, where a virtually amelodic progression of five-bar phrases yields an equally suspended and exotic quality, evocative of the musette.)

The minuet itself offers an emphatic contrast, but its improprieties are not far to find (Ex. 3–3). The *allegro molto* tempo (a most unusual marking in

EXAMPLE 3–3. *Symphony 28/iii, minuet, mm. 1–8*

Haydn's symphonic minuets, occurring again only in Symphony No. 94) and unison bariolage of stopped and open repeated notes are peculiar, for a start, and raucous in effect. Leaping lines and heavy-footed emphasis on the second beat of the measure bear no trace of courtly elegance: this dance sounds rather more like a country hoedown. All told, both minuet and trio would seem to justify complaints of indecorous manners.

"Abuses" of a decorum that preserves unity of *Affekt* are not merely conspicuous in the Poco Adagio of Symphony No. 28—they motivate the movement's very discourse. But while Haydn exploits the contrast of comic and serious styles, he also allows the two to influence each other in the progress of the piece. Even if the result is not an entirely convincing synthesis, the movement does illustrate the dramatic possibilities of such an attempt. The opening measures present the contrasting forces seen in Example 3-4, mm. 1–12. Here a broad legato statement of muted unison violins, lying low on the strings, moves in graceful counterpoint with the accompanying voices. Suspensions and appoggiaturas both enrich the harmonic progression and promote seamless continuity of the phrase. The entrance of high-pitched, staccato, harmonically static, and rhythmically nervous voices is thus not simply a non sequitur, it is a radical departure from the stately and somber character of the opening statement, and one that will repeatedly interrupt the proceedings. (By far the most intrusive is the entrance that subverts the dramatically prepared return in mm. 71–73.)

This movement would seem to be a prime example of Hiller's "odd mixture of styles, of the serious and the comic, of the lofty and the vulgar, so often found side by side in one and the same piece."[41] Yet despite a seeming incompatibility of manners in these opening measures, Haydn allows the comic style to impinge on the serious in ways that expand the formal and expressive dimensions of the movement. The influences of static repetition, parallel thirds and sixths, and staccato articulation are evident in the protracted closing passage to the first section (see Ex. 3-4, mm. 23–45). The approach to the cadence is first prolonged, then playfully sidetracked as more and more the comic voice obtrudes; to reestablish stability requires a substantial addendum. While the graceful style of the opening thematic statement prevails in the end, the formal design has had to accommodate the wayward voice, the imprint of which is audible (if subdued) at the close.

If Hiller found in Haydn's symphonies an unseemly blurring of boundaries between the comic and serious styles, there is an additional commixture that violated his sense of stylistic decorum. In an earlier issue of his *Wöchentliche Nachrichten* (1768), he had written: "Minuets and trios placed between the larger movements give to the whole an air of gaiety, which is better suited to symphonies than if a man wants to display his art inopportunely with retrograde canons and other harmonic artifices."[42] The inclusion of a minuet movement in the symphony appears to offend Hiller less than the use in such movements of learned techniques appropriate to the serious style. The minuet from the sixth work in the set reviewed, Symphony No. 3, is a case in point. Here the violins, doubled by oboes, are in canon at the octave with

EXAMPLE 3–4. *Symphony 28/ii, mm. 1–12; 23–45*

the violas and cellos throughout. Similar techniques are found in a number of minuets in early Haydn symphonies. In particular, Symphony No. 23 (1764), which Hiller may well have known, features another such canon in the minuet, as well as a three-part canon in the trio.[43]

The "retrograde canons" of which Hiller speaks are not present in any of these early symphonies of Haydn. It is interesting, however, that this procedure does appear in a minuet Haydn composed not long after the review of 1770. Symphony No. 47 (1772) contains the bizarre minuet and trio—both *al roverso*—used again by Haydn in his keyboard Sonata in A Major (Hob. XVI:26) of 1773.[44] The closing movement of Sonata in E-flat Major (Hob. XVI:25), also of 1773, is written as an invertible canon in "Tempo di Menuet." And, again, the minuet of Symphony No. 44 (c. 1771) features a *canone in diapason* throughout between violins and cellos. Haydn was experimenting in the early 1770s with fugal finales in string quartets as well, the most notable examples being the rigorously "learned" movements that conclude three of his Op. 20 quartets.[45]

It is possible, if ironic in view of the response of such critics as Hiller, that Haydn's experiments with canonic minuets were attempts to dignify this movement of the symphony—to transform its functional association into a patently artful one by infusions of the serious style. A similar impulse may account for the fugal finales of Symphonies Nos. 3 and 14. That any such effort would be regarded as an inappropriate mixture is implicit in our reviewer's remarks about minuet movements in general, as well as in the diehard assumption that learned manners should be reserved for more serious matters.

A revealing side to North German disdain for minuets in symphonies is the comparison of this movement by one of Hiller's reviewers to a "beauty patch" worn on the face of a dandy: minuets give symphonies a "foppish appearance and interfere with the manly impression that an unbroken succession of three related and more serious movements always makes."[46] Traditional associations of the minuet with the courtly manners of the ancien régime may have sat uneasily with the social and moral values of German burghers, as well as with the emergent nationalism in Hiller's day—a trend that he himself participated in as an important composer of *Singspiele* and promoter of German song. If, in the context of a lofty (and "manly") symphony, the minuet called up images of artificial and effete manners at the French court, there is scant evidence in Haydn's minuets of the preciosity this reviewer appears to associate with the movement.

Those critics for whom the inclusion of the minuet in the symphony constituted a departure from decorum—in particular, Germans considerably north of the Viennese orbit—responded to its appearance in the works of Haydn and other composers to the south as something of an intrusion. Minuet movements were not normally found in North German symphonies; those of C. P. E. Bach, for instance, are two- or three-movement cycles without minuets. Fellow Berliners, such as Hasse and the Graun brothers—much admired by Hiller—also wrote three-movement symphonies in the traditional fast-slow-fast arrangement. Around the middle of the century, the presence of a minuet in a symphony would be at least a novelty and, for the North Germans in particular, would bespeak a southern levity ill suited to a serious genre. As late as 1791, Spazier argued that minuets were unsuitable in symphonies because they

> simply recall at the wrong time the realm of dance, and thus misuse music; and if they are caricatured, as is often the case with those by Pleyel and Haydn, they provoke laughter. If this latter be the case, there can no longer be any question of whether minuets are appropriate in lofty symphonies.[47]

Thus the association of Austrian composers with the "comic style" might have particular force in a movement already regarded as beneath the dignity of symphonic composition. In this sense, Haydn's minuets would be heard as bearing the stamp of a national "humor."

While such musical manners are described as "humoristic," they appear to pose real—as opposed to playful—challenges to good taste and aesthetic standards for the "true" German symphony, and they prompt dismissive critical judgment as odd, tasteless, burlesque, mocking, vulgar. For these judges there can be no question of "the prosperity of a jest," of teasing wit, of ingenious revelations and discoveries: the incongruous is simply the incompatible, and the laughable simply the ridiculous.

If the Viennese taste posed an indecorous confusion of styles for some critics, Haydn's individual humor began to be noted by others. Among these writers, responses to Haydn's music in the 1770s and early 1780s reveal significant shifts in the taste for humor in instrumental music. The first to address the subject of musical humor takes Haydn as his exemplar, but takes issue with the "humorous" style in symphonies. Here the terms of earlier critics are radically transposed.

The Bias of Temperament

In the same year that saw the publication of Hawkins's *General History* and the first volume of Burney's, Karl Ludwig Junker recorded his impressions of some contemporary composers in his *Zwanzig Componisten: Eine Skizze* (1776). Interesting in itself, Junker's entry on Haydn becomes the occasion for a lengthy excursion on the subject of musical humor.[48] Citing William Congreve, Ben Jonson, and Lord Kames, among others, Junker follows the English lead, locating humor partly in "those tendencies of the mind by which a man views all things from a somewhat peculiar side," and partly in "those sorts of feelings in which he says what he thinks and does what he is inclined to do without holding back—things that other men would neither say nor do because they are restrained by custom or the opinion of others."

While Junker concludes that the humorist will be considered "somewhat bizarre and improper," he does not share Kames's view that the indecorous aspect of humor reduces esteem for the humorist and arouses the laughter of ridicule. Junker maintains, rather, that "impropriety" can be interesting, even important. One can recognize in this assertion a distinction between the aesthetic and the everyday encounter: framed by aesthetic interest, the bizarre departures of a humorist may be laughable without being contemptible.[49]

This said, it is the irrepressible dominance of a single mood or feeling, the one-sided *Empfindung* ruling the humorist, that Junker objects to in Haydn's music:

> No one will deny that the single governing . . . feeling in Hayden [sic] is marked, bizarre;—that it manifests itself without restraint. Does someone wish to refer to Hayden's *adagio*? Good, because it is serious, interesting humor [*Laune*]; like the tragic sentiments of a Shakespear. . . . But can anyone tell me one single work of Hayden in which *humor* would not always be a marked trait? One will find none.

> If a single, determinate feeling [*Empfindung*] can never be the subject of a symphony, then humor above all cannot be the true stamp of the same, and Hayden's symphonies, because his feeling is so one-sided, will be less than symphonies.[50]

Junker's concept of Haydn's musical humor suggests the wayward bias of the humorist we have encountered in English sources. He too assumes an intimate connection between the composer's personality and his musical style: deviant behavior must have its way in the behavior of the art. But in Junker's view, the music of a humorist becomes in a sense denatured in being too one-sided, deprived of the variety and complexity of feeling that are natural conditions of life: "Who knows the many-sided influence on the heart and the complexities under which a man of the world must labor; and who would want to assume that any one sentiment or feeling would dominate and be active always in the same way?"[51] It is the natural "ebb and flow" of humor, as of life, that Junker promotes as commendable in a symphony.

One senses here a rather different "psychology" of music from that promoted by earlier theorists of the affections, who required unity of emotion rather than continuous change and variety of contrasting moods. While Junker argues for the natural and spontaneous expression of feeling in music, his ideal of the universal and natural diversity and flux of sentiments to which art must appeal is incompatible with the overly particular bias of a humorist's nature.

Elsewhere in his *Skizze,* in the article on Dittersdorf, Junker levels a more direct attack on Haydn. Here he seconds earlier critics' distaste for the "new fashion" of Austrian music. And like them, he takes Haydn to task for musical trifling and for failing to elevate Viennese music to a level of refined expression:

> Since Hayden altered the tone of Viennese music, or set a new fashion, it is truly more characteristic than before, but it has sunk too much, from the dignity preserved by Wagenseil, to the trifling. Since Hayden, music has perhaps undergone the same change that the theater has endured, but it has certainly gained less in doing so.
>
> To arouse laughter, in whatever way, was the latter's aim. . . . The comic maiden, having been banished from the theatrical sphere, seems to have begged acceptance into music; the priest [Haydn], a man who seems to be made for humor, was softened—seized the droll thing—and shoved her into his temple;—and ever since, we laugh at Viennese music.
>
> But is the laughable the true, satisfying feeling of music? Is it not, rather, too wearisome, too one-sided to be a national music? Is it not beneath art, too base?[52]

Junker's colorful, if opaque, account suggests that Haydn accomplished at a stroke and single-handedly the unfortunate transfer of a comic, theatrical style to music that should serve a more lofty purpose. While it is here implicitly the church style that has suffered, in Junker's view, the dignity of Viennese music in general, preserved under Haydn's predecessors, appears to have fallen victim to fashion.

Notwithstanding Junker's progressive views in advocating a dynamic psychology of the affections, his attitude toward Haydn's symphonies suggests a stability of traditions and tastes under siege. In fact, however, midcentury attitudes in Germany toward instrumental music in general and the symphony in particular were characteristically ambivalent, far from stable;[53] moreover, the chief efforts of composers in the North focused on German opera and *Lied*. Within both movements, the appeal of *volkstümlich* melodies, simply accompanied, promoted a new aesthetic of the naïve and sentimental, and in opera the comic and serious styles were joined in a productive synthesis. The decidedly conservative bias that had informed North German reactions to Viennese instrumental music—especially its popular air—takes something of a turn in the early 1780s. Along with belated acceptance of Viennese currents in instrumental composition, North Germans take a more respectful stance in viewing Haydn's works. With the benefit of retrospective judgment, critics now make a distinction between his earlier style—viewed by some as undisciplined and trifling—and his current, mature manner. And they associate the development of his musical style with the maturation of his humor. The terms of changing tastes and audiences may be estimated in newly indulgent views of Haydn's "natural" humor.

Changing Views of the Musical Humorist

Friedrich Nicolai, in his travel journal of 1781, describes Haydn's impact on Viennese tastes in terms rather different from those of Junker and Hiller:

> The music [of the Viennese] conformed entirely to the sensual character of the nation. Cassations, little songs, minuets, and Styrian dances passed with high and low for works of musical art; serious and lofty ideas aroused boredom. Finally a man stood up whose like Austria had not known for a long time, a man of wide-ranging imagination, rich in invention, in new techniques, and in sublime song. Joseph Haydn started out, as his works show, in the taste of the familiar folk music. He knew how to make the goodness of these sources his own, but he soon went far beyond these. At times he reverted unexpectedly to the low style, formerly widely beloved, probably to please a part of his public—an indulgence that such a great artist had no need of. He has in great part transformed the taste of his nation, and he ought to strive to lead it even further.[54]

Even if Nicolai regrets with earlier critics the "low style" that indulges the popular taste, he sees Haydn as one who has transformed and elevated national folk idioms to artful ones. Increasingly recognized as individual, the personal humor of Haydn's music is identified with ingenuity of invention and more refined tastes.

The comments of an anonymous writer (whose style resembles Junker's) in the *Musikalischer Almanach auf das Jahr 1782* are indicative of the changing estimate of Haydn's humor. Separating the "high" comic from the low, burlesque variety, the author rescues Haydn from earlier criticisms of his role in promoting the vulgar inclinations of Viennese music:

[Haydn is] a musical jester, but as is Yorick [Laurence Sterne], not for bathos, but rather for the high comic, and this is desperately difficult.... Since it must be absolutely the result of one's own unique temperament complex [*Temperament-mischung*], young composers should be all the more wary of the perils of imitation.

Haydn composes in this way because he must, if he wishes to compose naturally.[56]

There are some obvious changes here: Haydn's compositional humor has become naturally imperative, his jests aesthetically elevated and subtle. In a retrospective move, the author goes on to note "two styles, or two epochs in Haydn's works"; in the first, the composer "laughs heartily," whereas in the works of the second period, "he simply has a smile on his face . . . the older man is more serious." Noting the difficulty of composing in the "high comic" manner—and the perils of trying to imitate a manner natural to Haydn—the author also comments that his subtle jesting eludes many listeners. Perhaps most significant is the very recognition that instrumental music can accommodate jesting manners as legitimate, artful means of engaging listeners.

Distinctions between Haydn's earlier and later humor are picked up by other commentators, among them Johann Reichardt, editor of the *Musikalisches Kunstmagazin* in Berlin. In the issue of 1782, Reichardt reviews Haydn's Op. 33 string quartets and six of his symphonies, both of which sets had been published in Berlin that year.[56] Unlike Hiller's reviewer, then, Reichardt is reviewing up-to-date compositions addressed to the public. And he has nothing but praise for the "most original humor, the most lively, most agreeable wit" of the works under review. Sounding a note that will be echoed by others, Reichardt hails Haydn for a style that while artful is also natural, charming, and popular. He too takes a retrospective glance "to observe with a critical eye Haydn's works in the order of their composition":

His very first works, which we got to know some twenty years ago, already show his characteristic, good-natured humor; at that time, however, he displayed mostly youthful mischievousness, and often exuberant merriment, with superficial harmonic treatment; gradually the humor becomes more mature and the work more thoughtful, until, finally, through elevated and controlled emotion as well as more mature study of the art, and above all, the careful handling of special musical effects, the mature, original man and confident artist is apparent in all his works.[57]

Many of these points are repeated as received truths in later reviews and biographical essays, along with Haydn's "invention" of a new minuet form, octave doublings, and novel integration of melody and accompaniment. But in labeling Haydn's "later style," that is, works of the late 1770s and early1780s, Reichardt marks a new species of the humorous, different from (and presumably more estimable than) the "mischievous" manner of his earlier works. Haydn's "original humor" is clearly respected: not only is his music charming and popular, it is good, interesting composition.

Retrospective comparisons of style, in which the estimate of Haydn's earlier works is adjusted to a more accepting tone, may have been attempts to reconcile critical judgments with the undeniable fact of the composer's suc-

cess with audiences outside Germany. In Paris, for example, where his symphonies and quartets had been performed and published from the mid-1760s
on, reviews from 1773–77 document enthusiastic reception of Haydn's music.[58] And in London, where the sale of his works began as early as 1765,
Haydn was a well-known composer by the time Reichardt wrote his review
in 1782.[59] It is not simply that the North Germans have revised their critical
views, but that a broader public has registered approval of Haydn's works:
charming and popular, witty and humorous, comic and serious, original and
natural—there are terms of engagement here to please a wide range of listeners and players.

Burney's perspective in 1789 suggests that as Haydn's music became more
widely known, his manner also became more "familiar"—in the eighteenth-
century sense of being at one's ease—with performers and critics alike:

> [I]t may be laid down as a maxim in music that "whatever is *easy* is *old*," and what
> the hand, eye, and ear are accustomed to; and, on the contrary, what is *new* is of
> course *difficult*, and not only scholars but professors have it to learn. The first
> exclamation of an embarrassed performer and a bewildered hearer is, that the Mu-
> sic is very *odd*, or very *comical*; but the queerness and comicality cease, when, by
> frequent repetition, the performer and hearer are at their ease.[60]

Prompting nervous reactions on first hearing, novelties and difficulties are
here synonymous with "funny-strange"—an estimate revised on repeated
hearings. Burney has the advantage of hindsight in applying his "maxim" to
early criticisms of Haydn's music, but in stressing the importance of repetition and familiarity, he locates basic elements of Haydn's success with listeners—elements that, as we shall see, are increasingly embodied in the works
themselves.

By the end of the 1780s the general acceptance of Haydn's style in Germany is such that a reviewer in the *Musikalische Real-Zeitung* can assert that
Haydn's "original manner of writing, his beautiful modulations, and his rich-
ness of idea are already all too well known that we should need to say any-
thing further in recommendation of the pieces under consideration."[61]
Rather than being classified with the aberrant Viennese, Haydn is elevated to
the status of standard bearer of an indigenous German style in instrumental
music—Berliners even put him on a par with their own C. P. E. Bach. And
in the next decade writers will move beyond the retrospective view of
Haydn's own stylistic development to place him as "the glory of our age"[62]
in the historical development of instrumental music in general. Whereas Junker had regretted the one-sided *Empfindung* of Haydn's symphonies, writers
from the 1790s on celebrate the natural, unaffected cheerfulness of his music
and its popularity with the general public. "Simple," "modest," "pious," and
"jovial" become ready adjectives for biographers of the "worthy patriarch of
composers."[63]

The persistent identification of style with temperament is as clear as are
signs of changing tastes in Reichardt's evaluation of "die drei echte Humor-
isten," Haydn, Mozart, and Beethoven. In letters that recount his trip to

Vienna in 1808 and 1809 (the year of Haydn's death), Reichardt records his impressions of an evening's concert devoted to string quartets of these composers at the palace of Count Andrei Razumovsky. He is moved to compare the manner in which "the three true humorists developed the genre, each according to his individual nature":

> Haydn created it from the pure, bright source of his delightful, original nature. Naïveté and gay humor are thus always his unique features. Mozart's more powerful nature and richer fantasy enabled him to express in many works the heights and depths of his inner being; he himself was a more accomplished virtuoso, and therefore demanded more of his players; he also valued artful modulations more highly and thus built his palace on Haydn's lovely, fantastic summer house. Beethoven himself was at home in this palace early on; thus it remained for him only to express his own nature in a unique way, in building defiant towers on which no one could place anything further without breaking his neck.[64]

If Reichardt's architectural image of stylistic development suggests a high rise erected on Haydn's shoulders, the significance for him of the *true* musical humorist is that each of these three expresses his own unique nature, or humor, in his music. The Romantic temper would find congenial the images of Beethoven as iconoclast and Mozart as melancholy genius—in whose company Haydn was consigned to the role of the jovial and naïve predecessor, or, in Reichardt's terms, the summer house to Mozart's palace and Beethoven's towers. "In the opinion of some judges, Beethoven is more sublime," wrote Charles Butler in 1818, but "on account of its greater simplicity, colloquial cast, good nature and incessant epigram, the music of Haydn will always be more popular."[65] Butler's prediction would prove a bit wide of the mark, yet he summarizes the qualities that contemporary listeners found in both the music and the man.

In the transition from private to public patronage that affected the composition of audiences (and music) during Haydn's long career, specific venues of music making have implications for his success with various listeners. But the recognition of Haydn's wit in his "careful handling of special effects," and of his humor as agreeable rather than trivial, is itself suggestive. That German critics of the 1780s distinguish a "mature" humor both original *and* serious in Haydn's newest works signals a certain maturity of musical style in general, of language and conventions sufficiently stable to invite the play of wit, as well as listeners responsive to that play. It is in this broader context of instrumental music as an entertaining medium, pleasurable in its own right, that Haydn's wit would prove to be an engaging strategy. In the chapters that follow, I propose four models for analysis of that strategy in Haydn's instrumental works. Each offers a particular frame of reference within which to explore the means and effects of "ingenious jesting with art" and to gauge the range of musical humor for listeners of his day.

II

Frames of Reference

4

Humorous Manners and the "Really **New** *Minuet"*

While late eighteenth-century critics disagreed about the aesthetic propriety of Haydn's symphonic minuets, they reached consensus in finding them original. Those favorably disposed to Haydn's personal stamp singled out his minuets as primary evidence. Saluting the uniqueness of each of Haydn's works, one reviewer from the Paris *Mercure* of 1779 maintained that "often one recognizes Haydn simply by his minuets"; another noted in the Leipzig *Musikalischer Almanach* of 1782 that "Haydn found for his minuets an almost entirely new form."[1] Charles Burney's opinion was somewhat equivocal in viewing the Haydn minuet as a "sportive, even grotesque" interlude, the purpose of which was to highlight the "serious business of his other movements."[2] But Ernst Gerber found them estimable in displaying "comic humor [*komische Laune*] . . . without any help from words."[3] Haydn himself, in asserting the artist's freedom from the constraints of "pedestrian rules," commented: "Such affectations are worthless. I would rather someone tried to compose a really *new* minuet."[4]

With at least one such movement in each of his nearly seventy string quartets, over one hundred symphonies, and vast number of assorted divertimenti, it is not surprising that Haydn should have noted the challenge of composing "a really *new* minuet." Nor is it surprising that contemporary listeners located his novel and humorous manners most often in this movement. For one thing, its modest scale and scheme of internal repetitions guaranteed that any irregularity, whether egregious or subtle, would be heard twice in fairly quick succession—and, in the minuet da capo, once and perhaps twice more.[5] Thus, while many of the incongruous procedures found here were used by Haydn in other movements, their appearance in the minuet would have been especially audible.

Underlying such perceptions, moreover, was the minuet's dual association

55

with art music and with the step patterns and gestures of an ongoing tradition of dance. Even though removed from a functional context, departures in the artful minuet from patterns normative in the dance might be especially striking to those involved as participants in that tradition. Writing in 1779, the composer, theorist, and pedagogue Abbé Georg Joseph Vogler captured something of the complex interplay for the listener of the "felt" and the

EXAMPLE 4–1. *Minuet,* in Vogler, *Betrachtungen der Mannheimer Tonschule* 4:118

"heard" minuet. Discussing the minuet (seen in Ex. 4–1) of a piano sonata, Vogler calls particular attention to its unusual phrase structure as a departure from what would be required of a danced minuet:

> One notices even in the first phrase—[which is really] the first and second taken together—a rhythm of five bars, within which the regular movement of the feet cannot settle into their prescribed steps. That such a contradictory rhythmic number as 5 can creep in here without distracting the listener's attention—much less shocking him—is owing to the particularly artful shift . . . [in measure 4 that] fuses an idea of four bars into three.[6]

Detailing the variety of artful devices in the minuet's second section, Vogler goes on to note that the rhythm of "normal minuets" serves "the animation of lively feet, the measurement of their steps, . . . and the adroit turns of all limbs of a lithe form." Artful imitation and active inner voices, on the other hand, are "novelties that make the listener ever more eager for newness." Engaging a double awareness—of the dance as a basis for physical expectations and of artfulness in departures from them—minuet movements might exert particular charms on listeners and composers, then, in the exercise of sensual and intellectual challenges.

Haydn's impatience with "pedestrian rules" points to a second context in which the minuet played a prominent role, namely as a didactic model in the pedagogy of composition. As such, it was an ideally compact prototype of normative compositional procedures in binary form: here simple patterns of melody and accompaniment, rhythm and phrase, modulation and cadence could be worked out on a metric and harmonic grid that derived from the eight-bar period structure of functional dance. Indeed, such a structure was sufficiently regular to support "chance" combinations, the arrangement of precomposed, formulaic modules being determined by a throw of the dice. The broad appeal of composition by the numbers is suggested by the title of Pierre Hoegi's *A Tabular System Whereby the Art of Composing Minuets Is Made So Easy That Any Person, without the Least Knowledge of Musick, May Compose Ten Thousand, All Different, and in the Most Pleasing and Correct Manner* (London, c. 1770).[7]

However "correct" the results of such entertainments for the would-be composer, they pleased more as parlor games than as original, artful inventions. But the minuet also served more serious pedagogical aims as a small-scale laboratory for trying out artful techniques of contrapuntal elaboration. In this context of ingenious artifice, traditions of patterned dance and contrapuntal artifice meet in an often incongruous overlap. The mixture displeased some of Haydn's critics, we may recall, who expected a clear separation of functional and artful styles.

Finally, there is the context of Haydn's own compositional development and his use of the minuet and trio movement as a vehicle for displaying incongruous novelties. For the historically distanced investigator, there is assistance from the minuets that Haydn wrote specifically for dancing. These provide a measure of the functional against which to judge the "dysfunctional" deviations that distinguish the artful minuet from its danced counterpart. Not surprising, it is those aspects of the minuet most intimately related to its tradition of courtly decorum that Haydn often chooses to manipulate, such that the incongruous is manifest in a radical transformation of the stately dance. *Allegro* tempos and pronounced "rustic" elements—drones, yodeling melodies, stomping syncopations—may be completely compatible with dance, but subvert the measured dignity and refinement that a proper minuet preserves. Here too we can consult Haydn's own output of *Teutsche*, or German dances, as models of what was considered folklike within the context of art music, however much or little it resembled the actual music of the *Volk*.[8] Against this background, changes in the status of the danced minuet itself are of interest as reflections of changing social patterns and fashions in the late eighteenth century.

Clearly, the "Haydn minuet" inhabited a range of intersecting contexts and traditions: courtly dance and decorum, pedagogical prototype, artful stylization of the dance in a full spectrum of instrumental genres, even combinatorial games of chance. During Haydn's long career, none of these remains a stable category untouched by others. Yet each contributes to the minuet's meanings for eighteenth-century listeners—a complex of associations that is remote from most concertgoers today. Quite apart from specifically historical speculations about the responses of eighteenth-century audiences, however, listeners today can appreciate disturbances of the "humors" in Haydn's minuets. For here the composer takes the very premises of dance as his "topic," surprising physical habits into recognition of humorous manners.

Devices most obviously incompatible with what is normative in a dance piece are those that unexpectedly interrupt, suspend, or confuse the regularly marked continuity and organization of time. An abrupt halt may be surprising in any piece, but it is an especially palpable arrest in patterned gestures of dance. Similarly disruptive is the confusion that results when the regularity of meter is obscured or actually displaced, or when the predictability of regular patterns of measures is thwarted by irregular or ambiguous phrasing. While such devices would be perverse in a minuet for dancing, they draw the listener's attention to artful means that suit the particularity of a given movement.

In both types of incongruous procedure—those that betray normal expectations of dance pieces in general and those that subvert norms of the courtly minuet in particular—there is a correlation with chronology in Haydn's works: in the later symphonies and quartets we find not only more frequent (and egregious) examples of a specific deviation, but also the combination of several incongruous elements in a single work. Thus Haydn's affinity for the incongruous and surprising—seen by his contemporaries as signal evidence of his original humor—constitutes in itself a compositional tradition of the "Haydn minuet."

However complex the interplay of various contexts in the minuet's associations for listeners in Haydn's day, it is against the backdrop of functional dance that the "really *new* minuet" becomes salient. Attention to the nature of the minuet as a dance and to features of the music Haydn composed to accompany it helps to clarify contemporary responses to his "original oddities" and complaints such as Spazier's, quoted on page 45, that Haydn's symphonic minuets "provoke laughter" as caricatures of the courtly dance.

Haydn's designation for the minuet movement varies: *Minuet* is rare, used only in the earliest works; *Menuet* and *Menuetto* are used interchangeably, without apparent significance, in early and late works. *Tempo di menuetto* is reserved for movements in $\frac{3}{4}$ meter (less often $\frac{3}{8}$) that may loosely resemble the form of the minuet. Such movements most often serve as finales in three-movement cycles, as in some of Haydn's early symphonies and, more frequently, in keyboard sonatas. (It might be noted that the use of such an indication suggests some common understanding of what the "*Menuetto*"'s tempo was—a matter whose complexities I will consider later.)

The Danced Minuet

While writers around 1700 speak of the minuet as a lively and fast dance, by midcentury it is described as a serious dance of "grave and noble simplicity."[9] Wye Jamison Allanbrook distinguishes two types of minuet in use around

1770: the first derived from the earlier, faster dance, and might be notated in $\frac{3}{4}$ or $\frac{3}{8}$; the second, more grave variety "admitted eighth notes to its figuration" and presumably slowed in pace to accommodate them.[10] This second type is heard in Mozart's famous collage of dances in the ballroom scene of *Don Giovanni,* a compositional tour de force that dramatizes the realities of a social hierarchy.[11] The minuet, representing aristocratic traditions, is the appropriate dance for the masked guests (and also their host, whose fall is prefigured in his decision not to join them); the German dance serves Leporello's purposes of distracting the peasant, Masetto; and the fashionable contredanse, mediating between court and country, offers a convenient middle ground for the Don to pursue his seduction of Zerlina. Thus participants in the more animated dances carry out the dramatic "actions" of the scene until its strained balance is ruptured by Zerlina's scream. In comparison with the lively dances in $\frac{3}{8}$ and $\frac{2}{4}$, whose swinging melodies reinforce the first beat of their respective measures, the minuet that supports them sounds strained, even stiff, its melody relatively static in two-bar phrases over a steady "walking" bass line. The tension of musical and social manners is suggestive of fashion's challenge to the minuet's courtly dignity, as it was overtaken (here literally on its own ground) by simpler steps and movements of the body in group and line dances.

The intricate nature of the dance explains in part its demise. Retaining the formality of courtly decorum, the minuet remained a couple dance throughout the century, often danced by one couple at a time while others looked on, appreciative of the subtle nuances and finesse required of the executants. Goethe captured the distinction of the minuet in describing it as a "work of art," performed only by those few properly tutored in its refinements:

> Nobody ventures unconcernedly to dance unless he has been taught the art; the minuet in particular is regarded as a work of art and is performed, indeed, only by a few couples. Such a couple is surrounded by the rest of the company in a circle, admired, and applauded at the end.[12]

Eighteenth-century dance manuals furnish detailed—though not entirely conformant—descriptions of its execution.[13] Two eight-bar periods of music were needed to complete the characteristic Z or reversed S floor pattern, within which figure the dancers repeated a pattern of four steps (two *mouvements*) to each two measures of music. What might seem an obvious placement of the four steps according to downbeat stress in $\frac{3}{4}$ meter (♩ ♩ | ♩ ♩) is not coincident with felt stresses of rising and bending motions of the body in executing the step pattern. Citing early eighteenth-century dance treatises, Wendy Hilton notes that "in the pas de menuet the accents made by the rises in the demi-coupés occur on the first and third quarter notes," and that the dance "derives enormous strength, beneath its controlled surface, from the hypnotic cross-rhythm" of contending stress patterns:[14]

Hilton's observation is of considerable interest in view of the frequent manipulations of metric pattern in Haydn's artful minuet movements. Eighteenth-century sources do not offer universal agreement on this point, however, as various possibilities are suggested for placing the steps within the two-measure pattern.[15] Lack of agreement in primary sources and among dance historians on the issue of hemiola points up the difficulties, and perhaps futility, of seeking a "common practice" of the minuet in various countries and locales. Most English and German dance treatises rely on French predecessors; as with documentation of eighteenth-century performance in general, local practices may have departed considerably from the prescriptions of earlier dancing masters. Regardless of step placement, however, the composer's chief responsibility was to maintain a steady quarter-note pulse in music that clearly articulated a two-measure unit for each step pattern of the dance.

Authors of manuals on the dance suggest, perhaps not without self-interest, that the motions accompanying the minuet's step patterns were sufficiently subtle to require considerable practice—and the tutelage of a dancing master. They also emphasize that mastery of the dance is a mark of refined breeding. The social distinction awarded to the minuet is widely noted in contemporary sources, especially those of dancing masters who promote the dance as an essential exercise of both moral and physical virtues. One such writer, C. J. von Feldtenstein, extols the merits of the minuet in palpably aristocratic terms:

> [The minuet] is well known over half the world, and in all classes, and although the greater part of men still considers it the easiest part of dancing, yet in the judgment of connoisseurs it takes the prize from all the others. And who can deny the minuet this honor? No one except the man who finds good taste only in the dancing of a boisterous peasant, and blindly admires the impetuous over the decorous in all movements of the body. The minuet is the queen of all dances; the test of every dancer who wants to acquire a reputation; ... and ... the best occasion for displaying everything beautiful and charming in nature which a body is capable of employing.[16]

Feldtenstein's complaint in 1767, that the minuet has suffered under the feet of negligent dancers who think it an easy affair, suggests some slippage in courtly decorum. Marking the distinction of "good taste" in refined dance, he also notes (with obvious distaste) the appeal for others of "boisterous" country dances.

While Vienna's aristocratic society may have preserved the noble bearing of a courtly style in the minuet, simplified versions may have emerged in public ballrooms. The "democratization" of Vienna's Redoutensaal was officially authorized in 1772 under Joseph II, admitting all who were appropriately masked and who could pay the entrance fee of two gulden.[17] As ballrooms in the late eighteenth century increasingly included the "mixed company" of nobility and those of lower station, some less tutored in courtly manners may have preferred the relative anonymity and simplicity of group and line dances such as the contredanse. These were dances enjoyed by aristocrats as well, of course, as were the *menuet en quatre* and *menuet en huit*, which involved broader participation in group figures. Still, refined execution of the courtly couple dance might be counted on to mark class distinctions among the masked guests. As reported in the *Neuesten Sittengemählde von Wien* of 1801, social pretenders were easy to spot: "[I]t was often very amusing to me to watch the strange turns and dainty bends with which many light-footed tailors wound through the grave minuet . . . entirely without propriety, without the proper step, without grace and dignity in their movements; . . . without fulfilling a single one of the conditions of the dance."[18]

It is tempting to speculate about the sort of dance the minuet may have become in its late stages, especially as most of the surviving minuets that Haydn composed for dancing were written in this period. If hand and body motions of the dance became less intricate, for example, the tempo of the dance could become faster, and its character less stately; and if the minuet as a dance was susceptible to stylistic modification, the music to accompany it would have changed in turn, becoming less "grave and noble."[19] In any case, by the turn of the century the single couple dance that Goethe admired had become something of a nostalgic relic, as a new generation of dancers took the floor to waltz.

Features of the music written to accompany a danced minuet in the late eighteenth century can be examined in a number of such pieces that Haydn composed for Viennese balls in the 1780s and 1790s.[20] Here, where the music must serve the dancers, regular articulation of an even quarter-note pulse in two–measure units is normative, as is the symmetry of balanced phrases within each eight-bar period.[21] Upbeat figures are common, serving to locate the first beat of the measure, and harmonies are simple. Major keys predominate, with trio sections most often in the same key and mode as their companion minuets. Frequently the trios offer contrasts of reduced scoring and dynamic level; typically, a smoother melodic contour distinguishes them from the fanfarelike dotted rhythms of melodies often found in the minuet sections.

Example 4–2, from the minuet that opens a collection of Haydn's "danceable minuets," *Raccolta de menuetti ballabili*, Hob. IX:7 (1784), illustrates some of these features. Straightforward harmonies and homophonic textures underscore a pattern of two-measure units in balanced symmetries of phrase; clear articulation of meter and pulse is secured by the regular motion of the bass and the upbeat figure that reinforces the downbeat of the measure. A moderate tempo is suggested by the regularity of harmonic change above a "walking bass" line and by the graceful, somewhat dainty articulation (present throughout the accompanying trio) of two-note slurs.

This minuet's deliberate quarter-note pulse is perhaps best felt in comparison with a typical folklike dance Haydn composed for the ballroom (Ex. 4–3). Although this German dance shares with the minuet basic features of triple meter and balanced phrases, a dotted half-note pulse is felt here, as each individual measure becomes a distinct unit in the repetitive patterning of melody, rhythm, and harmony. Insistent stress on the downbeat is

EXAMPLE 4–2.   *Minuet,* Hob. IX:7/i: mm. 1–8

achieved by a "springing" bass, with oom-pah-pah scoring that is suggestive of the waltz. We will find that with the infusion of country manners in
Haydn's artful minuets, the stately and measured quarter-note pace of a
courtly dance often gives way to an expanded unit of pulse.

Although artful traces are observable in Haydn's dance minuets, in touches
of imitation and subtle elisions of phrases, these do not attract attention as
disconcerting to dancers. Such is not the case in Haydn's minuet movements,
however, where both materials and procedures *do* call attention to themselves—often in marked contradictions of the dancelike. Even in Haydn's
early minuets we find evidence of the artful deviations and exaggerations of
gesture that become characteristic in later works addressed to public audiences. It is appropriate, then, to pay particular attention to minuets com-

EXAMPLE 4–3. *German Dance*, Hob IX:9/1, mm. 1–8

Ed. H. C. Robbins Landon. Copyright 1960 by Ludwig Doblinger (Bernard Herzmansky) K.G., Vienna, Munich. Used by permission of Music Associates of America.

posed in the 1760s and 1770s, when Haydn's humor was still a relatively private affair in works composed for the princely chambers of Eisenstadt and Eszterháza.

While some of Haydn's boldest experiments occur in the minuets of his string quartets, it is most often in his symphonic movements that contemporaries mark his deviant manners—whether for criticism or praise—and I will track "original oddities" in musical examples from this genre. I examine Haydn's artful departures in these minuets with a shifting focus and emphasis: on procedures that alter normative patterns of both the dancelike and the minuetlike and on materials that alter the nature of the minuet as an expression of courtly elegance, both ceremonial and galant. The minuet of Symphony No. 104, the last of the "London" Symphonies, serves as a summary illustration of the incongruous manners and exaggerated gestures that become typical of Haydn's public humor in his late works.

The Novelty of Artful Display

Given the ubiquity of the minuet as compositional model and Haydn's reservations about rules, one might imagine his taking a certain pleasure in displaying his own ingenuity in patently artful devices that challenged and transformed the prototype. In this light, the canonic minuet presented a special challenge to composer and listener. The incongruities of canonic procedure in a dance-related movement are immediately obvious: a linear and seamless continuity of overlapping imitation provides an unlikely medium for steps that rely upon clear metric and phrase patterns reinforced by regular melodic and harmonic articulations. Then too, the overall tonal structure of the minuet imposes formal constraints on canonic procedure: modulation, clear cadences, dominant preparation for tonic return—above all, the internal repetitions indigenous to the minuet scheme. But perhaps most incongruous within a dance-related movement is the exhibition of a thoroughgoing learned style. As noted in Chapter 3, Hiller regarded the combination as inappropriate, an unseemly display of artifice.

All of Haydn's canonic minuets do indeed invite recognition of this incongruous juxtaposition of traditions. For one thing, his scoring calls attention to the technique: unison doublings reinforce the two-voice texture of outer voices, and accompaniment by free voices is sparse; imitation proceeds at the interval of the octave and at the distance of one measure, with rests, repeated notes, and embellishments that promote audibility of the canon.

The canons in Example 4-4 illustrate the sorts of materials that Haydn used for this movement. Here we note additional features that advertise the technique even while departing from normative canonic procedure. Melodic and rhythmic articulations of the canonic voices tend to reinforce the downbeat of the measure; melodic materials are harmonically conceived, and the harmonic progressions themselves are rather limited—often repeated to the point of stasis. While these features promote audibility of the meter and of harmonic functions, as well as of the imitative technique per se, they also yield a stop-start quality that frustrates the linear continuity normative in both canonic procedure and dance. Especially conspicuous in this respect is the immediate repetition of a phrase; in canon this means, of course, a double repetition. These may be exact (as in Ex. 4-4b) or slightly varied (as in Ex. 4-4c; see also the voice exchange that promotes additional repetition in Ex. 4-4a). In open-ended canons such reiterations would seem gratuitous delays, but in the minuet they effect prolongation and emphasis of formal procedures and harmonic goals, affirming stability, sustaining tension, and reinforcing resolution.

EXAMPLE 4-4.   Canons in symphonic minuets

   a.   *Symphony 3/iii, mm. 1-5*

   b.   *Symphony 23/iii, mm. 1-6*

   c.   *Symphony 44/ii, mm. 1-8*

   The minuet of Symphony No. 44 in E Minor (before 1772) illustrates the
playful potential of such a device. Here a premature return of opening material in the tonic early in the second section (Ex. 4-5, m. 19) motivates a long
digression, during which Haydn manipulates the rules of his canon as well as
the expectations of his listener. Interrupting continuous imitation, the stalled
reiteration of dominant preparation in measures 26-31 breaks off in silence.
Instead of the expected tonic resolution, further delays prolong suspense:
the prevailing canon is given up as tentative-sounding entrances—now at the
distance of two measures—repeatedly frustrate resolution of the diminished-
seventh chord. A proper cadence will not be reached until measure 55, where-
upon the opening material returns, *piano*, in canon at the original one-mea-
sure interval. The abrupt *forte*, fully orchestrated cadence that cuts off the
movement five measures later is a reminder of what every student of canon
soon learns: the difficulty of bringing one to an end. In this case, the piling
up of extra entrances calls for forcible action.
   If strong closure is a potential problem in canonic procedure, so too is definitive arrival. Decisive articulation of thematic and tonic return, a character-

EXAMPLE 4–5.   *Symphony 44/ii, mm. 1–4; 17–41*

istic structural principle in music of the Classical period is bound to be complicated by a "double return" of overlapping canonic voices. Haydn handles
this moment in the minuet of Symphony No. 3 (before 1762) by switching
the roles of leader and follower; tonic resolution waits for the soprano entry,
by which time the canon is already underway. The earlier eighteenth-century
composer and polymath Johann Mattheson might have regarded such distor-

tions as misplaced or exaggerated punctuation. Using a rhetorical model of phrase structure within a sixteen-bar *paragraphus*, Mattheson discussed various degrees of closure as analogous to commas, semicolons, and periods.[22] A canonic minuet undermines the clarity of articulation in this model, as one voice is always catching up to the punctuation point, the other always going on.

In the minuet and trio of Symphony No. 47 (1772), on the other hand, Haydn displays the artifice of a different sort of canon (Ex. 4-6). Here the

EXAMPLE 4-6. *Symphony 47/iii*

riddle of retrograde construction—by its very nature a playful challenge to performers as well as listeners—poses the rhetorical absurdity that a speech will make as much sense going from the end to the beginning as from beginning to end. To demonstrate the seeming paradox that a piece of music can make as much sense read backward as forward is also a considerable feat for the composer, particularly in a style that relies upon the clear functions of tonal harmony. And indeed, Haydn broadcasts his ingenuity in this movement. The repeated measure of large leaps and accelerated dynamic contrasts (mm. 8–9) is especially prominent when heard back to back with its retrograde in the minuet: heard in reverse, the relationships of V and I and of downbeat and upbeat undergo surprising alterations that alert the listener to the hidden game.[23] As for the trio, the opening five measures present an imbedded retrograde phrase that is advertised by its scoring. In both sections the play of paradox is audible in odd accents that subvert both metric hierarchies of upbeat and downbeat and harmonic function of progression. The manifest appeal to the listener in this movement is a real departure from the tradition of the *cancrizans* canon as concealed art. Here explicit play with artifice in the composing of the riddle extends beyond the fraternity of the learned in inviting discovery of its solution.[24]

The learned techniques in the minuets of Symphonies Nos. 44 and 47 represent in unique fashion a more general stylistic trend in Haydn's works, which Gerber noted in his *Lexikon* of 1790. Gerber's estimate of Haydn's success with contrapuntal techniques is a far cry from the attitudes of early critics:

> Every harmonic means, be it even out of the Gothic age of the old contrapuntists, is at his disposal. But as soon as he dresses them for our ears, they take on a pleasing way instead of their former stiffness. He possesses the great art of seeming familiar [*öfters bekannt zu scheinen*] in his pieces. Thereby, in spite of all the contrapuntal means that are found therein, he has become popular and accepted by every amateur. . . . Both the beautiful young lady and the contrapuntist grown gray over his scores, hear his works with delight and approval.[25]

Earlier writers such as Hiller assigned complex contrapuntal textures to the serious style, deemed appropriate for the church but lacking the direct appeal of accessible melodies simply accompanied. This view lingers in Gerber's image of the aged contrapuntist. But Haydn's "great art of seeming familiar" makes contrapuntal means palatable to the uneducated listener and transforms formerly "stiff"and "Gothic" procedures.

Itself grounded in convention as both functional dance and pedagogical model, the minuet movement was ripe for the novel transformations of artful play. The minuet of Symphony No. 70 (1779), a movement in which Gerber's "every harmonic means" takes on new meaning, might be consulted for a demonstration of play with the reiterative scheme of the form itself (Ex. 4–7). In something akin to minimalism, the simple melodic pattern of its opening two measures is repeated in various contexts, initiating both antecedent and consequent phrases, and fitted out with a variety of harmonic realizations and scorings. Even the tonic return is reinterpreted (and destabilized) in a new harmonization. But only in the coda, heard at the very end of the movement, does the proper consequent phrase finally "get it right."

Haydn's procedures in such a movement recall eighteenth-century notions of wit as sleight of hand, as a subtle recasting of something long familiar. In Locke's terms, though, the discriminating listener will be called upon to exercise judgment in detecting the differences of things seemingly alike. And Haydn extends that challenge in his own play with extremely simple material within the symphony's most redundant of forms.

EXAMPLE 4-7. *Symphony 70/iii, minuet: reduction*

Courtly and Rustic Airs

Gerber's remarks make it clear that he appreciated the art required in seeming artless. He also marked an aspect of Haydn's works that Charles Butler would call his "colloquial cast" and Johann Karl Friedrich Triest his "artful popularity, or popular (intelligible, penetrating) artfulness."[26] Recent scholars have written variously about Haydn's so-called popular style, in some cases collapsing the distinction between style and reputation.[27] But one aspect of the style frequently noted as *volkstümlich*, or folklike, can already be distinguished in Haydn's early minuets, and is especially salient as incongruous when measured against the elegant restraint of a "grave and noble" dance.

Transformation of the courtly minuet by the emphatically dancelike but informal air of the country may have disconcerted some contemporaries, but the infusion of folklike elements is not easily reduced to the simple "caricature of the dance" that Spazier regretted. For the rustic manner takes many shapes in Haydn's minuets. It can be heard in more extreme form in movements featuring very fast tempos, heavy-footed emphasis on (and off) the downbeat of the measure, springing leaps in the melody, and droning pedal points. The graceful, waltzlike lilt often heard in trio sections, on the other hand, offers a counterpart to the mincing grace of trios in the courtly mode. This polite-pastoral version of country dance is characterized by spare accompaniment, often pizzicato, and a graceful downbeat stress; solo wind instruments featured in flowing melodies reiterate simple rhythmic patterns, and harmonies are straightforward in four-bar phrases. The German dance seen above in Example 4–3 is a fair example of the country manner that serves as a point of departure for artful play in many of Haydn's symphonic minuets.

The minuet of Symphony No. 58 (1766–68) is rather less graceful, as its title *alla zoppa* ("limping") indicates (Ex. 4–8a). As noted in the example, irregular agogic stresses in the melody create a constantly shifting and elastic meter above the bass line's steady quarter notes. The melodies of this and the minuet of Symphony No. 38 (1766–68) (Ex. 4–8b) suggest the second-beat stress pattern of Hungarian folk (or folklike) dance, heard in Haydn's *alla Zingarese* minuet of the String Quartet Op. 20, No. 4.[28] At a leisurely pace, this second melody might take on a somewhat more graceful lilt, but at the *allegro* tempo indicated, the second measure of each two-bar pattern delivers a syncopated stomp. Its trio mixes in a whirling triplet figure—here too, an acceptably elegant courtly gesture at a slower pace—but exaggerated leaps in the oboe line of measures 11–14 support the impression of a "boisterous peasant." The courtly dance is as thoroughly displaced in this movement as it is in the similarly heavy-footed *allegro molto* minuet of Symphony No. 28 (see Ex. 3–3).

Most commonly noted among sources that Haydn undoubtedly drew upon in affecting the *volkstümlich* is the Austrian Ländler. A number of early nineteenth-century collections preserve the melodies of Ländler, some harmonized in arrangements for piano. While collectors of such tunes may well

EXAMPLE 4–8.   Minuet melodies
  a. *Symphony 58/iii, mm. 1–8*

  b. *Symphony 38/iii, minuet: mm. 1–10; trio, mm. 11–14*

have altered their original sources, certain features might be taken as reflections of Bavarian and Austrian folk melodies—and certainly as distinguish-
able from courtly minuets. The melodies in Example 4–9 are representative
of Ländler found in the earliest of these collections.[29] Nearly all fall into two
eight-bar reprises and feature hypnotic repetitions of simple rhythmic and
melodic patterns. "Yodeling" melodies, often involving the rising sixth, are
prominent, as are drones that anchor a rarely varied alternation of tonic and
dominant harmonies. The anticipations seen in Example 4–9a give a characteristic lilt to melodies that lack rhythmic variety, as do the lightly orna-
mented downbeats of Example 4–9b. In the introduction to this second melody, a bagpipe effect is imitated in the leading-tone slides to the repeated
tonic notes; in the continuation, as in the others, the melody becomes self-
sufficient in providing its own harmony. Of particular interest in the second
and third examples is the suggestion of duple rhythmic and melodic patterns
(indicated in brackets) that play against the prevailing triple meter. This becomes an artful technique in emphatic displacements of triple meter, notable
especially in Haydn's late minuets; we will find evidence of such manipulation in early symphonies as well.[30]

EXAMPLE 4–9.   Ländler melodies

Melodies in Ländler style are met with most often in Haydn's trio sections, which are themselves generally more regular than their companion minuets and often set off from them by additional contrasts of reduced scoring and dynamic level. Nearly always marked *piano*, they feature solo winds in chordally motivated eighth-note motion, with bare chordal punctuation in the strings, often pizzicato. Governed by harmonies that are more likely to change with the measure than within it, such trios have a pronounced downbeat emphasis and frequently a secondary stress on the third beat.[31]

Graceful Ländler-like trios, the best known of which are found in Haydn's "Paris" and "London" Symphonies, are heard in some of his earliest works; examples from the early 1760s include the trios of Symphonies Nos. 5, 25, 9,

22, and 24 (1764). But the Ländler style also offered opportunities for bold experiments that exaggerate the exoticism of its rusticity. Among several such trios, that of Symphony No. 67 (c. 1775), shown in Example 4–10, is

EXAMPLE 4–10. *Symphony 67/iii, trio*

most bizarre in its scoring. Here two solo violins play *con sordino*, the second with its G string tuned down to F; this low drone of the scordatura accompanying voice is remote from the upper regions explored by its partner. Thus anchored over the persistent tonic pedal, the melody wanders oddly in a continuous eight-bar phrase that threatens to ascend off the fingerboard. Lacking harmonic direction, the tune fails to define a distinct balancing phrase to the opening four measures; its altered return (mm. 38–40) is both seamless and irregular, in part because there has been no real departure. The extension in measure 39 of the repeated four-bar phrase to five bars permits some dominant articulation for a tonic "return," but elision cuts short the eight-bar confirming phrase to seven. The eerie sound of this static, hurdy-gurdy-like trio furnishes maximum contrast to the courtly manner of the minuet sections that frame it.[32]

In the trio of Symphony No. 69 (1778), Example 4–11, Haydn makes more explicit reference to the melodic patterning of the Ländler as a basis for irregular departures. Here eighth-note motion prevails in a melody that is given to repeating itself. The reiterative habit of Ländler melodies, noted above in

EXAMPLE 4–11. *Symphony 69/iii, trio*

anticipation figures, is exaggerated to a stuttering effect in this tune; the stasis of a repeating fragment in measures 37–38 duplicates this pattern at the level of the phrase. Moreover, the interpolation of extraneous repeated measures impedes—and prolongs—expected progress to the dominant: either measures 2–3 or 4–5 could be omitted to make up a more regular and direct eight-bar first section. An additional irregularity is felt with the displacement of triple meter by duple patterning in measures 41–42, where the compression of hemiola (reinforced by a quickening of harmonic rhythm in the accompaniment) urges the melody along, suppressing its pattern of reiteration.

Described in Haydn's day as a dance in which the couples "hop and turn themselves continuously," the Ländler is generally regarded as a predecessor of the waltz. Indeed, Heinrich Koch furnished nearly identical definitions for the two dances in his *Musikalisches Lexikon* of 1802: the *Ländler* is "the melody to a German dance of the same name, set in ⅜ time, and is performed in a moderately fast tempo. Its character is hopping joy." The *Walzer* is "a familiar dance whose character is hopping joy. The melody is set in triple meter, has a lively movement, and generally two reprises of eight measures." One wonders if the tempos of these couple dances were comparable to the late minuet: for Koch the minuet was "moderately quick."[33] The question of tempo is obviously problematic—after all, the aristocrat's "moderately fast" could be the peasant's "fairly slow"—but there does seem to be relative agreement here. (Of course, Koch might simply have preferred all of his dances in the "moderate" range.) Taken up as fashionable by upper- and middle-class city dwellers, the domesticated Ländler may have lost some of its rustic vigor in accommodating the more studied movements of polite society. So too, in public ballrooms the reserved minuet may have been invigorated (if debased, according to some) by dancers untutored in its refined nuance of gesture.

For performers today, the issue of tempo in Haydn's symphonic minuets is no less vexed than that of the dances themselves and deserves a comprehensive study. I wish only to point out its relevance to matters of interpretation addressed here and to acknowledge the precarious nature of such interpretation. The current trend in historical performance practice favors faster tempos in minuet movements of the Classical period, although the evidence adduced is not altogether convincing.[34] Neal Zaslaw notes that in light of recent scholarship, "too slow minuets should become a thing of the past," but he is also quick to caution against a too general reform. He characterizes the minuet as "a moderately flowing, dignified if cheerful courtly dance, with emphasis and articulation tending to the allegro rather than the adagio style of playing."[35] Such a description seems to leave the way open to a fairly broad interpretation of "faster" minuets.

As with any sweeping reforms, the rush to "correct" tempos in the direction of faster minuets runs the risk of treating all as alike. In the minuets of his symphonies and string quartets, Haydn was increasingly specific in marking some *allegretto*, some *allegro*, some even *presto*. (Nonetheless, on a recent recording of Symphonies Nos. 93 and 99, the former's *allegro* minuet is played more slowly than the latter's *allegretto*.) Each case offers an opportunity to take the composer at his "word," and to evaluate features that distinguish the characters of individual minuets within this wide range of tempo markings for guidance in those movements lacking any indication.[36] In short, one might hope for tempo decisions that are particular rather than general.

That said, the relation of tempo to humorous effects is particularly elusive, entailing a thicket of historical and subjective issues in interpretation and performance. Not least of these is the extent to which tempo itself becomes a source of humor in Haydn's minuets—in his day and ours. A decided circularity arises in asserting the humor of exaggerated manners, in that the manner of performance (including imagined ones in the ear of the analyst) can prejudice the case in favor of the interpretation. But many of the minuets that Haydn marks *allegro* have pronounced irregularities; in others marked *allegretto* (or lacking any indication), more subtle incongruities are flattened out at a too-fast "one beat to the bar." In this second category of minuets, Haydn's commentaries on the manners of both contrapuntal and courtly models may best exhibit their "original oddities" in performances that honor the "moderately" of Koch's "moderately quick."

Interruptions, Disorders, and Delays

If recognition of incongruous manners in the minuets examined thus far relies upon eighteenth-century traditions of dance as courtly and pedagogical paradigms, excessive gestures in others of Haydn's minuets provide more immediately felt disturbances of the humors. The Englishman Thomas Robertson observed in 1784 that Haydn's "abrupt and unexpected stops upon Discords, the application of which he has greatly extended, if not invented, excite the happiest disorder and surprize."[37] While it is not possible to determine which works Robertson had in mind, the surprising effect he notes is conspicuous in Haydn's use of interrupted cadences at moments where strong tonic resolution is expected. And it is here as well that the composer is likely to heighten the deception by disrupting temporal continuity. Such surprises have a somatic force in minuet movements, where regularity of pace and pattern is the rule. But to experience disorder as an *agreeable* surprise requires a compensatory shock—of recognition that the seeming dysfunction is uniquely functional in context.

Symphony No. 53 (c. 1778/79), a work of considerable renown in England, is one that Robertson may have heard in 1781 at the Bach-Abel concerts in London.[38] Its minuet, shown in Example 4–12, provides an excellent example of the productive work of surprise. The simple tunefulness of the melody, with its frequent note repetition, triadic construction, and rather heavy-footed accompaniment, sets up a swinging dotted-half-note pulse throughout; scoring, upbeat patterns, and appoggiaturas ensure an emphatic regular-

EXAMPLE 4–12. *Symphony 53/iii, minuet*

EXAMPLE 4–12. (*Continued*)

ity of stress on downbeats, and the persistence of tonic pedals thoroughly
grounds the harmonies in D major.

Under such conditions, the interrupted cadence *cum* fermata at measure
24 is especially startling. Furthermore, the timing of the surprise guarantees
maximum effect, coming as it does where continuity into the final cadence
would seem to be a foregone conclusion. The gradual chromatic unwinding

that follows, *pianissimo*, explores new dimensions of orchestral and harmonic color unsuspected in a movement seemingly straightforward, even a bit square. In the course of this digression, Haydn expands the dimensions of the movement itself: instead of the expected eight measures, the return lasts for twenty-six.

On closer examination, this codalike passage reveals additional functions as a "harmonic fermata," providing a counterbalance to the weight of tonic pedal stasis and allowing time for further development of the descending fifth tentatively explored in measures 9–12 (D–G in the subdominant over a tonic pedal; now A–D, over a dominant pedal). The seemingly capricious incongruity of an abrupt discontinuity and shift of harmonic direction is more than compensated by this extension of time, harmonic dimension, and mood. Haydn thus asserts the function of surprise not only as a dramatic device that forces our attention but also as a structural means that provokes expansion of the movement in several domains.

While the surprising interruption in this minuet proves to be an agreeable disorder, the prolonged delay it generates does not strike the listener as a playful jest. Though clearly ingenious and artful, Haydn does not here announce his intentions to dally with seemingly gratuitous repetitions as he does in the finale of the "Joke" Quartet. In the minuet of Symphony No. 61 (1776), on the other hand, the surprise of an interrupted cadence effects a playful delay. Here the deceptive harmonic progression and abrupt silence interrupt a continuation that is itself unexpected. Indeed, the combined incongruities of irregular phrasing, a deceptive cadence, and a grand pause follow the presumed conclusion of a minuet that has been a near model of regularity.[39]

The passage shown in Example 4-13 begins with the return of the minuet's opening material, measures 31–38 being identical with the first section of the movement. The seemingly superfluous addendum of measures 39–40 interrupts the silence that normally follows a final cadence. In the afterthought that begins as if to echo the foregoing close, a single note deflects tonic resolution and forces continuation. But Haydn delays further, with silence that is newly charged—and provocatively prolonged—before reapproaching the tonic in an expanded and forceful closing progression. As in Symphony No. 53, the return is extended (here from eight to twenty bars), and the proportions of the movement are balanced thereby.

An essential difference between the two minuets is that the play with tonic resolution in this coda is anticipated by "gratuitous" repetitions earlier in the movement: first in passages that involve cadencing in the dominant, and then in the dominant preparation of the retransition that follows, Haydn both prolongs this section and playfully delays its progress. Here and in the more explicit interruption of measures 39ff, Samuel Johnson's definition of *amusing* is a fitting reminder of deceptions that divert in order to "gain" or "waste" time. The payoff of Haydn's wit is that his diversions gainfully extend time while seeming to waste it in forgetful delays.

EXAMPLE 4–13.   *Symphony 61/iii, minuet: mm. 31–50*

If in this minuet Haydn displays irregular manners akin to saying something after you've finished—in seeming distraction saying the same thing over again—his tactic in the minuet of Symphony No. 66 (c. 1778) is that of explicit dallying. Again, as seen in Example 4-14, repetition figures in the

EXAMPLE 4-14.   *Symphony 66/iii, mm. 9–28*

intent to delay. The reduced scoring and dynamic level, like the prolonged dominant tension, are common features of Haydn's approach to thematic and tonic return. Fermatas and grand pauses are also frequent means by which he dramatizes this structural resolution. But here he suspends arrival with repetitions that exaggerate delay and tease anticipation of the obvious. Overplaying the displacement of F as downbeat and offbeat, Haydn prolongs its anticipatory function for a total of eleven bars before the appropriate upbeat signals return.

The effect of measures 23–27 is comparable to a fermata that undermines the listener's sense of when resolution and return will occur. Unlike the ad libitum fermata, however, the length of this delay is patently under the composer's control (especially if conductors don't attempt to improve on Haydn's sense of timing), and it is the listener's awareness of that control that Haydn engages and plays upon. In so doing, he points toward the moment of tonic and thematic return, yet throws the listener off balance with one measure too many (or too few).[40] Both set-up and surprise seem particularly humorous in the context of this minuet, which has a certain ceremonial bearing in its dotted rhythms, figuration, and deliberate bass line. Upon its return, even the opening material will seem to have picked up a reiterative habit as it expands from eight measures to an irregular nine.

The interruption of metric pattern is a discontinuity only slightly less disturbing in a minuet than an abrupt silence or unexpected delay. Displacement of $\frac{3}{4}$ meter by other metric groupings disturbs established patterns of phrasing as well. While such devices as hemiola and shifts of accent, which contradict a regular ordering of upbeat and downbeat relationships, can introduce surprising disorders, they are not necessarily experienced as delays. Indeed, shifts of meter may give the impression of increased momentum, as in the trio of Symphony No. 65 (before 1778), seen in Example 4–15a. Overlapping hemiola patterns drive the sixth-chord sequence in measures 36–40 with an urgency that is in marked contrast to the static opening. This momentum is effectively braked by a playful confusion of meters (mm. 40–43), where a repeating $\frac{2}{4}$ melodic pattern "marks time," mediating between the $\frac{3}{2}$ hemiola and the $\frac{3}{4}$ that must confirm the cadence (Ex. 4–15b).

Three measures of $\frac{4}{4}$ time in the opening section of the minuet (Ex. 4–16a, mm. 7–10) similarly suspend time and direction. Here the repeating irregularity interrupts and provokes a detour, prolonging what had promised to be a straightforward consequent phrase of four bars (Ex. 4–16b). The $\frac{4}{4}$ melodic figure that waylays the anticipated phrase requires two repetitions before a proper downbeat in $\frac{3}{4}$ is reached; as in the trio, delay emphasizes the goal of the cadential progression to the dominant. And here too, the metric disturbance lingers in a modified return of the opening section.

In both minuet and trio Haydn makes his intent to delay especially conspicuous by isolating and repeating the melodic fragment that has caused the metric disturbance. The effect is one of falling out of step yet continuing to run in place, distracted in "superfluous" repetition. In movements that invite associations with the patterns and continuity of dance, such seemingly absentminded repetitions are especially salient as isolated, frozen gestures, and all the more humorous for their seeming detachment and stasis.[41] But as artful strategies, these incongruous irregularities deliver more than simply

EXAMPLE 4–15.

a. *Symphony 65/iii, trio, mm. 33–44*

b. Schematic of mm. 37–44

comic subversions of dancelike norms. While we might sense the composer's humor in such deviant manners—indeed, feel them as physical disturbances—we are also made highly conscious of the compositional procedures Haydn chooses to dramatize in this way. Thus displayed, his ingenuity in manipulating conventional patterns forces attention to their potential for renewing and expanding the dimensions of the minuet. It was perhaps this

EXAMPLE 4–16

a. *Symphony 65/iii, mm. 1–14*

b.   Predictable 4-bar consequent phrase vs. delay, mm. 5–14

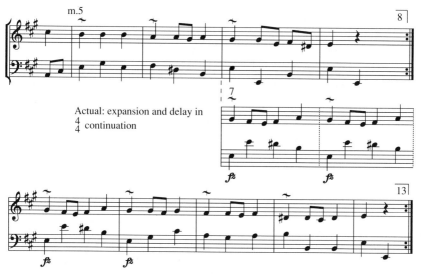

renewal that Dittersdorf recognized in admiring Haydn's "gift of trifling without surrendering art."[42]

Theatrical Gestures and the Display of Humor

Haydn's theatrically eccentric manipulation of conventional gestures is best
illustrated in late works intended for the public. None is a better candidate
than the minuet of Haydn's last symphony. (As this is a readily available work,
I quote only brief excerpts, citing measure numbers for reference to passages
not given in the musical examples.) Like the humor in many of Haydn's minuets, that of Symphony No. 104 relies on the surprise of excessive gestures,
but here the focus of attention is on gestures most basic to tonal music and
patterned dance: those that articulate upbeat and downbeat functions and
define cadence. As can be seen in Example 4–17, the opening section juxta-
poses ceremonial instrumentation and folklike manners: narrow in compass,
the securely harmonized tune is fully scored and defines its tonic directly in
balanced four-bar phrases. The *allegro* tempo marking, unsuitable for a
courtly minuet, fits the regularity and simplicity of this material, which would
be ponderous at an *allegretto* pace. Certain features of the theme, however,
undermine its regularity and seeming stability. Sharp accents and slurs over
the barline give the upbeats an exaggerated prominence and create the ambiguity of potential downbeats. The persistence of a tonic pedal for six measures (horns, trumpets, and timpani) is another kind of exaggeration that
seems incongruous in the presence of a strong rhythmic and melodic pro-

EXAMPLE 4–17. *Symphony 104/iii, mm. 1–8*

file—one expects harmonic change to support the phrasing of four-plus-four bars, as well as to clarify upbeat-downbeat relationships within the measure.

But the minuet's most unusual feature is its full-measure trill for the entire orchestra. The cadential trill is a standard convention of formal articulation in tonal music, and prolonged trills are often used to mark major cadence points in large-scale forms such as the concerto. In the context of this unprepossessing minuet, such a gesture is clearly excessive, exaggerated in duration, and ungainly in execution. The approach to the leading tone is conspicuously awkward: prepared by an upward leap that is accented against the meter, the "compensating" downward leap of a minor seventh lands with force on the downbeat of the trill. The sound of this fully orchestrated dominant-seventh shake (including horns and timpani), unprecedented in Haydn's works, overcompensates for the theme's irregularities; as a seemingly misplaced and excessive gesture, this distortion of a familiar formula alerts the listener to an eccentricity that will return with telling effect at the close of the movement.

While the written-out repeat subdues the dynamic force of the theme's metric ambiguity (suppressing the *forzando* accents), the second section takes metric conflict as its subject in more extended development, isolating the familiar upbeat triad figure and relocating it in displaced duple patterns (mm.

21–24). Over a prolonged dominant pedal that prepares the tonic return, this same upbeat fragment loses its metric bearings in an extended pattern of eighth notes that outline the dominant triad (mm. 30–34); seemingly unable to find its function against the *forzando* syncopation that is its counterpoint, the repeating figure tries the upper octave. But it is the grand gesture of the timpani roll that defines arrival in a five-bar crescendo of dominant to tonic, upbeat to downbeat.

If the cadence formula sounded odd in its first (and second) hearing, its return (Ex. 4–18) extends to comic exaggeration, as Haydn manipulates expectations that are specific to this context as well as those that apply more generally to dance, minuet protocol, and cadential gestures. As Gerber noted, "joy turns to mischievousness," in Haydn's music, suggesting to him "the image of a man who shivers and shakes in the ease and charm of mirth."[43] In addition to isolating the trill formula as a stylistic cliché, Haydn now repeatedly frustrates its function, at the same time turning upbeats into ineffectual afterbeats. Motivating these alterations is the *over*leap from the *forzando* B to the seventh of the dominant chord (m. 41) rather than the leading tone; proper voice leading requires descent to the third of the tonic chord, a pitch heavily emphasized in the scoring. This relatively unstable conclusion prompts the *reculer pour mieux sauter* that proves even wider of the mark, as a move to the subdominant forestalls any confirming tonic. And what might logically be the anticipated final cadence in the next two bars is suspended by a two-measure grand pause. The D/B upbeat is left hanging and becomes ambiguous: should it be heard as upbeat or afterbeat—*reculer* or rebound? (In retrospect, the same might be asked of the D on the third beat of m. 42.)

Deprived of a definitive upbeat, the trilled dominant-seventh chord enters tentatively, its dynamic level *piano*, its scoring reduced; in length, however, it fully compensates for the two measures of silence. And four bars of cadential confirmation dispel any doubt of finality, as upbeats and downbeats are given firm harmonic definition. All told, these twelve measures constitute a manifold expansion to outrageous proportions of an incongruous two-measure cadence formula. The attentive listener will be alert to changes leading up to the sudden silence and what follows. As in the finale of the "Joke" Quartet, each move becomes slightly more exaggerated than the last, yet all are heard as manipulations that delay the inevitable final cadence.[44]

That Haydn's teasing manner was recognized in his own day as a salient trait in his compositions suggests listeners attuned to the playful in manipulations such as those that delay the conclusion of this minuet, and it is not surprising that the "Haydn minuet" provoked more comment among his contemporaries than any other movement. It is also understandable that startling departures from functional norms of the minuet and the dancelike—notable, as we have seen, in some of his earliest works—vexed some critics. For viewed in their historical context, Haydn's minuets offered an especially broad range of challenges to compositional decorum and listening readiness.

Eighteenth-century perceptions of social and stylistic decorum aside,

EXAMPLE 4–18.   *Symphony 104/iii, mm. 33–52*

Haydn's minuets remind us of the physicality of that readiness, and of the original sense of the word *humor*. When expectations are grounded as habits and tendencies in patterned motions and gestures, discontinuities of motion and disturbances in metric and phrase patterns can have a visceral impact, taking the body by surprise. Whereas Haydn's contemporaries might have felt the surprises of his artful minuets in a more immediate connection with gestures and patterned steps of the dance, the humorous manners of this movement are playfully dysfunctional for today's listeners too.

Haydn's minuets also remind us that whereas the pleasures of discovering wit rely on succession, on music's temporal sequence of events, humorous incongruities can be entertained simultaneously—can oblige the listener to "say yes and no at the same time," as Sulzer put it. One can actively feel $\frac{3}{4}$ meter in play with and against $\frac{2}{4}$ patterns, for example, or the play of canonic voices against the measure of a minuet's regular phrase patterns. This immediacy of the "humors" has particular force in music, alerting the listener to strategies in play and prompting attention to their implications. Seen thus, humorous incongruity, by giving an impulse to discovery and recognition of ingenuity, activates the wit of jesting.

5

Engaging Wit
in the Chamber:
Opus 33 Revisited

In his *Treatise on the Art of Music* of 1784, the Reverend William Jones dismissed Haydn as a "wild warbler of the wood," whose chamber works "differ from some pieces of Handel as the talk and laughter of the Tea-table (where, perhaps, neither Wit nor Invention are wanting) differs from the oratory of the Bar and the Pulpit."[1] A partisan of the music of the "Ancients," Jones apparently considered conversations at tea to be frivolous titters in comparison with the (manly) speeches of the judiciary and the church; Handel could be counted on to deliver more substantial messages than those purveyed by the wit and invention of the flighty "Moderns." In marking his preference for the stirring rhetoric of public address, however, Jones sets inappropriate terms for instrumental music in the chamber. The informal amusements of witty exchange among familiars presumed a more intimate discourse. Indeed, the enduring contemporary estimate of Haydn held that "[i]n the genre of the quartet, no one managed better than he the piquant surprises and the animated banter of musical conversation."[2] Among many who agree, Charles Rosen has noted: "The eighteenth century was cultivatedly self-conscious about the art of conversation: among its greatest triumphs are the quartets of Haydn."[3]

The metaphor of conversation is obviously attractive in characterizing the voices of the string quartet as listening and responding to one another—agreeing, contending, even changing the subject. Understood in these terms, the conversation of a quartet is heard by its players, whose intimate exchange may or may not be "overheard" by others. Theodor Adorno noted this aspect of chamber music's conversation: "In its initial import, at any rate, it is dedicated at least as much to the players as to an audience whom the composer seems at times scarcely to have considered."[4]

But why not extend the metaphor precisely to bring the audience into the conversation? Here the model of discourse may be more inclusive: even if the most immediate conversation is that between the players, themselves primary and requisite listeners, the audience of contingently present listeners is also engaged in dialogic interaction with the work in progress. One might also imagine that the composer figures in the conversation that rehearses his own dialogue with established conventions of genre and style. In this scheme, listeners are engaged in mediating multiple dialogues, both immediate and "historical." The more broadly inclusive concept of conversation suggested here makes room for listening that is more than eavesdropping, for quartets that address listeners in the overt manner of a performance.

With this extended metaphor of a quartet's conversations in mind, I will examine procedures in Haydn's Op. 33 string quartets that suggest to me a new conception of the genre as self-consciously addressed to an audience. By this I do not mean to imply a move out of the chamber onto the stage—string quartets were rarely heard on public concerts in 1781, most especially in Vienna.[5] Rather I am concerned with features of musical discourse *within* the chamber that extend beyond a self-sufficient private exchange to provoke awareness of dialogue in play between listeners and players. The finale of the "Joke" Quartet of Haydn's Op. 33, discussed in Chapter 1, is an especially salient example of such provocation. Haydn's procedures in this and other quartets of the Op. 33 set seem to me to challenge Adorno's notion that "in chamber music no provision is made for any difference between player and listener."[6] Indeed, the marking of that difference in Op. 33 suggests the strategies of a composer addressing a newly extended audience in the chamber. The particulars of Op. 33's significance in Haydn's career will be taken up in due course. First, however, the metaphor of conversation might be examined more closely in terms of listeners in eighteenth-century chambers.

"Models" of Conversation

From early roots in the broadly generic category of divertimenti suited to accompany conversations in the chamber, the string quartet rose to distinction as the analogue of conversation itself in many late eighteenth-century characterizations of the genre—a development in which Haydn was acknowledged to be preeminent.[7] Haydn's early biographer Carpani offers a more embroidered version than most through the agency of a "friend, who imagined in listening to a quartet of Haydn that he was in attendance at a conversation of four amiable people":

> It seemed to him that he recognized in the first violin a man of spirit and affability, middle aged, well spoken, who was sustaining the major part of the discourse. . . .
> In the second violin he recognized a friend of the first who was seeking in every

way to enhance him, . . . intent on sustaining the conversation more by agreeing with much of what he heard from the other than [by presenting] his own ideas. The bass was a solid man, learned and aphoristic . . . supporting the discourse of the first violin with laconic but secure maxims, and at times . . . [he] predicted what the principal speaker would say, and gave force and regulation to what was said. The viola, then, seemed to him a somewhat loquacious matron who did not really have much of importance to say, but all the same wanted to inject herself into the discussion; at times she seasoned the conversation with grace, and at other times with delightful chatterings that gave the others a chance to take a breath. In the end, she was more the friend of the bass than of the other interlocutors.[8]

Whatever one might think of the gendered roles in this description, Carpani's "friend" imagines a rather less than equal-opportunity ensemble. German writers inclined toward a more sober appreciation of the craft required in equal-voiced part writing. Heinrich Koch, for example, noted the difficulty of alternating the melodic prominence of each part such that those supporting and enhancing the melody would not obscure it, and he credited Haydn with having set the example for others in diligent cultivation of the genre.[9]

In his mastery of contrapuntal procedures in quartets of the late 1760s and early 1770s, Haydn realized the potential of the medium for both homogeneity of ensemble and independence of voice. The traditional texted model for learned counterpoint was the equal-voiced polyphony of vocal music for the church, the connotations of which infused instrumental works with the authority of an august and rule-bound tradition. Exclusivity of elevated discourse in the chamber is perhaps nowhere better illustrated than in the fugal finales that Haydn wrote for three of his Op. 20 quartets of 1772. Driven by the linear, cumulative premises of fugal procedure, such finales assured full equality of participation in a strict four-voice texture. Internally governed by its compositional rigor and admitting no additional voices, the fugue might be an object of admiration for connoisseurs, its conversation a self-sufficient and "learned" one. Even if others might be invited to listen in, the pleasures of private exchange—here among four accomplished players—did not presume additional auditors.

In elevating the expression of a chamber genre whose early associations were simply diverting, Haydn borrowed additional means to serious ends from a rather different model of texted music, namely, opera seria. The slow movements of Op. 17, No. 5, and Op. 20, No. 2, invoke the highly charged style of recitative and arioso in monologues for the chamber that are both private and theatrical. Commonly acknowledged as accommodating both connoisseurs and less sophisticated music lovers, the theatrical style might attract a broader audience than the fugue, but *seria* characters moved the spectator from a distance in grand solo numbers of reflection, and rarely in polyphonic ensembles.

The mixed company of opera buffa staged more immediate conversations in diverse voices and gestures paced for intrigue and dramatic action more wide-ranging than in its serious counterpart. Ensemble finales in particular offered a variety of encounters and manners of address among characters less leisurely and remote, ultimately requiring extended (and *presto*) affirmations of the happy resolution to their intrigues. In the relatively informal atmosphere of comic opera, characters might enlist spectators as co-conspirators in asides seemingly free from the scripted conversation of the dramatis personae. Commentary expressly addressed to the audience called attention to the permeable frame of comic opera, suspending the illusion of self-enclosed conversations to invite self-consciousness of formal conventions of drama. While similarly provocative devices in Haydn's string quartets are most notable in late works composed for public performance, the finale of the "Joke" Quartet serves again as a reminder of comic gestures that exceed the frame of an exclusive conversation.

In the learned and theatrical styles, then, Haydn had a range of texted models for instrumental discourse. In addition to these, however, he might also have found a model in conversation itself—that is, in conversations that fall short of polished etiquette and decorum. While denizens of the chamber cultivated conversation as an art, Haydn's discourse brings into play its more realistic features: equivocation and disagreement, non sequiturs and gratuitous addenda, uncomfortable silence, stubborn insistence on an irrelevant point, stuttering and stalling, even rude interruption. While these are common enough malfunctions in everyday communication, they are used to advantage as artful strategies of jesting in Haydn's quartets. Here seeming impediments to continuous and lucid discourse function as mechanisms of engagement that provoke the participating voices as well as the community of listeners for whose pleasure the conversation is played out.

The metaphor of conversation as it is traditionally applied to the string quartet does not call up notions of dysfunctional discourse, nor does it suggest strategies of engaging an audience. Most often the conversation paradigm is invoked as a matter of texture in the easy exchange of motives among the instrumental parts. Frankly provocative aspects of jesting, however, make different sorts of claims on listeners. In speculating about the pleasures of jokes, philosopher Ted Cohen locates an essential feature in the space of play allowed to the listener.[10] Recalling Aristotle's recommendation of the *enthymeme* (an incomplete syllogism) as an effective rhetorical device, Cohen describes the listener's effort to identify its implied but unstated premise as a "mental scramble . . . undertaken *before* the legitimate arrival of the conclusion," that "augments the persuasion implicit in the validity of the completed argument." In the delivery of both jokes and arguments there is, in his view, "a sense of having done something meant to move your hearer, of having created a momentum which now moves to him":

> but for the argument your expectation is more a demand, while for the joke it is much less a demand and far more a hope. When you tell a joke you lose control in a way in which you don't when you tell a sound argument. You leave extra room for the hearer.[11]

Distinguishing the jester as a playful rhetor, Cohen acknowledges both freedom and risk in granting play space to the listener: some will fall short of the "active complicity" essential to the success of a joke.

The effect of insider jokes on those in the know is thus a double pleasure:

> [T]he audience collaborates in the success of the joke—the constitution of inti-
> macy—just as the audience for an enthymeme collaborates in the construction of a
> valid argument, with the difference that the audience of the joke derives additional
> intensity of feeling from knowing that the success is due to them specifically, that
> other groups would fail.[12]

Few would deny that the recognition of musical jokes delivers a certain ca-
chet to the intimacy thus achieved. In eighteenth-century chambers, jesting
strategies might well reinforce the distinction of a connoisseur's pleasures.
The false ending of the "Joke" Quartet might thus be a double pleasure for
the insider catching out the inattentive and naïve listener.

But the theatricality of gesture in Haydn's finale extends "extra room," as
we have seen, to engage a wide range of participants. Cohen's attention to
the open invitation of the jest and the uncertainty of its success underscores
the double focus of play in a musical conversation. If a composer who proposes a jest "loses control" of its success with listeners, he does not forfeit
control of the conversation among its players—though their skill is certainly
a factor in realizing it. In a literal sense, the players are the insiders in the
quartet's exchange, the most privileged of its listeners—and the most likely
to succeed in a joke's transaction. Addressed to an audience of listeners, the
joke of the players' conversation is retold, delivered to an uncertain reception.
An ingenious jest has a dual function, then, in challenging listeners to attend
to the players' conversation and to discover the point of the composer's jest
in their conversation.

Theatrical display intersects with the conversational in the staging of jests
in performance. Familiar gestures made strange in seemingly contradictory
poses call attention to themselves as eccentric—humorous, in the eighteenth-
century sense of the word—and as prods to the discovery of wit in unsuspected similarities. Cohen's "play space" makes explicit the role of the listener in this discovery.

New Prospects and Strategies

In a larger sense than Cohen implies, Haydn "loses control" of the jest to the
public in his Op. 33 quartets. Marking an important juncture of private and
public patronage in the composer's career, these works are particularly suggestive of new terms of engagement in the chamber. They might also be
judged something of a risk on Haydn's part. Secure in the employ of a patron
whose musical establishment was lavish and whose tastes were educated,
Haydn enjoyed a particularly favorable position, as he himself reported to his
early biographer Griesinger:

> My Prince was content with all my works, I received approval, I could, as head
> of an orchestra, make experiments, observe what enhanced an effect, and what

weakened it, thus improving, adding to, cutting away, and running risks. I was set apart from the world, there was nobody in my vicinity to confuse and annoy me in my course, and so I had to be original.[13]

Despite the restricted ambit of his employ, Haydn acknowledges the considerable advantages of private patronage. In such a protected environment, where experiments and their effects could be tested and revised, "running risks" would be less than hazardous.

Far greater uncertainties attended the success of works in the public domain, as attested by early reviews of Haydn's works—the criticisms of which he knew well. The earliest evidence of Haydn's sensitivity to critical response in less favorable quarters is contained in his "Autobiographical Sketch" of 1776, where he makes explicit reference to critics in Berlin:

> In the chamber-musical style I have been fortunate enough to please almost all nations except the Berliners; this is shown by the public newspapers and letters addressed to me. I only wonder that the Berlin gentlemen, who are otherwise so reasonable, preserve no medium in their criticism of my music, for in one weekly paper they praise me to the skies, whilst in another they dash me sixty fathoms deep into the earth, and this without explaining why; I know very well why: because they are incapable of performing some of my works, and are too conceited to take the trouble to understand them properly.[14]

This statement is evidence not simply of Haydn's sensitivity to criticism (perversely misguided in the North, by his lights) but also of his awareness of the broad dissemination of his chamber music—or, more properly, his music in the "chamber style." For the court composer, this broad category included most instrumental music: symphonies, sonatas, trios and quartets, divertimenti for various combinations of instruments, and the like—in short, instrumental genres played and heard in princely chambers.

Even if Haydn's relationship to players and listeners under the Eszterházys was enviable by any standards of eighteenth-century patronage, his right to address a wider audience was restricted under the terms of his original contract of 1761. The compositions required of him were to be the sole property of his prince:

> The said Vice-Capellmeister shall be under obligation to compose such music as his Serene Highness may command, and neither to communicate such compositions to any other person, nor to allow them to be copied, but he shall retain them for the absolute use of his Highness, and not compose for any other person without the knowledge and permission [of his Highness].

In Haydn's service contract of 1 January 1779 this restriction is conspicuous for its absence.[15]

Haydn's status at court had clearly risen in the nearly twenty years since his original contract, as had his reputation in the world outside Eszterháza. For regardless of their origins in the daily round of musical events in the Eszterházy domains, Haydn's works found a much wider audience in the

1770s, as witnessed by his own and others' reports. Although only a single printed edition before 1779 is known to have been prepared under Haydn's supervision, his works circulated widely in unauthorized prints and in manuscript copies.[16] Aware of the demand for his music abroad, Haydn would have had good reason to press for the right to deal directly with publishers in his own behalf. The change in Haydn's compositional circumstances during the years that separate Op. 20 from Op. 33 helps to explain, in my view, both his marketing strategy and the stylistic and formal departures in his new set of quartets.

Granted official permission to compose with an eye to a much wider audience (and greater financial gain), Haydn was not long in exercising his entrepreneurial independence. He moved quickly in the early 1780s to enter into direct negotiations with a number of publishers, chief among them the newly established Viennese firm of Artaria. He satisfied this publisher first with the types of pieces most favored by amateurs: with twelve *Lieder*—a new genre for Haydn—and a set of six keyboard sonatas. Apprehensive about critical reaction to his sonatas, Haydn, in a letter to Artaria, insisted on a printed disclaimer as foreword to the collection "in order to forestall the criticisms of any witlings [*Witzlinge*—i.e., pretenders to wit]":

AVVERTISSEMENT

Among these 6 Sonatas there are two single movements in which the same subject occurs through several bars: the author has done this intentionally, to show different methods of treatment.

For of course, I could have chosen a hundred other ideas instead of this one; but so that the whole *opus* will not be exposed to blame on account of this one intentional detail (which the critics and especially my enemies might interpret wrongly), I think that this advertisement or something like it must be appended, otherwise the sale might be hindered thereby.[17]

Clearly testy about hostile critics who might fault him for a lapse in originality, Haydn offers an explanation that sounds a bit disingenuous. What he fails to mention in the letter to his publisher is that among the sonatas he has sent, one (the Sonata in C Minor, Hob. XVI:20) had been composed nearly ten years earlier; it is not unlikely that others in this collection were works ready at hand for quick publication.[18]

In his next project with Artaria, however, Haydn turned to the genre he had abandoned for nearly a decade, and he adopted a bold strategy in approaching potential buyers directly with assurances of the currency and originality of his new works. On 3 December 1781 he took it upon himself to solicit subscribers for manuscript copies of the Op. 33 quartets in advance of their publication by Artaria. In letters addressed to various influential music lovers, he promises quartets of an "entirely new and special kind, since I have written none for ten years."[19] In speculating about the actual nine-year gap that separates this set from the earlier Op. 20 quartets, scholars have advanced various interpretations of this phrase. Some take Haydn at his word in announcing an "entirely new and special" *style*. Ludwig Finscher, for example, locates in Op. 33 the arrival of a fully "classic" style, an arrival that Charles Rosen characterizes as a "revolution" in comparison with Haydn's earlier quartets.[20] More mundane, but certainly plausible, is Jens Peter Larsen's explanation that in announcing his quartets as "gantz neu," Haydn has seized a phrase common in the musical marketplace;[21] here the composer gives notice that these works are recently written and up-to-date, rather than pieces on the shelf for nearly a decade and dusted off for sale in 1781.

Aside from the wording of Haydn's letter, though, the very fact that he should promote his new quartets in this manner is worthy of attention. The market for string quartets was more select than that for piano sonatas and songs; enjoyed as elevated self-entertainment for well-trained players, the string quartet was held to be a connoisseur's genre, sociable but demanding, and suited for the pleasures of the musically elite in private chambers. Haydn's promotion of his new quartets to potential subscribers abroad is understandable, then: in appealing first to a community of patrons not unlike his own prince, he addressed men of influence and sophisticated tastes who might themselves commission future works. He may also have imagined that a list of prominent patrons would enhance sales of the printed edition.[22] Nonetheless, the printing of his quartets for sale in the public marketplace would release them to a much wider audience of unknown players (and critics). The success of these and future quartets would rest with discriminating buyers: sales pitch or no, the art of persuasion would ultimately fall to the works themselves.

In view of his new contractual freedoms, it is reasonable to suppose that Haydn would take up the quartet with the resolve of fashioning a "new and special" approach to the genre—as he surely did in announcing the results of his efforts. Obvious departures from the Op. 20 set have been widely noted: the concision and clarity of sonata-form procedures in opening movements; the designation of "Scherzo" or "Scherzando" for the minuet movements; a recasting of finales as tuneful and dancelike movements in reiterative forms rather than closely argued sonata forms and fugues; a more distinctive casting of character for each of the four movements; and, overall, an ease of style that breathes a more "popular" air.[23] In comparison with Haydn's quartets of the early 1770s, these features might be viewed as concessions to less sophisticated listeners in a now broader and anonymous audience. Rather than asking whether Haydn's strategies in these quartets were an accommodation, I want to focus instead on the manner of address to the listener as remarkable in itself. For in making overtures to his audience, Haydn extends something akin to Cohen's incomplete argument and leaves room for play in its completion.

Evidence of Haydn's new self-consciousness in addressing a more diverse audience is most apparent in opening and closing movements of the Op. 33 quartets, and it is these movements that I will consider in detail, in particular their manners of initiating conversation and signaling closure. The intimate form of address, *piano* and seemingly *in medias res*, that characterizes the openings of several of these quartets belies their audacity in manipulating the most familiar of conventional gestures. A counterbalance to these singular beginnings is the familiar manner of the finales, whose endings play out closure in extended delays and theatrical gestures. If such manners suggest that Haydn was hedging his bets by appealing to different kinds of listeners, a more subtle interplay of dialogues is heard within and between these movements.

(De)Parting Gestures

Commonly known as "No. 5" of Op. 33, the G Major Quartet was in fact the opening number in the original edition of the set by Artaria.[24] Haydn's point of departure in this work might be taken as symbolic of new beginnings—and endings. At once intimate and impertinent, the first two measures conflate the function and syntax of opening and closing remarks (Ex. 5-1). "Con-

EXAMPLE 5-1. *Op. 33/5/i, mm. 1–10*

Joseph Haydn Werke, XII/3: Streichquartette "Opus 20" und "Opus 33," edited by Georg Feder and Sonja Gerlach. Copyright 174 by G. Henle Verlag, Munich. Used by permission.

fusion" of opening and closing phrases is a ploy in many of Haydn's works, but only in his late quartets does such a bold gesture propose a syntactic contradiction from the outset—a beginning that *sounds* like an ending, rather than an opening that in the end proves to be ambidextrous.[25] Musical jests about beginnings and endings go back at least as far as Machaut's *Ma fin est mon commencement*. Even if here the text signals a musical palindrome, the wit of invention in such a composition is not immediately manifest as play with structure; retrograde canons are discernible only over time—for even the most perceptive of listeners, a complete statement must precede its *cancrizans*. To effect a playful reversal of expectation at the beginning of a piece, the composer must rely on an explicit contradiction of musical gestures that distinguish openings from closings.

Acting simultaneously as initiating motive and closing cadence, the opening quip of the G Major Quartet is provocative not only because it is isolated and seemingly misplaced in its function, but also because it is understated, even nonchalant. Seemingly superfluous to the "proper" beginning of the work, the contradiction of opening-and-closing proposes an immediate ambivalence.[26] If this gambit signals a piece about conventions of beginning and ending, the formal implications of its anomaly remain to be played out, for it is in the nature of sonata form that the subject will come up again. In retrospect, the listener discovers that Haydn's "epigram," as Finscher describes it,[27] has both introduced and summarized the basic subject matter of the movement. Both motivic and cadential uses of the opening gesture are heard throughout, but its functional ambivalence undermines major points of articulation in the formal structure of the movement.

The duality of closing-as-opening is especially conspicuous at the point of recapitulation (see Ex. 5–2). Whereas the initial two measures of the movement are "barred" from the exposition proper (confirmed for the listener in

EXAMPLE 5–2. *Op. 33/5/i, mm. 166–85*

Joseph Haydn Werke, XII/3: Streichquartette "Opus 20" und "Opus 33," edited by Georg Feder and Sonja Gerlach. Copyright 1974 by G. Henle Verlag, Munich. Used by permission.

its repeat), Haydn includes them here. And he prepares their return with a tentative-sounding retransition that is extended by a grand pause. Dramatiz-

ing the tonic return as both imminent and delayed, the two-bar silence appro-
priates the introductory function of the opening measures of the movement
and sets up the cadential gesture. It is as if, after much jockeying for position,
the participants ignore the closest seat and regroup, only to take up their
original (root) positions—seemingly firm in a move of resolution. Nonetheless, the return isolates and subverts both opening and closing functions: pre-
empting the recapitulation, the opening measures interrupt, both registrally
and harmonically, the "proper" return in measure 184, anticipating and thus
weakening its structural function. Acting true to form, the gesture equivo-
cates.

As might be expected, the ambivalence of the opening measures compli-
cates matters at the close of the movement as well. Following a coda that
recalls the opening gesture's motivic presence throughout the movement, its
legitimate closing function would seem to be at hand (see Ex. 5–3). Measures

EXAMPLE 5–3.   *Op. 33/5/i, m. 286 to end*

Joseph Haydn Werke, XII/3: Streichquartette "Opus 20" und "Opus 33,"
edited by Georg Feder and Sonja Gerlach. Copyright 1974 by G. Henle
Verlag, Munich. Used by permission.

301–2 provide the appropriate formal context for a literal return of measures
1–2, but the association of this gesture with opening functions undermines
the stability expected of a final cadence: the emphasis of repetition is needed
to confirm the close. Stripped of its harmonies, however, this bare unison
version confirms as well the identity of the opening gesture as a generative
motive. Thus the duality of opening and closing is summed up as surely—
and as paradoxically—at the end as at the beginning. Indeed, the rising-fourth
motive may be recognized as superfluous, after all, to the straight cadential
function of the opening gesture; the movement itself could have "done"
without these measures (the recapitulation, too, would have been a more

straightforward affair without them). Their role in signaling play with conventions of style and syntax is the more apparent, then, in the excess of this seeming superfluity.

Haydn preserves an artful equilibrium throughout this movement: between the signifying power that adheres to a convention, even when displaced from normative functional contexts and the novel ambiguities of procedure and formal articulation that such displacements entail. By revealing this interaction of novelty and convention to be essential to his invention, he dramatizes a process of closure that is specific to this movement—one that is provoked and governed by the "double take" of its opening.

Play with closure is not confined to the opening movement of this quartet. Echoes of the cadential motive are heard at the close of the Largo, now in a grave manner and in the minor mode; and reminders of its nonchalance heighten surprise at cadence points in the Scherzo. But it is in the finale that the motivic material of the opening movement's coda is recalled and its unfinished business dramatically resolved. Having displayed the viola and cello in a variation of elaborate passagework, Haydn abandons strict variation treatment of his Allegretto theme. The abbreviated statement that follows, *presto,* launches an extended coda of parting gestures reminiscent of the accelerated action in an opera buffa finale (see Ex. 5–4). In repetitions that prolong (and forestall) closure, the accompanying voices assert new independence. First in the second violin and then in the cello, the tonic pedal ostinato figure undermines cadences in measures 87 and 94. And disagreements between C sharp and C natural, then F sharp and F natural, produce dissonant cross-relations as the original tune is all but given up. Even the unison focus of the ensemble in measures 100ff is diverted by voice exchanges and registral repositioning. If the additive structure of variation movements poses the (theoretical) possibility of infinite addition, this coda flaunts its unexpected continuations: all told, six approaches to a final cadence are tried before a decisive and fully orchestrated close imposes an ending. A familiar convention in opera numbers, the procedure of repeated closing gestures (dubbed by Janet Schmalfeldt the "OMT," or "One More Time" convention)[28] is here playfully excessive. In an obverse of the equally extended close of the "Joke" Quartet's finale, stalling tactics signal closure in a protracted display of leave-taking.

The manners of opening and closing in the first and last movements of the G Major Quartet suggest an interplay of private and public gestures suitable to drawing room wit on the one hand and humorous theatrics on the other. These distinctions draw attention not only to the range of listeners who might be engaged in the quartet's conversation but also to Haydn's task in defining openings and closings for an audience of contingent listeners—present by invitation, so to speak, of the primary participants. Whereas opening remarks in the chamber might be heard even if understated, a breach of decorum could be counted upon to attract attention. Initiating conversation in an intimate manner, Haydn provokes attention to the beginning of this quartet

EXAMPLE 5–4.   *Op.* 33/5/iv, m. 79 to end

Joseph Haydn Werke, XII/3: Streichquartette "Opus 20" und "Opus 33,"
edited by Georg Feder and Sonja Gerlach. Copyright 1974 by G. Henle
Verlag, Munich. Used by permission.

with a gesture that is both familiar and odd, and whose inherent contradictions are not readily reconciled with the rhetorical protocol of opening, return, and closure in sonata-allegro form. The simple theme of the finale, on the other hand, furnishes an amiable subject for varied elaboration that might continue "indefinitely." Here hyperbole reinforces closure as a demonstrative event of consensus. That the work has ended is not in doubt. That the extended play of its ending also resolves the uncertainties of its beginning would amuse and instruct those most attentive to the more subtle artfulness of wit.

Haydn's appeal to the listener in signaling play with beginnings and endings in the opening quartet of Op. 33 is manifest in the opening movement of the last quartet as well. In a gesture reminiscent of the opening of the G Major Quartet, the first movement of the B-flat Major ("No. 4") pushes off from a V^4_3 chord to take cadencing as its chief subject (Ex. 5–5). The first twelve measures do little else, in fact, trying out versions of I and V in various locations within the phrase, measure, and beat, testing register and dynamic level. The tune in measures 7–11 proposes to bring this subject to its point (and cadence), but the stubborn three-note motive forces a new start.[29] (Two false starts will precede the proper recapitulation as various tonal locations for the opening cadence are tried.) Returning to the opening once again at the close, Haydn offers a condensed version of these twelve measures in a brief coda (Ex. 5–6); this time he "gets it right." A listener wise to the devious strategies in this and other movements might well question the finality of the last word. However emphatic, the final cadence is suspect by association: though both shoes have dropped, one half expects a playful third.

The surprising moves that call attention to beginnings in the opening movements of the first and last quartets find parallels throughout the Op. 33 set; only in the D Major Quartet do the voices proceed without hesitation, addressing the subject in various textural combinations. In others, openings are called into question, whether by flat contradiction or by stubborn reiterations of wayward voices that interrupt and delay continuation. Indecision is particularly audible in the B Minor and C Major Quartets, both of which prolong the ambiguity of indirect approaches to the tonic; uncertain beginnings in both movements provoke due compensation in extended closing sections, and in each of these movements an apparent contrast of emphatic stability is accompanied by reminders of unstable beginnings.[30]

The opening of the B Minor Quartet (Ex. 5–7)—tentative and seemingly in D major—yields by degrees to the proper tonic. Even though the $V^{6\text{-}5}$ progression in measure 2 confirms B minor for the attentive listener (a move to A in the second violin would have confirmed D major), conflict between A natural (cello) and A sharp (viola, then first violin) sustains disagreement.[31] In repeated gestures toward resolution, the upper parts fail to persuade the cello until D major's leading tone is inflected to C natural for a Neapolitan assist to the cadence in B minor. Thus delayed by competing voices, the tonic is unanimously confirmed (m. 11) as a dramatic arrival—now a point of departure as well. The equivocation of the movement's beginning is retained in

EXAMPLE 5–5.   *Op.* 33/4/i, mm. 1–13

Joseph Haydn Werke, XII/3: Streichquartette "Opus 20" und "Opus 33,"
edited by Georg Feder and Sonja Gerlach. Copyright 1974 by G. Henle
Verlag, Munich. Used by permission.

the exposition's closing material, emphatically *buffa*, and elsewhere in the
work the D major/B minor ambiguity is conspicuous for its surprising turns:
in the retransition of the finale (mm. 90–109), in the approach to tonic return
in the Andante movement (mm. 52–55), and in the abrupt semitone shifts
needed to redirect voices stalled by reiteration in the *scherzando* minuet. The
automatic tendency to regard works in the minor mode as deeply solemn

EXAMPLE 5–6.   *Op. 33/4/i, m. 85 to end*

Joseph Haydn Werke, XII/3: Streichquartette "Opus 20" und "Opus 33,"
edited by Georg Feder and Sonja Gerlach. Copyright 1974 by G. Henle
Verlag, Munich. Used by permission.

EXAMPLE 5–7.   *Op. 33/1/i, mm. 1–12*

Joseph Haydn Werke, XII/3: Streichquartette "Opus 20" und "Opus 33,"
edited by Georg Feder and Sonja Gerlach. Copyright 1974 by G. Henle
Verlag, Munich. Used by permission.

might be questioned here: overall, Haydn's humor in the B Minor Quartet seems more playfully quixotic than *Sturm und Drang*.[32]

The opening of the C Major Quartet is similarly tentative, but marks out tonic territory in increasingly decisive terms, which are then undermined by new beginnings. The circuitous route through the supertonic and the minor dominant suspends a definitive cadence in C major until measure 18. As in the B Minor Quartet, the confirming cadence is elided in marking the beginning of a related, more stable subject with balanced phrases. Devices that undermine stability persist, however, most particularly at the recapitulation and in the coda's reminder of the opening material that has informed the entire movement.

Even if provocatively framed, the manner of address in these movements projects an air of easy informality in comparison with their counterparts in the Op. 20 quartets. The motivic play that characterizes Haydn's more confident handling of form and medium in Op. 33 promotes an equality of voices consistently focused on the developmental potential of simpler materials. Haydn's opening moves, while surprising expectations of proper beginnings, also challenge those on familiar terms with the formal conventions of opening movements to speculate about the implications of such manipulations. Attentive to the consequences of paradoxical and ambiguous beginnings, connoisseurs in Haydn's audience might enjoy the insider's privilege of discriminating wit.

Haydn's approaches to closure in the finales of Op. 33, on the other hand, extend a more inclusive invitation in manifestly playful manners that delay and heighten expectation of the inevitable. His procedures here are particular to closing movements that are "new and special" by design. In favoring reiterative forms—variation and rondo—to close five of the six quartets, Haydn departs significantly from the finales in earlier sets: three of the Op. 20 group close with fugues, three with sonata-form movements; all six of the Op. 17 finales are in sonata-allegro form, as are five of the six in the Op. 9 set. László Somfai has argued that Haydn's turn to finales that are distinctly different in form and character from opening movements, and his experiments with the weight and internal order of movements, were efforts to achieve a new balance in the cycle overall.[33] Experimenting in Op. 20 with fugal finales, Haydn had displayed his craft in rigorous, thoroughly contrapuntal movements, whose learned terms suggest a self-absorbed and self-sufficient discourse.

The concluding movements of Op. 33 are vastly different in conception and effect. These finales propose frankly simple subjects—four of them *presto*—with sharp rhythmic profiles and homophonic textures. With the exception of the B Minor Quartet (the only finale in sonata-allegro form) all present symmetrically balanced tunes, easily taken in, and primed for variation and rondo procedures. Unlike their counterparts in opening movements, these beginnings do not pose explicit paradox or ambiguity, but they do suggest different strategies for defining closure of the movement and

work. Since, in reiterative forms, the listener cannot be certain of which itera-
tion will be the final one, Haydn's choice of rondo and variation finales offered opportunities for extended anticipation and delay. Here the process of
closure itself becomes thematic.

Whereas in the "Joke" of the E-flat Major Quartet Haydn exploits this
uncertainty up to and including the "end," in others of the Op. 33 finales he
plays with the delay of emphatic consensus. Four of the finales close with
decisive cadences that are fully orchestrated: the closing chords of the G
Major Quartet, discussed above, have counterparts in the finales of the D
Major, B Minor, and B-flat Major Quartets. In the Op. 20 quartets, such gestures define closure in the open-ended fugal movements; the sonata-form
finales in that group, on the other hand, are subdued at the close, descending
to "weak" final cadences over tonic pedal points.[34] These are not less satisfying endings, of course, but they are certainly less emphatic gestures. By comparison, flourishes of triple and quadruple stops make a theatrical display of
closure.

Whether or not final cadences in the finales are dynamically emphatic, the
manner in which they are approached is sufficient notice of their function.
The nickname awarded the finale of the E-flat Major Quartet might as justly
be applied to that of the C Major Quartet, a movement described by Donald
Francis Tovey as "one of Haydn's most comic utterances."[35] In the coda of
this Presto rondo the ludic becomes frankly ludicrous in extended mimicry
between paired voices that makes a mockery of imitation and inversion as
artful contrapuntal devices (Ex. 5–8).

EXAMPLE 5–8.   *Op. 33/3/iv, 146–56*

Joseph Haydn Werke, XII/3: Streichquartette "Opus 20" und "Opus 33,"
edited by Georg Feder and Sonja Gerlach. Copyright 1974 by G. Henle
Verlag, Munich. Used by permission.

This conversation has obviously stalled. That it was likely to do so is suggested by the movement's unpromising beginning, shown in Example 5-9. Despite animated "variation," the opening of the theme is both static in its repetition and unstable in its foundation on a tonic chord in second inversion. Moreover, the abrupt move to firmer ground in measure 5 is graceless in its voice leading, as the prominent G's in the outer voices (here viola and first violin) leave an impression of having committed parallel octaves. (The contrasting section that follows is similarly repetitive and grounded over open-fifth drones.) However lively the chatter of this ensemble, its limited range of rhythmic, melodic, and harmonic material confines the dancelike to rather mechanical turns.

Overall, the finale of the C Major Quartet suggests a comedy of errors in which the lowborn attempt to imitate (or perhaps mock?) the witty conversation of their betters. A case might be made for the first movement as its model: thematic and harmonic correspondences are audible in the openings of the two movements despite their very different settings. But it is in the grace of motivic play with the opening material that urbane manners are most clearly displayed as a world apart from those of the finale's coda (Ex. 5-10). Even in diminution, the opening motive becomes the subject of relaxed exchange among these voices, the play of inversion a gracious rejoinder.[36] In the finale, on the other hand, parody reduces grace to comic distortion. One might, of course, wonder about the target of this parody—the insiders versus the outsiders, in Cohen's terms. The matter hangs dubious between the model and the listener. While the less sophisticated listener would likely find comedy in the broad strokes of the finale and perhaps enjoy a spoof of artificial manners, the connoisseur would more likely discover the wit of its relationship to the opening movement and might derive special satisfaction in confirming the privilege of polished manners and discriminating taste.

EXAMPLE 5-9. *Op. 33/3/iv, mm. 1-8*

Joseph Haydn Werke, XII/3: Streichquartette "Opus 20" und "Opus 33," edited by Georg Feder and Sonja Gerlach. Copyright 1974 by G. Henle Verlag, Munich. Used by permission.

EXAMPLE 5–10. *Op. 33/3/i, mm. 140–50*

Joseph Haydn Werke, XII/3: Streichquartette "Opus 20" und "Opus 33," edited by Georg Feder and Sonja Gerlach. Copyright 1974 by G. Henle Verlag, Munich. Used by permission.

In its combination of understatement and display, the ending of the last work in Op. 33 is a fitting counter to the opening of the first work in the set. As in the G Major Quartet, the first movement of the B-flat Major Quartet takes opening and closing as its subject, and its finale also closes with no lingering uncertainty. Haydn's manipulations of material and listener in this rondo-variation are as manifest as his demands on the performers. From the outset, playful signals are heard in the distracted octave displacements (mm. 5–6) that stray from a seemingly straightforward theme—and point up the stalling quirk of its consequent phrase (Ex. 5–11).[37]

In the course of this movement, the theme's melodic contour is wildly distorted by extensive displacement of register. The coda (Ex. 5–12) begins by restoring its integrity, but suspends closure with exaggerated delays. Here the quirk of measures 5–6 is dramatized in a nine-bar interruption (mm. 197–205) that seems to ask, "Do you remember how this went?" As in the "Joke" finale, silences offer the listener "play space" to recall and predict the possibilities. Thus prepared, the last and simplest version of the theme enters, *pianissimo* and pizzicato. The very novelty of fully scored pizzicato might well have impressed the reviewer Reichardt as a humorous "special effect," but it is in the recasting of the theme's character that the wit of Haydn's dramatic flair is most ingeniously displayed. Reaching "balanced" consensus in a nine-bar answer to previous indecision, a unanimous ensemble exhibits the theme in its barest essentials. At once intimate and theatrical, simple and exotic, this display of closure is a fitting conclusion to both work and opus.

EXAMPLE 5–11. *Op. 33/4/iv, mm. 1–8*

Joseph Haydn Werke, XII/3: Streichquartette "Opus 20" und "Opus 33," edited by Georg Feder and Sonja Gerlach. Copyright 1974 by G. Henle Verlag, Munich. Used by permission.

EXAMPLE 5–12. *Op. 33/4/iv, m. 182 to end*

Joseph Haydn Werke, XII/3: Streichquartette "Opus 20" und "Opus 33," edited by Georg Feder and Sonja Gerlach. Copyright 1974 by G. Henle Verlag, Munich. Used by permission.

"Gli scherzi"

Each of the Op. 33 quartets presents a sequence of four distinctly characterized movements, typically framed by a provocative gambit and a theatrical closing. While such manipulations are most salient in the opening and closing movements, Haydn called special attention to the minuet movements in designating them *Scherzo* and *Scherzando*. In strictly formal terms, these movements do not depart from earlier minuets, nor does Haydn use this label for later ones. But in marking four of them *allegro*, (in the G Major, E-flat Major, B Minor, and D Major Quartets) he assures an immediately audible departure from minuet norms.[38]

Appropriately, the minuet of the opening quartet has the most audibly deviant manners. Beginning with an immediate conflict of metric identity (Ex. 5–13), this Scherzo takes the misplaced downbeats and overextended upbeats of hemiola as its subject. Displacement of the cadence in the first section is answered in the larger form by a seeming return that is aborted (mm. 17ff), and eccentricities of the opening material are augmented in further development. Haydn's procedures here offer a microcosm of incongruities that surprise expectations of decorum in a dance-related movement: distortions of rhythmic, metric, and phrase patterns, sudden stops and prolonged delays, ambiguity of continuation, and patent miscontinuation. The full-measure upbeat that coincides with tonic resolution in measure 32 is a fitting irregularity to launch the return of the opening section—exact but for the *pianissimo* dynamic of its unstable close.

Aside from *allegro* tempos, other minuets of this set display less egregious differences from those of Op. 20. Whereas the minuet of the G Major Quartet features an errant soprano voice and that of the B Minor a stubborn one, the Scherzando of the C Major Quartet, marked *allegretto*, promotes equality of voices in a fully homophonic chordal texture, low and continuous in first-inversion harmonies; the trilling "birds" of its two-voice trio is a thorough contrast—a characterization that the Reverend Jones might have adduced as wild warbling in the chamber. But one might wonder if Haydn consciously recalls the C major/D minor juxtaposition of the first movement in the opening phrases of the minuet; the trio also recalls the opening movement's clock-like upper-voice duet in the closing material of the exposition. While the minuet of the D Major Quartet and both minuet and trio of the B Minor Quartet distribute motivic fragments throughout the texture in a more democratic contrapuntal exchange, the B-flat Major Quartet's *allegretto* Scherzo reverts to the octave doubling of first and second violins characteristic of the early quartets. Overall, these movements do not give the impression of a radical departure from Haydn's previous minuets in the genre. Perhaps in labeling them as "jesting" he signals a manner of ease, advising performers to approach the *allegrettos* as rather more playful than sedate, the *allegros* more relaxed than driven.

Although the nickname of *Gli scherzi* attached to Op. 33 probably derives

EXAMPLE 5–13. *Op.* 33/5/iii, mm. 1–33

Joseph Haydn Werke, XII/3: Streichquartette "Opus 20" und "Opus 33,"
edited by Georg Feder and Sonja Gerlach. Copyright 1974 by G. Henle
Verlag, Munich. Used by permission.

from the composer's titles for the minuet movements, Haydn signals the jesting manners of his new quartets from the outset of the opening work. The
wit of subtle correspondences between movements (noted earlier in the G
Major, B Minor, and C Major Quartets) that link seemingly disparate conversations might be appreciated only by the most discriminating of listeners, but
the audibility of playful procedures throughout the collection distinguishes
Op. 33 as deserving of its acquired title.[39]

While the easy intimacy of diversions in private chambers might have encouraged Haydn's witty, conversational approach to the string quartet in

1781, the dramatic and theatrical elements in Op. 33 suggest the additional influence of his activities in opera during the late 1760s and 1770s. An increasingly heavy burden of responsibility for productions of his own and others' operas followed completion of the opera house at Eszterháza in 1766; composing aside, Haydn's energies must have been pushed to the limit in selecting, coaching, rehearsing, and conducting operas, of which there were ninety-three performances in the year 1780 alone.[40]

Rosen has called attention to the fundamental importance of comic opera for the mature styles of Haydn and Mozart.[41] The demands on the composer of extended ensemble finales, in particular, promoted a dramatic pacing of continuous action and clear articulation of structural events in instrumental music. Haydn's experience in composing and directing operas may well have fostered the tighter continuity and more emphatic punctuation in the Op. 33 quartets, providing as well models for "staged conversations" in the chamber. The finales in particular suggest the syllabic diction of comic opera; so too the endings that recall parting gestures of the theater. But here, as in the opening movements of Op. 33, Haydn accommodates demonstrative manners of address to the intimacy of the chamber. He also distinguishes the tastes and abilities of its occupants in inviting listeners to recognize not only the conventions of a style but also the ludic potential of invention within that style.

To single out the Op. 33 string quartets as evidence of Haydn's first maturity in the Classical style is, as James Webster has pointed out, to put undue emphasis on these works as a point of arrival.[42] Privileged status might as well be claimed for the Opp. 17 and 20 sets, in which the expressive power of the genre and equal-voiced texture of the medium are new and special achievements in comparison with Haydn's earliest quartets. Or, looking to the Op. 50 quartets of 1787, one can assert as new Haydn's thorough mastery of motivic development in more extended works that recall the contrapuntal intensity of Op. 20. On the other hand, to regard the Op. 33 quartets as aimed low to amuse the unsophisticated is to slight the significance of their claims on the listener.[43] Beyond simply diverting the *Liebhaber* as capricious reversals, "twisted" conventions are displayed as artful devices that challenge routine responses to the familiar and alert listeners to the play of alternative meanings in progress. In proposing frankly tuneful and seemingly artless materials, Haydn makes irregular manners all the more salient. And in strategies that render familiar gestures ambiguous in function, that prolong anticipation and thwart arrivals, he gives surprise dramatic point. The playful wit that infuses these works is one of profound consequences in calling attention not only to musical events and procedures but also to the roles of performers and listeners in that play—and ultimately to the composer as *magister ludi*.

Offering challenges and delights to the connoisseur as well as the amateur, the Op. 33 quartets found a responsive market. Numerous printings of the collection appeared throughout Europe and in London, as did a large number of arrangements of the works for other instruments.[44] The chronicle of critical response to specific works of Haydn is sparse in the early 1780s, but Reichardt's favorable review of the Op. 33 quartets was seconded by another prominent editor and reviewer, Carl F. Cramer:

> These works have been praised and cannot be praised enough, in view of the most ingenious humor and the most lively, most agreeable wit that prevails in them. I understand that Bach in Hamburg, an artist of quite fastidious taste, who nevertheless refrains from issuing harsh, pedantic, and injurious criticism of lesser talents, has expressed extreme satisfaction at these works of Haydn.[45]

Cramer's notice of C. P. E. Bach's endorsement—whether or not firsthand information—is a significant indication of the rising status of Viennese instrumental music.

The response of Mozart to the Op. 33 quartets was perhaps Haydn's greatest tribute, however. In a letter of dedication he attached to his "Haydn" Quartets, Mozart acknowledges that they are the result of "a long and laborious effort," and he expresses in moving terms his debt to the older man as a spiritual father, sponsor, and friend. Composed between 1783 and 1785, the six quartets published by Artaria as Mozart's Op. 10 (K. 387, 421, 428, 458, 464, and 465) followed a hiatus in quartet composition comparable to Haydn's own. And like the earlier quartets of Mozart that reflect the influence of Haydn's Op. 20, these works demonstrate the younger composer's absorption of Haydn's new mastery of the medium in motivic play. Stanley Sadie marks the change as one in which "textures [are] conceived not merely in four-part harmony but as four-part discourse, with the actual musical ideas ineluctably linked to a freshly integrated treatment of the medium."[46]

More specific correspondences are heard in several movements, most especially in the finales,[47] but the differences in Mozart's compositional temperament are even more audible. The finale of the A Major Quartet, K. 464, offers a particularly good example of the chromaticism and dissonance that distinguish Mozart's musical discourse—and for which he was often criticized by contemporary listeners. Specific mention of this movement by Gerber affords a look into the chamber and private music making among "educated friends." Gerber quotes passages of the finale without mentioning the name of its composer:

> There is a most artistically worked out and abundantly penetrating finale that is built out of the following principal theme:

> I hardly need say that if by chance the first violinist allows his finger to slip or to drag these notes, and the other players follow his example, the entire theme, however artistically it is interwoven throughout the whole finale, will sound like a pitiful meow. . . . Moreover, not only is this chromatic passage extended even further in the course of the movement, e.g.,

but it is also supported with the most cutting, most dissonant harmonies in the other instruments. Such music can only succeed with musicians whose ears have become to a certain extent dulled and desensitized by constant study and playing . . . or with those educated in the art who listen merely with the intellect and seek no enjoyment other than that which springs from any gratification of the mind. Indeed, this is why the honorable composer wrote this finale not for public performance by a full orchestra, but rather for the private music making of a quartet for musicians and educated friends of art: thus this art piece of his, in the setting where it belongs, is not only blameless but praiseworthy as an exercise and wonderful effusion of humor.[48]

Making a sharp distinction between what is appropriate fare for the general public and that intended for private music making by expert players, Gerber judges Mozart's "art piece" to be an exercise in extremes. Its humor appeals to connoisseurs, whose enjoyment is suspiciously intellectual.[49]

Turning to his second example with obvious relish, Gerber reproduces the theme of the opening movement of Haydn's Symphony No. 104, distinguishing its constituent motives. "Hear it as often as it truly returns in the piece, only always newly formed, and say if I am wrong when I maintain that each portion expresses clearly: Now I am happy! all cares vanish; joy laughs, what more do I want?" His final counsel to composers is that they seek to express the spontaneous cheerfulness of such a work, for "whoever makes men happy also makes them better; and whoever makes them better is their benefactor."[50] Beyond exhorting others to emulate Haydn in addressing the feelings as well as the intellect, Gerber asserts both the social role of instrumental music and a moral dimension of the composer's responsibility to listeners in the public domain. Haydn's "art of seeming familiar" and his "popular artfulness" would impress critics such as Gerber and Triest most forcibly in the public style of his late works, but the composer's self-conscious mode of address to new listeners had roots in the first set of quartets he composed for the public.

6

Extended Play in Eccentric Finales

Unlike most solo and ensemble genres of the chamber, the symphony of the middle to late eighteenth century could claim a range of public functions and venues. In addition to being heard in private chambers and in church, symphonies served as overtures to both comic and serious operas, as incidental music to spoken plays, as introductions and entr'actes for oratorios, and as opening and closing pieces that framed the varied fare of public concerts of the day, in which concertos and vocal numbers figured as the choice items. In many of these contexts the symphony served an introductory and subordinate role in calling attention to the main events that followed.[1]

In his entry on the symphony for Sulzer's *Allgemeine Theorie der schönen Künste* (1774), J. A. P. Schulz notes distinctions of function and style in theatrical and chamber settings:

> The symphony is excellently suited for the expression of the grand, the festive, and the noble. Its purpose is to prepare the listeners for an important musical work, or in a chamber concert to summon up all the splendor of instrumental music. If it is to satisfy this [former] aim completely and be a closely bound part of the opera or church music that it precedes, then besides being the expression of the grand and festive, it must have an additional quality that puts listeners in the frame of mind required by the piece to come, and it must distinguish itself through the style of composition that makes it appropriate for the church or theater.[2]

Elaborating further, Schulz notes that opera symphonies need not be as carefully worked out as those for the chamber, "because the listener is more attentive to that which is to follow than to the symphony itself." (In Schulz's account the Italians are happy with a "nice sounding noise" in such overtures, the French with an alternation of "trivial and bombastic" passages.)

The chamber symphony, on the other hand, which "constitutes a whole

116

in and of itself and has no following music in view, achieves its end wholly through a full sounding, brilliant, and fiery style." For such pieces to command attention and sustain interest, he advises the use of strong and startling contrasts of harmony, texture, and dynamics and artful connections of voices to ensure coherence. Chamber symphonies as described by the Berliner Schulz are three-movement cycles, lacking the minuet typically found by this time in Austrian and South German symphonies. While he certainly admits the dramatic element into symphonies of the chamber, Schulz prescribes an equivalent style and content for opening and closing movements.[3]

The symphonies Haydn was composing in the 1770s, at the time of Schulz's writing, depart radically from this model, not simply in including minuets, but in finales that are distinctly unlike opening movements and in which the dramatic style is defined in rather different terms. In exploring that difference, I focus in this chapter on intimate and theatrical manners in Haydn's symphonic finales, with attention to formal procedures that promote the success of jests. While novel strategies of engagement might be expected in symphonies composed specifically for public performance, the relationship of theatrical and chamber styles to performance setting is more complex in earlier works intended for a more restricted audience. As evidence of the problematic issues of style and venue, I turn first to a finale with theatrical connections.

Overture/Finale: A Distinguishing Connection

Among the six symphonies printed by Jean Julien Hummel in 1781 and reviewed with favor by Johann Reichardt, two, Symphonies Nos. 62 (c. 1780) and 63 (1777–80), have opening movements that originated in a theatrical context as opera overtures. The first movement of Symphony No. 62 has the more complicated history and is of particular interest here. Serving first as overture to an opera that remains unknown, the movement appeared in slightly revised scoring as the finale ("B") to one of several versions of Symphony No. 53 (before 1777).[4] One implication of such recycling is that during a period of heavy responsibilities for opera productions at Eszterháza, Haydn hastily assembled pieces composed for theatrical use to do double duty as symphonic movements.[5] Such a practice, at least in the case of Symphony No. 53, also suggests that in function and style there was little to distinguish an opening from a closing movement. Schulz, we recall, claimed as much with respect to chamber symphonies. Symphony No. 62 provides a model for investigating both the relationship of a symphonic opening movement to its theatrical source and that of a first movement to a finale.

Haydn's revisions of the overture (Hob. Ia:7) for use as a finale in Symphony No. 53 involved only slight alteration: aside from adding a flute to the scoring, he omitted the thirteen-bar transition that linked the overture to the

beginning of the opera.[6] In its later appearance as the first movement of
Symphony No. 62, however, the opening section of the overture-finale is
modified to make a broader statement. Example 6–1 compares the openings
of both. The original Presto's three-bar phrases are expanded to five in the

EXAMPLE 6–1.

   a. *Overture*, Hob. Ia:7, mm. 1–12

Edited by H. C. Robbins Landon. Copyright 1969 Ludwig Doblinger
(Bernhard Herzmansky) K. G., Vienna/Munich. Used by permission of
Music Associates of America.

EXAMPLE 6–1 a. *(Continued)*

b. *Symphony 62/i, mm. 1–14*

b.   *(Continued)*

Allegro, as Haydn recomposes a more leisurely and continuous version of measures 2–3; the repeating fragment in measures 11–14 of the latter version, drawn from measures 9–10 of the overture, is more audibly static for refusing to change. Whereas the earlier movement proceeds to a half cadence only to repeat its opening twelve measures, the symphony moves on in measure 15, jumping to measure 24 of the original and expanding its dimensions once again; for the remainder of the movement, the only significant departure from the overture is a double bar with repeat sign after closing material in the dominant, the normative procedure for movements in so-called sonata-allegro form.

Despite these alterations, the symphony's Allegro contains many of the elements of Haydn's overtures: a triadic fanfare opening; rapidly changing textures of full and reduced scoring and dynamics; constant pulsing subdivisions of the beat; and a penchant for repetition. It also resembles overtures in having a distinctly different second-key theme. Less typical is the development section common to both overture and symphony, which is doubly striking for exploring material new to the movement (though assisted by a familiar figure) and for its leisurely yet bold modulations. As seen in Example 6–2, Haydn takes as his subject a simple arpeggio figure and traces a slow-moving and continuous sequence over sustained pedals. In an extended progression (mm. 77–93) from B minor (vi) to F-sharp minor (iii), root movement is by third. Prolonged dominant preparation for return of the opening theme in F-sharp minor (at m. 104) gives the mediant key particular emphasis as a mediating tonic between the dominant, A major, and the tonic, D major (reached with the proper recapitulation in m. 110).

I draw attention to this section because its material is related to that of the symphony's finale, which is striking in its opening move (Ex. 6–3). The shifting diminished and minor harmonies of this oblique beginning, give the im-

EXAMPLE 6-2. *Symphony 62/i, mm. 69–82*

*) ♩ ♪ so in thus in Hummel, Basso

EXAMPLE 6–3. *Symphony 62/iv, mm. 1–12*

*) Cor. I, 7-20, in den Quellen = Cor. II; nach T. 129 ff geändert
   Cor. I, 7-20, in the sources = Cor. II; changed on basis of bars 129 ff

pression of a displaced passage more at home as a transition to the return of an opening theme than as the opening theme itself. By commenting on similar material heard previously in its appropriate context (a development section), Haydn jests with contradiction in an uncertain start that is both eccentric and strangely familiar.

Varied in subsequent appearances in the finale, the strange beginning increasingly takes on developmental characteristics, first in the imitative voice added to its repetition in measures 29–34, then in the transition passage that follows. But confirmation of its rightful function comes only at the end of the development section. Following prolonged stasis in the minor tonic (mm. 95–119) and tentative attempts to recover the opening material, the seventh of the dominant chord finds resolution in a thoroughly transformed version of the movement's beginning measures, as shown in Example 6-4. At once ushering in the return of his opening material and disguising it as additional development, Haydn displays the functional context of his dysfunctional opening as appropriate preparation for the tonal recapitulation.

The wit of this extended play with incongruity links procedures and materials shared by both opening and closing movements. In that the opening movement is a close relative of a preexisting overture, its theatrical origin is clear. But if in Symphony No. 53 Haydn was content to use the same source as finale, in Symphony No. 62 he makes an obvious distinction between opening and closing movements. Here the finale could scarcely be exchanged for the opening movement, nor would it suit the opening of a theatrical work: its understated beginning, if heard at all, would be simply strange, its point without reference.

Off-tonic beginnings are rare in Haydn's symphonies,[7] and none appears at the very beginning of an opening movement. When Haydn does approach the tonic obliquely in the principal theme of a first movement, it is after a slow introduction has established the tonal center of the work (as in Symphonies Nos. 86, 90, 92, and 94). Such introductions provide not only the tonal reference point for the movement but also the broad gestures needed to announce the beginning of a public work. On the other hand, there are several instances of off-tonic openings in Haydn's string quartets, one of which we have noted in the ambiguous opening of the B Minor Quartet in Op. 33.[8] As a provocative gesture in the chamber, this might suit the opening movement of a quartet, but would be an unlikely choice for an overture or the opening of a symphony heard in public performance.

Even so, the connecting link in Symphony No. 62 is a rather recondite allusion. In his late symphonies Haydn makes audible the relationship of opening materials with distinct functions. The *adagio* introduction of Symphony No. 98, for example, begins with material that is shortly taken up in the principal theme of its Allegro. Example 6-5 compares these beginnings. Appropriately dramatic in outlining the minor tonic triad, the introduction proceeds by indirection, recasting the gesture as a major triad not of the tonic but of the submediant, thus sustaining expectation of B-flat minor. The rela-

EXAMPLE 6–4. *Symphony 62/iv, mm. 123–30*

EXAMPLE 6–5. *Symphony 98/i, mm. 1–8; 16–21*

tionship of the Allegro's theme is unmistakable, as is the surprise of its major difference.

Heinrich Koch, who reprinted whole paragraphs of Schulz's article in his *Versuch einer Anleitung zur Composition*, vol. 3 (1793), and *Musikalisches Lexikon* (1802), acknowledged that by this time differences between chamber and theater styles and character were difficult to locate in instrumental genres:

> [T]he theatrical manner of writing, because it is meant not simply for connoisseurs and amateurs of music, but rather for a larger and mixed public, should distinguish itself from the chamber style more through simplicity of expression and through less art, although now it is difficult to draw a distinct boundary line to separate it from the chamber style.[9]

Departing from the chamber, symphonies heard in public concerts might command attention by relying on theatrical devices. But to sustain that attention in contexts independent of theatrical functions would require more rather than "less art."

While the simplicity that Koch notes was a key element in the public address of Haydn's late symphonic style, the "great art of seeming familiar" praised by Gerber was achieved in a synthesis of theatrical and chamber styles. Part of that synthesis lay in the potential of an expanding orchestral medium for a wide range of contrasts—in color, texture, and dynamics—in the handling of both dramatic and intimate effects. Although this was a powerful and flexible resource in all movements of the symphony, Haydn found in the finale an ideal vehicle for artfully extended play with seemingly simple materials and surprising procedures. Evidence of humorous manners that become characteristic in late works can be found in much earlier symphonic finales, among them those specifically marked *scherzando*.

Symphonic Scherzandi

Many have noted the highly charged dramatic style—often assigned the catchall label *Sturm und Drang*—that is conspicuous in several of Haydn's symphonies of the late 1760s and early 1770s.[10] Focusing most often on works in the minor mode, writers have located features of "storm and stress" in intensely contrapuntal textures, in disjunct melodic lines shaded by chromaticism, in abrupt contrasts both harmonic and dynamic, and in driving rhythms agitated by syncopation. Dramatic surprise is an undeniable element in this style.

Play with surprise, on the other hand, is not generally treated as such under the *Sturm und Drang* rubric. Nonetheless, several of the finales in Haydn's symphonies of this period propose dramatic surprise in playful terms, most notably those of Symphonies Nos. 35 (1767), 42 (1771), 43 (before 1772), 46 (1772), 47 (1772), 50 (1773), 51 (before 1774), and 55 (1774). Among these, two movements, from Symphonies Nos. 42 and 46 are specifically marked

scherzando. Haydn used such an indication for only three symphonic movements—the third in Symphony No. 66 (c. 1778)—all of which are *presto* finales.[11] It might be argued that in using such a term he simply meant to
direct musicians to perform these movements in a light and playful manner:
if *scherzando* is taken as an indication of compositional jesting, why are only
three among many allegedly playful finales so marked? To this I have no
ready answer. Shared features in these three finales suggest, however, that
scherzando signals more than a performance direction: audible in each movement are surprising interruptions and miscontinuations, reversals that frustrate closure, the stasis of repeating fragments seemingly lost in time, and the
recasting of thematic materials in unexpected settings. Variation procedure
is conspicuous in the hybrid forms of all three, and in each a codalike episode
recollects the eccentricities of earlier materials in extended commentary.
Overall, these *scherzandi* exemplify the playful manners of reiteration and
exaggeration—whether of overstatement or understatement.

The earliest of these, the finale of Symphony No. 42 (1771), can be sche-
matically shown as follows, each section containing the internal repeats typical of two-reprise binary structures:

A	B	A var1	C	A var2	Coda (C + A)
DM: I	I	I	i	I	I
mm. 1–20	21–36	37–56	57–97	98–117	118–48

Following Koch, Elaine Sisman suggests the term rondo-variation as appropriate for hybrids of this type that combine variation and refrain elements.[12] In
the coda of the movement Haydn compresses remnants of the refrain and
resolves unfinished business of the *minore* "C" section that stands at its center. Example 6–6a shows the opening reprise of this, the longest of the finale's
sections. The first *forte* marking in the movement reinforces the chromatic
neighbor of the dominant; upon return (Ex. 6–6b), these disturbances are
extended and defused, as upbeats and afterbeats find a tentative resolution.
In the nonchalant close that links this section with the reprise of the A section that follows, disruptive voices are brought into conformity with the
theme.

Recalling the disparate elements of the *minore* episode, the coda requires
more definitive capitulation to the task of closure. As can be seen in Example
6–7, a number of devices extend play with previous material and with closure
of the work. Taking up a fragment of the theme's closing phrase—itself an
inversion of the penultimate phrase—Haydn reduces the continuation to a
repeating three-note motive stalled over dominant anticipation of tonic
resolution. Teased by delays of fermatas and silence, the descending-
appoggiatura motive confirms its relationship—by inversion—to the "C" section's frustrated upbeat figure in the *forte* passage that follows, the conclusion of which is again interrupted. Subverting the tonic resolution expected

EXAMPLE 6–6.   *Symphony 42/iv*

a.   mm. 57–64

b.   mm. 84–97

in measure 136, Haydn pauses for one final recollection of the D minor section, reducing its chromatic disturbance to playful voice exchange about the
augmented-sixth chord before giving over closure to material derived from
the "A" theme.

In character and style, the finale of Symphony No. 42 closely resembles
Haydn's divertimenti for winds and strings of the 1760s. Fine details in articulation, texture, and scoring, together with the prevailing *piano* dynamic level
and modest dimensions of this movement, suggest the intimacy of diversions
in the chamber, where the wit of variation is subtle in its play.

The finale of Symphony No. 46 (1772) is more overtly eccentric in its gestures and decidedly peculiar in its form. Noteworthy for a start is its key, B
major, which is unique among Haydn's symphonies.[13] Focused almost exclusively on variants of its opening two measures, this sonata-form Presto e
scherzando reveals motivic affinities with prior movements (see Ex. 6–8). A
verbatim and extended quotation from the minuet in the coda is its most

EXAMPLE 6–7. *Symphony 42/iv, mm. 106–48*

irregular feature, and one that makes the relationship between the two movements abundantly clear. But there is more to the affinity of these two movements than a motivic correspondence, for from its beginning this finale is
disposed to instant replay.

Throughout the movement intensive and audible reworking of the opening subject gives new meaning to the words *thematische Arbeit*—thematic or
motivic "work," or developmental working-out, in the German, but more
often rendered in English as "motivic play." Both senses are appropriate to
the procedures and effects of this Scherzando. As revealed in Haydn's treatment, the figure in measures 1–2 contains two motives: the first, labeled *x* in
Example 6–9, is a simple closing gesture; the second, *y*, is a gesture that resists
closure. Both are heard in various guises in their respective functions
throughout the exposition, as well as in combination (see Ex. 6–10). In succes-
sive restarts and progressively extended periods, the opening of the movement is repeatedly disrupted by variations on the afterbeat of *y*. Decisive
arrival in the dominant key follows an extended review of variants on the
opening descending-fifth motive, in canon and in augmentation, above variants of the *y* motive. The compulsion of the latter to reiterate undermines

EXAMPLE 6-7. *(Continued)*

EXAMPLE 6-8. *Symphony 46*
   a. i, mm. 1–4

   b. iii, mm. 15–18

   c. iv, mm. 1–2

EXAMPLE 6–9. *Symphony 46/iv, 1–8*

decisive closure even at the end of the exposition, as superfluous and fading afterbeats fade into silence.

Not surprising, the excess of inconclusive gestures toward closure at the end of the exposition is recalled at the end of the movement for further manipulation, to which low pedal tones from the horns (in B) offer a novel and amusing answer (Ex. 6–11). Thus grounded, one last *pianissimo* variant of the opening material wavers between tonic and subdominant before being cut off by a resounding full close.

The events that intervene between these two versions of closure are at the heart of the finale's jesting wit. Following an intensive examination of his fitful theme, Haydn abandons the development proper after twenty-four measures (though not without exploring the remote regions of D-sharp major and its dominant) and turns to a straightforward recapitulation with the barest of preparation. If the return of opening material was inadequately signaled, more than enough dominant preparation precedes the unexpected return of the minuet, whose appearance is an interruption that puts all previous eccentricities in the shade. Occupying a full thirty measures of the movement's coda, and replacing agitated stops and starts with graceful play on the descending motive in slow motion, the minuet poses as the model of decorum. But the manner in which the dance movement is recalled exhibits a fundamental kinship with the finale: quoting first measures 15–26 of the minuet and then its entire second section, Haydn replays the original's forgetfulness of its own beginning as well as its propensity for reiteration (Ex. 6–12). Displaying similarities between the two movements that exceed a motivic bond, the incongruous juxtaposition reveals in the end a congruity of musical character and of compositional procedure.

Combining elements of the theatrical and chamber styles, this *scherzando* finale offers a broad range of play with motive, syntax, form, and style. (One imagines that Schulz would have been hard pressed to find an appropriate

EXAMPLE 6–10.   *Symphony 46/iv*, schematic of mm. 1–71

EXAMPLE 6–11. *Symphony* 46/iv, m. 189 to end

category for such a finale—perhaps he would have found its manners altogether undeserving of the name *symphony*.) Landon aptly compares its effect to "a scene out of *commedia dell'arte*, with Columbine and Harlequin enacting some kind of pantomime in front of us: basically very amusing but with queer overtones."[14] However amusing and theatrical, the formal surprises and exaggerated gestures of the movement also direct attention to more subtle peculiarities of local details and to the compositional wit that reveals their relationships. Moreover, in displaying his materials as capable of ever-changing shapes and uses, Haydn animates his subjects as seemingly autonomous. Even though given to distracted repetitions, however, these motives do not become automatons. They seem, on the contrary, to take on a life of their own—unpredictable and surprising in their capricious manners.

   In comparison with its earlier counterpart in Symphony No. 42, the Scherzando e presto finale of Symphony No. 66 (c. 1778) is a considerably expanded rondo-variation movement with a wider range of intimate and theatrical play. Its formal structure is also unusual in combining rondo, variation, and concerto procedures, and its coda expands to include all three in a solo

EXAMPLE 6-12. *Symphony 46/iv, 148–88*

133

134   FRAMES OF REFERENCE

"cadenza" and tutti ritornello *cum* variation. The form of the movement might be shown as follows, "A" representing varied refrains, with intervening developmental episodes on refrain material:

A	Episode	A var1	Bridge + partial A	Episode	A var2
I	→V	I	→IV	(ii)→V/	I→
1–28	29–66	67–94	95–112	113–48	149–76

Coda: Bridge→"cadenza" A var3 (confirming tutti)
        177–84   185–207   208–42

Less boldly eccentric than the finale of Symphony No. 46, this is a movement similarly given to intensive development of its opening theme and to contrapuntal play with its motives. Above all, the finale of Symphony No. 66 is a model case of Haydn's subtle play with rhythm and phrase.

The astute observer Triest regarded as the "quintessence" of Haydn's greatness his "exceptionally facile handling of rhythm, in which no one else equals him."[15] Few early writers comment on Haydn's imaginative use of rhythm. Cramer, in his *Magazin der Musik* of 1787, does mention this feature and its potential for surprising effect. With respect to the Piano Trios Hob. XV:9, 2, and 10, issued by Hummel as Op. 27, the reviewer notes:

> In the Allegro of the second, in F Major [XV:2], the shortening of the rhythm in the sixth measure surprises the listener, taking many unawares, no doubt. The theme of the final Adagio with four variations becomes very original by means of the expansion of the rhythm in the seventh measure.[16]

The "shortening of the rhythm," shown in Example 6–13, compresses two bars into one (in m. 6), thus foreshortening a normative eight-bar period (4 + 4) to one of seven measures (4 + 3). The theme of the last movement features a similarly asymmetrical period, here of nine (5 + 4) measures. What Cramer views as an "expansion of the rhythm" is perhaps the syncopation of measures 6 and 7. But, as seen in Example 6–14, the real irregularity precedes this four-bar phrase: the paired two-bar phrases of the opening four measures have a dangling participle in the incomplete repetition of measure 5. In both cases, Cramer has pointed out the surprise that accompanies a departure from the symmetrical periodic phrasing normative in music of the Classical period.

Such asymmetries are manifest in the finale of Symphony No. 66, in which motivic play joins with rhythmic and formal expansion. The prototype for irregularities of "scansion" and expansion throughout the movement is the opening dance-like theme (Ex. 6–15a) that dominates every episode. Among various possible versions, Example 6–15b would do as a more direct (and pedestrian) four-bar route for each of these five-bar phrases. In Haydn's artful expansion, the upper voice turns back and marks time to allow the lower voice to catch up.

EXAMPLE 6–13.

   a. *Piano Trio*, Hob. XV:2/i, mm. 1–7

   b. Hypothetical 4 + 4 version

EXAMPLE 6–14. *Piano Trio* Hob. XV:2/iv, mm. 1–9

    The reiterative tendency of the accommodating leading part is audible as delay at important structural points throughout the movement. Repeating afterbeats in measures 15–18, for example, precede the upbeat to the return of the opening reprise of the theme, expanding a three-bar phrase to four—in this context, an irregular-sounding extension. Extended play with the afterbeat-upbeat relationship previewed in these measures serves elsewhere in the movement, most conspicuously in the passage that confirms F major as the secondary key (Ex. 6–16). Here the outer voices are in canon, seemingly stuck in repeating ever-shorter fragments:

EXAMPLE 6–15.

  a.   *Symphony 66/iv, mm. 1–19*

  b.   Hypothetical 4 + 4 version of mm. 1–10

EXAMPLE 6–16. *Symphony 66/iv, mm. 36–51*

EXAMPLE 6–16.   *(Continued)*

two bars, one bar, one-half bar. One last delaying quirk in measure 49 makes of an
expected four-bar phrase a five-bar close to this extended approach to the cadence.

The contrapuntal play of motives notable in the above examples is present
from the beginning of this finale and is carried on throughout the movement
in textures that range from intimate two-part exchange to fully orchestrated
canonic episodes. In preparing the tonic return of the refrain in measure 149,
here an event that resembles a large-scale recapitulation, Haydn displays his
artful invention in revisiting the delay of measures 17–18 (Ex. 6–17). After
prolonged and emphatic dominant preparation, the *pianissimo* chromatic ascent sounds relatively indecisive, although its reduced scoring provides an
appropriate transition of five bars to the theme's opening phrase. The relationship of the two figures is given playful emphasis in the accented appoggiatura that alters the theme's original shape, as it answers the tentative figure
with an incisively diatonic inversion and is answered in turn by the lower
strings. In this subtle alteration of the melody, Haydn points up the contrapuntal line that has accompanied the theme from its opening entrance.

The chamber-like intimacy of voice exchange at this point of structural
articulation answers the requirements of the thematic materials and calls attention to their elasticity upon return. Focusing on the subtle irregularities
of simply stated materials, Haydn exploits the full range of his ensemble in
revealing their potential for private and public effects. Decidedly theatrical
(and generically incongruous in this setting) is the tutti gesture that prepares
a cadenzalike passage of wind and string dialogue on fragments of the theme
toward the close of the movement. Yet even the fully orchestrated *fortissimo*

EXAMPLE 6–17. *Symphony 66/iv, mm. 138–51*

"ritornello" that closes the work preserves a chamber-like dialogue in its hocketing exchanges of theme fragments in their final appearance. Inventive in its play with rhythmic, motivic, textural, and formal variation, this *scherzando* is also a finely tuned balance of the intimate and the theatrical.

It is not surprising that finales would be fitting vehicles for such effects. Relieved of the opening movement's responsibility for broad, attention-getting gestures, the closing movement can begin in an intimate manner, *piano* and in reduced scoring, with an informal air of familiarity, and the reserves of the tutti ensemble can be counted upon for commentary on the waywardness of individual voices, as well as for appropriately definitive conclusions. In mapping the itinerary from opening to close, Haydn draws upon a variety of formal procedures, as the three *scherzando* finales demonstrate. Recognition of the witty interplay between local eccentricity and overall formal structure is particular to the materials in each of these movements, but all share a tendency to repeat and exaggerate peculiar features: in the eighteenth-century sense, these movements display their humors.

Deceptively Familiar Finales

Not always charitable to the efforts of literary wits and their drawing-room counterparts, Samuel Johnson located an essential hazard of jesting in its effect on listeners: "the hapless wit has his labour always to begin; the call for novelty is never satisfied, and one jest only raises expectations of another."[17] Suggestive of the general expectation that attaches to one who is typecast as a wit, Johnson's statement is relevant in more particular ways to the formal procedures that promote continued jesting in music. In the large-scale returns of tonal and thematic patterns that are characteristic in sonata and rondo forms, extended preparations for previously heard subjects offer opportunity for teasing the listener's anticipation. So too, subtle alterations of the subjects can themselves be a test (and object lesson) for the attentive listener in recalling the details of previous appearances. Additive, open-ended structures that combine rondo and variation procedures, such as that of Symphony No. 66's finale, are well suited to the playing out of incongruous features: tonally stable refrains that alternate with contrasting, often episodic and developmental sections allow progressive variation of both returning materials and the preparatory passages that anticipate them. In rondo finales of the middle to late 1770s Haydn often chooses to begin with the most simple and regular of themes, concentrating eccentric manners in subsequent appearances of the refrain and in exaggerating the delays of its return.

In presenting opening subjects with decidedly eccentric features, however, he calls attention to their incongruities from the start. To counteract increasing familiarity (and waning surprise) with each return, the composer must compound the oddity of his subject, progressively exaggerating its humorous character. An alternative to using reiterative rondo forms in finales was to display an eccentric opening theme as seemingly at odds with normative syntactic functions, a strategy we have noted in several opening movements of the Op. 33 string quartets. A notable example is the finale of Symphony No. 80 (c. 1783–84), whose opening theme is heard as deceptively simple, an

EXAMPLE 6–18. *Symphony 80/iv*
  a.   mm. 1–8 (as heard)

  b.   mm. 1–15 (as notated)

uninspired "tune," squarely on the beat (Ex. 6–18a). But things are not as they sound, and the listener soon discovers that this is indeed eccentric material posing as square: the notation of these eight bars, as Example 6–18b shows, is thoroughly off-beat. The first clue to the syncopation is heard with the chord change on the (proper) downbeat of measure 11. Here the harmonic rhythm of the continuation collides with the expected pattern (the "heard version"), producing a temporary kinesthetic imbalance. Firm metric confirmation of the dominant as the goal of the phrase in measure 12 requires an adjustment in hearing the melody as the syncopated element in measure 11—and, retrospectively, in measures 1–11. When it is repeated, the theme is heard as Haydn wrote it—thoroughly syncopated and animated by a governing pulse of eighth notes rather than the flat-footed quarter notes first perceived in the opening bars.

While syncopation is felt throughout the movement, the subject's eccentricity makes a peculiar fit with its subsequent formal functions—an incongruity used to explicitly playful effect at the moment of recapitulation. There are in fact two such "moments," the first of which is a ruse. A series of deceptive maneuvers begins with the preparations for this first return: a stasis of repeating anticipatory gestures on the presumptive dominant, a dominant pedal (the syncopated element here), a dramatic pause on the repeated dominant chord—squarely on the beat—followed by a rest with fermata. The continuation in the violins, seen in Example 6–19, is doubly deceptive. The fermata has undermined the downbeat's placement, such that the repeated B's sound at first as an echo of the preparatory gestures rather than as the syncopated beginning of the awaited theme. With the entrance of the lower strings, the thematic return is confirmed, but the anticipated harmonic goal (E major) is not. Instead, the insistent B is simply appropriated as the third in G major. Thus, not only is the return false with respect to the overall tonal scheme normative for such a movement, but the anticipatory gestures themselves are denied a proper local resolution. There is an added twist in this deception: in that the syncopated tune began on the third of the tonic, the repeated notes of the returning theme do in fact "fit" the unexpected resolution.

The modulating sequence of measures 171ff reveals the deception of the reprise, as the harmonies are directed toward a new goal with renewed dominant preparation. The anticipatory gestures are restaged with some significant differences (Ex. 6–20): the repeating I–V formula is stated twice, heard now as a cadential six-four, above the syncopated dominant pedal (now with added horns); the repeated dominant chord is stripped to a single tone, F sharp; and the twice-repeated octaves are heard, now syncopated, as an eccentric version of the conventional anticipatory gesture. Here the syncopation sounds incongruous, but is entirely appropriate as a rhythmic anticipation of the theme. The repeated F sharps are picked up without a fermata delay by the first violins, at once echoing and compressing the anticipatory gesture while ushering in the true recapitulation. Again the harmonic preparation has been deceptive, as the presumed dominant, F sharp, is taken over as the third in D major. It is perhaps Haydn's ultimate jest, however, that the prominent F sharps of the theme's beginning define as major the mode of this concluding movement to a D minor symphony.

Disguised as overly familiar, then revealed as frankly odd, this finale's theme is typecast as humorous from its first appearance. Adjusting formal

EXAMPLE 6-19. *Symphony 80/iv, mm. 157-72*

procedures to suit his eccentric material, Haydn underscores the theme's
own idiosyncracies. At the same time, he reveals the demands that unconventional materials make on conventional gestures of articulation in sonata
forms—and in turn on the interpreting listener.

Many of Haydn's later finales exploit the listener's expectations of formal
procedures commensurate with the ingenuous simplicity and format of rondolike opening materials. The effect on contemporary listeners was noted in
an account of the finale of Symphony No. 95:

> Haydn chooses for his final movement a theme to which he accords a coloring of
> ease and gallantry, but which, for all its simplicity, has much dignity and particu-

EXAMPLE 6–20.   *Symphony 80/iv, mm. 182–90*

larly allows for the most powerful and varied development. He presents this theme lightly and delicately, like the theme of a customary rondo; he thus deceives the audience, which expects a typical rondo; but he suddenly seizes the principal idea of his theme, states it loud and full, and then even develops a beautiful fugue out of this material.[18]

Haydn's procedures in this finale might well deceive on many counts. But the writer's expectation of a "typical rondo" would be justified by the first

EXAMPLE 6–21.   *Symphony 95/iv, mm. 1–8*

section of the movement and the theme that opens it (Ex. 6–21). Beginning his fugue in the passage that initiates transition to the dominant key, Haydn draws upon the first five notes of the theme for continuous and rigorously contrapuntal episodes throughout the movement. Such procedures reveal in seemingly artless tunes an unsuspected potential for developmental and textural complexity, challenging the listener to adjust predictions as to the implied direction and design of the movement, as well as the implied mood of the undertaking.

Melodies that might encourage expectations of rondo form were typically in two-reprise format with balanced and symmetrical phrases; simple, dance-like, and streamlined for *presto* delivery, these were tunes designed to be direct and easy to take in as a whole. Abundant repetition and patterning on all levels (melody, rhythm, phrase structure, and formal repeats) promote the listener's recognition of the theme and awareness of deviations upon its return. Example 6–22 shows the opening periods of themes from Haydn's rondo-variation finales of the middle to late 1770s. These spirited tunes, whose features are typical of finale openings in later symphonies as well, do not pose as dramatic, nor is there the suggestion of enigmas to be solved (although the tune from Symphony No. 68 does seem oddly repetitive). Even so, the most unprepossessing beginning may give way to extraordinary digressions. The finale tune of Symphony No. 55 in E-flat Major, for example, would not lead one to expect its altered return in G-flat major—nor the astonishing interruption that precedes it and the extended recovery that follows (mm. 80–125). Similarly, the gigue-like opening of the finale of Symphony No. 61 in D Major does not seem likely to stray into F major (mm. 35–50), nor to lose metric bearings, marking time in three measures of $\frac{4}{4}$ (mm. 158ff). In these rondos Haydn chooses the simplest of subjects and maximizes the ensemble's potential for both startling dynamic contrasts and playful echoes in developmental episodes that animate an otherwise stable, reiterative structure.

Haydn's preference for simple and symmetrical dance tunes is conspicuous in finales of the 1780s and 1790s, as is his integration of sonata-form and rondo procedures. Both are important sources of strategic play with intraopus expectations in closing movements. Rondo structures ensured the tonic stability and ready recognition of materials that a reiterative form promotes—features that accord well with the symmetrical, tuneful melodies and fast tempo appropriate to a closing movement. On the other hand, an additive, sectional structure limits the potential for internal expansion and long-range harmonic tension that characterizes the drama of sonata-allegro form in opening movements. A closing movement that fuses sonata-form and rondo characteristics has the advantages of hybrid vigor. The finales of the late symphonies have sufficient weight and length to balance extended opening movements, yet they provide the mood of relaxed stability that Haydn comes to favor in the thematic materials of his concluding movements.

Certain of Haydn's general habits made the sonata-rondo structure a likely choice for his closing movements. His fondness for so-called monothematic procedure in sonata-form opening movements finds a natural outlet in the sonata-rondo finale. Similarly, the recycling of opening material at the close of a sonata-form movement can be heard as a normal procedure in rondo form. And the developmental excursions Haydn so often embarks upon after

EXAMPLE 6–22.   Finale themes

   a.   *Symphony 55 (1974)*

   b.   *Symphony 68 (c.1774/75)*

   c.   *Symphony 69 (1775/76)*

   d.   *Symphony 61 (1776)*

the proper recapitulation in sonata-form movements are accommodated as
normal episodes in sonata-rondo designs. Formal articulations of closure and
return may be manipulated to deceive the listener's expectations in opening
movements, but the hybrid nature of sonata-rondo structures may itself entail
interpretation and reinterpretation in progress. The unbuttoned, familiar address of rondolike themes, coupled with formal ambivalence, offered promising grounds for playful defeat of expection.

The two events in the finale that Haydn most frequently manipulates by prolonged delay and by avoidance of the anticipated goal are the return of the refrain or the moment of recapitulation, and the approach to the final cadence of the closing section. As both require a decisive tonic resolution, the means of delay includes extended dominant preparation such that the harmonic goal is sensed as imminent. The tension of withheld resolution is greater in the former case, however, for here the tonic is anticipated after an extended development or episode. In addition, of course, the thematic return that accompanies harmonic resolution will mark the beginning of a new section in the overall design. The formal structure generates its own suspense here, and Haydn capitalizes on that tension. In the case of a delayed final cadence, on the other hand, he chooses to create suspense where harmonic tension is normally lower. Here expectation of closure is thwarted by continuation.

Manipulations of both return and closure are conspicuous in the finale of Symphony No. 88 in G Major (1787). Here preparation for the recapitulation is prolonged to the point of playful exaggeration. As is so often the case in Haydn's finales, the listener's expectations are teased by manipulation of an upbeat figure (Ex. 6–23). Gestures of dominant preparation are begun in measure 136 with all of the familiar apparatus of dominant pedal, repeated figures, and holding pattern on the repeated dominant note. The two-measure pattern of the octave leap is echoed, *piano*, by alternating first and second violins. Expectation of an imminent resolution and thematic return is thwarted, however, as the harmony drifts toward a new and more insistent dominant seventh, now involving the lower strings; suspense is prolonged and intensified by the addition of a minor ninth. At this moment of extreme harmonic tension Haydn makes some strategic adjustments: at measures 150–51 an extra repetition breaks up the predictable two-measure pattern; the upbeat function is toyed with as the figure expands to four eighth notes and the stress of the measure shifts to the second beat. Though the horns insist on the appropriate dominant pedal, a seeming impasse is reached and sustained for six measures.

A shift of focus to the isolated upbeat, now the appropriate melodic anticipation, generates new momentum. But the stalling tactics of the previous six measures disorient the listener as to placement of the downbeat in this attenuated upbeat. The scoring of measures 156–58 provides a clue, as flute and bassoon repeat the appropriate upbeat. And it is their third attempt that initiates the recapitulation. In the prolonged anticipation of this moment, the listener's expectation has first been directed toward the wrong tonal goal, then redirected and intensified, and finally confused by manipulations of the upbeat function itself.

This movement also contains several instances of surprising continuations where closure is expected. The most dramatic of these occurs with an interrupted cadence at the end of the refrain section whose return was so tantalizingly delayed (Ex. 6–24). Tutti chords—*forte*, syncopated, and followed by a rest with fermata—change the climate of the proceedings to one of dramatic

EXAMPLE 6–23.   *Symphony 88/iv, mm. 132–61*

expectancy. The continuation is unruffled by the incongruous intrusion. While the digression is thus reduced to the status of mock-heroic, it has provided an impetus for the extended closing passage that follows.

In retrospect, one realizes that expansion of the form by unexpected departures and delayed arrivals is foreshadowed in the opening section of this finale. The first digression from the expected route occurs in measures 7–8, as seen in Example 6–25. The normal progression in this context would be a move to V/V—V in the second four-bar phrase. Instead, the bass takes an unexpected turn to the mediant. From this unconventional arrival, the setting up of the dominant as a solid plateau from which to approach the tonic

EXAMPLE 6–24.   *Symphony 88/iv, mm. 183–96*

EXAMPLE 6–25.   *Symphony 88/iv, mm. 1–26*

EXAMPLE 6–25. *(Continued)*

return will require expansion in the succeeding section. Solid plateau aside, to abandon the imminent return for a sudden excursion to the minor side of the intended tonic is a delaying tactic—and sounds like one. As we have seen, this quirk and the brief manipulation of the upbeat pattern by contraction of the phrase in measures 15–16 have implications beyond local disturbances.[19]

Griesinger noted that Haydn's "allegros and rondeaux are especially often planned to tease the audience by wanton shifts from the seemingly serious to the highest level of comedy, and to be tuned to an almost wild hilarity."[20] Haydn's teasing strategy of exaggerated suspense invites the listener's interpretive strategies in predicting its outcome. If after prolonged delay the anticipated goal is denied, the listener will have been outwitted, surprised in a position of false intelligence. In addition to the obvious dividend of dramatizing and particularizing formal procedures appropriate to his subject, the composer gains additional time—play is extended by a local digression and by the new approach undertaken to set things right. While the point of recapitulation and the final cadence of the finale offered the most dramatic possibilities for the manipulation of anticipatory gestures and their supposed goals, such strategies could be used elsewhere in the movement to tease and deceive expectations. And an environment of playful deception set up in the opening section of the finale will be fair notice of more to come. Thus alerted, the listener can delight in the surprise of subtle as well as outrageous incongruities and in the discovery of ingenious, unsuspected congruities. However autonomous and wayward the isolated musical gesture may appear, the listener is repeatedly reminded that its changing and cumulative implications oblige attention and active engagement in the composer's play with his art.

7

The Paradox
of Distraction

As noted in the preceding chapter, several movements of Haydn's symphonies published in the early 1780s can be traced to prior lives in the 1770s as overtures to operas.[1] Only one complete symphony has been documented as composed in its entirety to serve a dramatic function, however, and that as incidental music to a comedy. With rich documentation of its theatrical past, Symphony No. 60, "Il distratto," is a useful model for investigating comic materials and procedures in instrumental music with a dramatic function. Various scholars have speculated about specifically programmatic aspects of the symphony as they relate to specific characters and incidents within the play, an effort that is considerably enhanced by a lengthy review of the work in an early performance in Salzburg.[2] In addition to these local associations of the comic, however, I wish to locate features that can signify jesting intent in the absence of a controlling theatrical context. Some background information about the play for which Haydn composed this work will be helpful, in any case, in clarifying comic procedures and contemporary accounts of the music's comic effects.

"Il distratto"

Unique in having six movements, and bearing the title "Per la Commedia intitolata il Distratto," Symphony No. 60 originally served as overture, entr'actes, and concluding piece to a German prose translation of Jean-François Regnard's five-act comedy of 1697 *Le Distrait* ("the absentminded one"). First performed at Eszterháza in 1774 by the famous Karl Wahr troupe resident there, *Der Zerstreute* subsequently traveled with Haydn's music to be heard and reviewed in nearby Pressburg and in Salzburg. As we shall see, Haydn's

music for the production attracted favorable comment from reviewers, particularly his successful rendering of the distraction that drives the play's plot
and main character.

The comedy turns on the familiar formula of arranged and rearranged marriage plans of an ambitious mother (Mme Grognac) for a daughter (Isabelle)
whose affections lie elsewhere. At the center of the play is the unbelievably absentminded Leander, whose misadventures extend well beyond the Freudian
slip. Not only does he misaddress letters to two female rivals and usher both into
the same closet, but he forgets that he has married one of them in the end—
and must tie a knot in his handkerchief lest he forget that it is his wedding night.
A strong presence in the cast of supporting players is the engaging reprobate
Chevalier, whose exuberant manner wins Isabelle's heart but offends her mother's sensibilities; adamant in rejecting a match with the laughing, dancing, singing cavalier, Mme Grognac is prepared to overlook Leander's oddness in view
of his favorable financial prospects. In the final act, the simple device of a dramatic and false announcement of Leander's disinheritance persuades Mme
Grognac that he will not do after all as a husband for Isabelle, and she accedes to
her daughter's choice of Chevalier. Leander is thus free to marry his intended,
Clarice, whose future one imagines will be full of distractions. Assisting in the
intrigue and resolution of the lovers' dilemmas are the ever-resourceful servants, Lisette and Carlin, and Valère, the uncle of Clarice and Chevalier.

With ample opportunity for musical characterization in instrumental pieces
that reflect and enhance the comedy, Haydn seizes upon disjunctions of exotic
and mundane materials and plays out the theme of absentmindedness in a variety
of temporal and harmonic disorders. Early reviews of the production note particulars that serve as relevant indices of the music's effect on Haydn's listeners. Features most often noted as musical analogues to the play's theme are the composer's
manipulations of time, the juxtaposition of folk melodies of various national
origins, and suitably distracted digressions of thematic materials. While the motivation for such eccentricity is pointed in a theatrical context, we will find that the
comic devices most salient to contemporary listeners as musical distraction are
party to a more subtle wit that serves the coherence of the work overall.

In the first notice of the play's performance, a correspondent for the *Preßburger
Zeitung* noted that connoisseurs regarded the music as masterful, and that in matters of comic absentmindedness Haydn and Regnard vied for top honors. Notice
of a second performance referred specifically to unmistakable evidence:

> [T]he finale had to be repeated in view of the insistent applause of the listeners. Particu-
> larly well handled in this movement is the reference to the distracted man who forgets
> that it is his wedding day, and who must tie a knot in his handkerchief to remind himself
> that he is the bridegroom. The musicians begin the piece with great pomposity and re-
> member shortly that they have forgotten to tune their instruments.[3]

In proposing that in the end even the musicians have fallen under the influence of the drama's theme, Haydn breaks the musical frame with the shock-
ing intrusion of "realism" seen in Example 7–1. The writer of a third and
lengthy review of the Salzburg performance registered its effect: "The

EXAMPLE 7–1.   *Symphony 60/vi, mm. 1–34*

absentmindedness of the orchestra is surprising, amusing, a hearty good effect. One must laugh out loud at the idea."[4] The clearly errant pitch is the violins' low scordatura F, a prominent mistake-on-purpose. As the violins retune to G, the proper dominant, an appropriately theatrical effect is achieved in an excruciating slide up to the correct pitch. In syntactic terms, Haydn has not violated sense, however: the tuning interruption, sounding at first as an absurdly *un*deceptive cadence from an emphatic V to a hollow vi, accomplishes a vi–ii–ii⁶–V progression by means of the seemingly mistaken F.

Although the false tuning passage in the finale is the most outrageous of Haydn's musically rendered distractions, it is not unrelated to others in the work. The Salzburg reviewer noted a similarly distracted passage in the overture as excellent and appropriate to the play's theme. Here the effect is a gradual losing of one's way and falling into dreamy inaction. As Example 7-2 shows, Haydn specifically marks *perdendosi* to indicate this prolonged suspension of forward momentum. F natural is again an agent in the delay, here undermining the local tonic, G major, of the second theme group. Also salient in this context of sturdy diatonic action is the distracted indecision of chromaticism in the D sharp that alternates with the third's upper neighbor. Lacking the appropriate leading tone, the melody loses direction in a twelve-measure impasse on G major's subdominant: in seeming disregard for the rule of time, the passage becomes harmonically regressive in lingering on the original tonic of the piece.[5] In the abrupt *fortissimo* corrective, F sharp is appropriated by the bass to motivate a downward resolution of the now unstable C.

Emphasis on the subdominant in delay about the tonic is prominent early on in this movement in the first theme of the *allegro* section. The relationship of this principal theme to the *perdendosi* passage is a telling one (Ex. 7-3). As is frequently the case in Haydn's works, the second-key theme is a varied restatement of the first—in this instance an augmented version that retains the eighth notes of the original upbeat as an ornamental subdivision of its larger upbeat pattern. While Leander may lose track of time, Haydn only seems to. In the theme of delay that is signaled in measure 27, augmented in the second-key theme, and played out on a grand scale in measures 71ff, a leading role is played by the three-note upbeat. Initially heard in eighths, then in quarters, the upbeat eventually expands to fill three bars in measures, 80–82. In the "recovery" of the closing material that follows (mm. 87ff), two levels of upbeat are playfully manipulated in repetitions that thwart continuation and force expansion of the phrase.

As seen in Example 7-4, the *perdendosi* passage serves in a rather different context in the retransition of the development section. With assistance from the oboes, subdominant (in vi) stasis is turned toward dominant preparation. Here the delay heard first in measure 27 is reenacted "on pitch" in the first violin's persistent F; free of chromatic distractions from the tonic goal, the expanded upbeat anticipates the theme's beginning and can be elided with that of the recapitulation. Comically intended in the dramatic context of this work, the *perdendosi* passage exaggerates rhythmic and melodic features that

EXAMPLE 7–2.   *Symphony 60/i, mm. 67–90*

waylay the thematic material from the start. And overlong emphasis on otherwise normative pre-dominant harmonies similarly delay large-scale resolutions. In playing out the implications of distraction, Haydn demonstrates the essential interplay of harmonic and rhythmic expansion in these seeming digressions and felt delays.

Instability of modal degrees, suggested in the forgetful passage of the first movement, is far more common in other movements of Symphony No. 60 and is no doubt related to the prominent use of "exotic" tunes in the work. The Salzburg reviewer makes note of "Polish, French, and somewhat Turkish

EXAMPLE 7–2.   (Continued)

melodies" in the second movement, and comments further: "Doesn't this springing up of the melodies of such different nations brought together in a single piece seem too dense, this musical absentmindedness too unnatural? Does it not seem a parody of the taste of these nations?—Yet it only seems so!"[6] While Leander is ever-present throughout the play, whether in fact or in the accounts of his absentmindedness by others, the unstable Chevalier is a dominating presence in Act II of the play, which the Andante second movement introduced. Perhaps, too, the opening scene between the servants motivated this first appearance of folklike melodies. In any case, exotic scales, drones, and rhythms of the "folk" are pronounced in movements 2, 3, 4, and 6.

It is in this last movement that the most topical reference is made to an identifiable folk tune. Apparently well known among Haydn's contemporaries as "The Night Watchman's Song," this melody has been identified in several of his works.[7] Its appearance in the last movement of "Il distratto" may be a musical comment on Leander's wedding night, but the melody itself is a microcosm of both melodic and rhythmic irregularities heard throughout the symphony. Haydn's use of the tune in the middle of the Prestissimo finale not only effects a striking shift in mode, pace, and texture but also accomplishes the single modulation in the movement (Ex. 7–5a). In this latter role, features of the familiar tune appear altered, however, as comparison with Ex. 7–5b shows. Seemingly more "exotic" versions exhibit both instability of the fourth scale degree and ambiguity of meter in the asymmetry of

EXAMPLE 7–3. *Symphony 60/i, mm. 25–91, upbeat expansion*

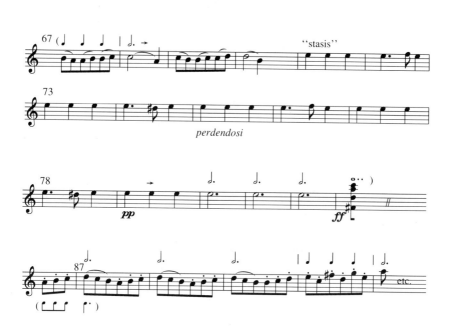

the tune's consequent phrase—features that Haydn preserves in this finale of his Divertimento in C Major, Hob. II:17 (before 1766). In Symphony No. 60 the tune is bent to serve modulation and concludes with a rather routine cadence in E flat. The Salzburg reviewer doesn't comment on this melody, but one wonders if listeners familiar with the tune would be more amused by its reference to the night watchman or by the seeming distraction of imperfect recall. In any case, the very technique of quotation invokes a kind of realism that might serve humorous ends in the absence of a specific theatrical context.

In the second movement Haydn engages the folklike in more subtle variation of thematic material and manipulation of its rhythmic shape. The melody that dominates the "development" section of this movement is labeled *Ancien chant français* in an early manuscript copy, lending credence, perhaps, to the Salzburg reviewer's report of "French melodies."[8] Here too one might find a basis for the reviewer's sense of parody in contemporary notions about national "humours" that we have noted in other writers of the period.

EXAMPLE 7-4. *Symphony 60/i, mm. 145-60*

Whether or not the tune is in fact old or French, it recasts the opening theme in a minor-mode version (or presents the full version of the melody from which the opening theme is derived?), now in a more extended melody with a strangely stiff and ceremonial posture (Ex. 7-6). Haydn's procedures in this movement recall the absorption of disparate voices in the Poco adagio movement of Symphony No. 28.[9] But here the materials are responsive to dramatic characterization. In suggesting an opposition of Leander's wandering indecision and Chevalier's more boisterous brand of instability, Haydn's musical

162

EXAMPLE 7-5.

   a. *Symphony* 60/vi, mm. 61–72

   b. *Divertimento à 9 in C Major,* Hob. II:17/viii, mm. 1–5

commentary underscores differences and similarities between the two in an artful process of progressive variation.

These techniques are particularly audible in his treatment of the second-key theme, in which artful devices of canon and diminution absorb the Andante tune in a sequence of variation that seems to digress (Ex. 7-7, mm. 22–31). The third of these variations, which serves to stabilize closure of the exposition, is both familiar and strange in its transformation. Expanding upon his model, Haydn presents a newly flexible melody in which a marchlike setting yields by degrees to a triple-meter polonaise. (In view of Haydn's use of such folk melodies as the "Night Watchman's Song," one wonders whether this dance was the model for his canon.)

Chevalier's song in Act II of the play may have motivated Haydn's treatment of a French folk song in this movement. The text of the play's song refers to the solace that drink offers the unsuccessful lover, and in interrupting his song to comment on it, Chevalier points out the effective move to B minor: "Isn't the B minor tender? Doesn't it pierce the heart?"[10] In Haydn's rendering, B minor becomes a point of several measures' fixation for the knight-errant (Ex. 7-8), such that the return to the movement's opening theme is tonally unprepared. On the other hand, the juxtaposition makes more audible the relationship of the (alleged) folk song to the opening material of the movement. Haydn's manner of shifting into an unsettling resolution by appropriating a common tone of third-related keys, here B as the third in G major, is a device that motivates further development before a stable tonic is confirmed.[11]

The modal instability of the finale's folklike tune recalls that of others heard in the fourth movement and in the trio of the preceding minuet move-

EXAMPLE 7–6. *Symphony 60/ii*
   a.   mm. 1–5

   b.   mm. 64–70

EXAMPLE 7–7. *Symphony 60/ii*
  a.   Reduction of mm. 1–5

  b.   Schematic of mm. 22–31, 43–50

ment, both of which take C minor as tonic (Ex. 7–9).[12] In the fourth movement of "Il distratto" such melodies succeed one another in a dizzying collage, promoting an appropriate atmosphere for Act IV, in which the intrigue
is escalated by various confusions of an increasingly distraught Leander.
Abrupt juxtapositions of key and mode promote an impression of exotic melodies as independent entities—as characters, perhaps, that flash by in self-
absorbed action.

The symphony's minuet may have had a more directly pantomimic function as accompaniment to the dance in Act III of the play that features the
unlikely pairing of the imperious Mme Grognac and the rather flighty Chevalier fancied by her daughter. If its humor is linked to situational comedy,
the movement is nonetheless a useful point of reference for features that
undermine the minuetlike (Ex. 7–10). Beginning in a convincingly ceremonial
manner, the movement soon drifts toward the ineffectual: a tentative and
wandering "fugato" that returns prematurely (m. 12) to the tonic, an abrupt
return of the opening material in D minor (m. 18), a perfunctory transition

EXAMPLE 7–8.   *Symphony 60/ii, mm. 71–81*

back to the proper tonic, and an entirely gratuitous resolution (mm. 29–30) in advance of a proper restatement of the opening material. In the abrupt contrasts of this second section, even the learned and stately styles lose their bearings.

The trio (see Ex. 7–9a) exaggerates the ceremonial and the folklike in juxtaposing a *forte* unison passage in the minor with a mincing answer of modal indecision, thoroughly grounded by a sustained (minor) dominant harmony. Non sequiturs and square phrasing heard in the second sections of both minuet and trio would suit the composer of Mozart's *Ein musikalischer Spaß*. As in the minuet of that work, the incongruous mixture of materials and procedures in this movement subverts the elegance and ease of gestures appropriate to the courtly dance, as well as the clarity of its regular two-measure step patterns.

In the Salzburg reviewer's opinion, the most successful movements of Symphony No. 60 were the first and fifth. The "excellent Adagio" in F major that followed Act IV combined not folk melodies, but "ideas that are pleasing, joyful, partly sad, partly absurd, yet thoroughly suitable as humorous in their succession one after another in the mind of an absentminded person."[13] Perhaps heralding the announcement in Act V that will resolve the lovers' dilemmas, a six-measure fanfare in C major interrupts a lapse of the theme in C minor. And in the recall (from the second movement) of Chevalier's military

EXAMPLE 7–9. *Symphony 60*

   a. iii, trio, mm. 1–10

   b. iv, mm. 1–8

   c. iv, mm. 61–72

   d. iv, mm. 82–92

EXAMPLE 7–10. *Symphony 60/iii, mm. 1–31*

motto that follows, *forte*, in the oboes, horns, and trumpets (Ex. 7-11), pizzicato string doublings mimic the pretense of his gestures. Resuming its wandering excursion in C major, the theme of the movement strays into its subdominant—an absentminded reversion to the tonic of the movement that recalls a similar harmonic preoccupation in the opening movement. Subdominant deflections throughout the Adagio (*di Lamentatione*) fifth movement lend it a meandering quality that suits Leander.[14] Perhaps this movement in

the subdominant key of the work is his lament over the confusion he has brought on in the previous act. That there will be a happy resolution is signaled in an *allegro* close that literally winds up the movement and anticipates the triplets that will dominate the finale.

Recognizing Haydn's intention in the music for *Der Zerstreute* as that of "heightening the absentmindedness of the actors," the earliest reviewer

EXAMPLE 7–10. *(Continued)*

found in its "musically comic humor [*musikalisch-komischen Laune*] the same spirit that enlivens all of Haydn's works."[15] Even if most effectively realized in the company of its comic characters, Symphony No. 60 found success with listeners independent of Regnard's play.[16] In settings where theatrical jests relied on purely instrumental resources, Haydn's more subtle means of achieving coherence in this work would be of special consequence. Unifying threads that bind seemingly disparate materials in larger schemes of rhythmic, motivic, and harmonic relationships are heard from first movement to last, just as inventive variation procedures transform simple materials within individual movements. The comedy of distraction was thus assured an afterlife in concert settings. So too, Haydn's jesting strategies in other purely instrumental settings would draw upon means of characterizing musical distraction as humorous.

In consulting other symphonies of the early 1770s, we find theatrical gestures that may indicate origins similar to those of Symphony No. 60. The slow movement of Symphony No. 65 in particular suggests the theatrical staging of a whimsical character at odds with a Chevalier-like presence and with the ensemble overall; the symphony's other movements are similarly suggestive of a comic drama.[17] But whether or not Haydn was writing music specifically intended for use in the theater, gestures at home in theatrical comedy—surprising stops and starts, disjunctions and reversals, prolonged delays and teasing anticipations, forgetful repetitions, and "twisted" quotations—could

EXAMPLE 7–11. *Symphony 60/v, mm. 35–42*

be appropriated as signals of jesting intent in instrumental music independent of such a context. Echoes of Leander, heard throughout Haydn's works,
suggest a rich source of humor in the paradox of seeming distraction.

The Attraction of Distraction

Perhaps because absentmindedness is a familiar (and generally harmless) human foible, it is a ready source of humor in comic characterization and inci-
dent. Characters oblivious to their surroundings and to the passage of time

can live a charmed life in comedy. Naturally inattentive and destined to re-peat peculiar behavior, the eccentric is flawed but not fatally; though forget-ful of time and place, he will be rescued from serious consequences by the miracles of timing that avert disaster. The misadventures of such characters bring into sharper focus for the audience the very things that their distraction shuts out: the open manhole in the path of the daydreamer; the perilous angle of a gravy boat passed by the smitten suitor; the absent trousers of the absentminded professor. The seeming suspension of time and heightened suspense of the moment in time that this double view isolates is inherent as well in the enterprise of distraction that drama itself undertakes.

Musical distractions effect a similar enchantment in curiously detached absorptions of the moment. Seeming to waste time, and focusing attention on aberrant patterns, humorous distractions in music are audible in excessive repetitions that seem increasingly dysfunctional in their immediate context: preoccupied by an isolated motive, a displaced meter, a misplaced upbeat, an imperfectly recalled quotation, indecisive harmony, or simply silence, the mu-sic appears forgetful of its past and indifferent about its future. The attention of the listener, on the other hand, is sharpened by such anomalies. The effect might be likened to the freeze frame in a motion picture—an incongruous and patently artful device that unexpectedly isolates a fragment of the whole, freezing gestures and forcing attention to what they may signify.

In music, unlike film, the "frame" is animated even while static in its repe-titions, and would seem to answer Henri Bergson's notion of the comic as something "mechanical encrusted upon the living."[18] In his view, such a con-junction arouses laughter for its automatism, its rigidity in violation of per-ceived laws of nature. Wary of the dehumanizing effects of increasing mecha-nization in the modern world, Bergson argued that the comic serves as a social corrective to the "easy automatism of acquired habits"; laughter itself, "by the fear that it inspires . . . restrains eccentricity" and "pursues the utili-tarian aim of general improvement."[19] The exaggerations and distortions of time and gesture in Haydn's prolonged anticipations and delays might also fall under Aristotle's understanding of the laughable as "some blunder or ugli-ness that does not cause pain or disaster" because it is framed by comedy.[20] Both theories would suit the distortions of Mozart's *Musikalischer spaß*. But as artful strategies, deviant manners reveal more than comic distortion: while we might sense the composer's humor in absentminded repetitions, we are also made highly conscious of the local detail that Haydn chooses to drama-tize in this way, and attracted to consider its implications for the music's unfolding—past, present, and future. Thus, in the seemingly static moment, the listener is invited to a more elastic play of the imagination.

Haydn's intentions in such manipulations are often audible as means of raising expectations the better to tease them, forcing consciousness of playful delay. They also point up the connections between seemingly isolated events, thus confirming the coherence of larger patterns within a work. The means and effects of humorous distractions range from intimate play to theatrical display, commensurate with medium and genre and particular to the materials of an individual movement. But they characteristically exaggerate delay in the repetition of seemingly superfluous gestures that digress from and suspend expected patterns of continuation. Moreover, the exaggeration of distracted manners will be increasingly manifest over time, as repetition at the local level is played out in varied returns within larger structures.

The minuet movement of Haydn's Piano Sonata in G Major, Hob. XVI: 27 (before 1776),[21] provides a model example of playful—and progressive—distraction appropriate to the intimacy of the chamber. Excessive repetition is first heard in a prolonged approach to the dominant cadence at the first double bar (Ex. 7–12). Upon return of the opening measures in the second section, the delay is extended in registral, harmonic, and temporal variations of the theme's second measure. Indeed, it is this measure that is the source of distracted repetitions in both sections. The subject of obsessive preoccupation is a satisfactory resolution of the diminished fifth/augmented fourth dissonance that pervades the piece. In that the bass refuses to cooperate with support for a tonic resolution (m. 34), the repetitions of the first section are replayed in various configurations of the dissonance and resolution. Dallying in the keyboard's upper register, the figure continues to resist easy resolution in approaching the close. In what might have been a simple affair of four-bar antecedent-consequent periods in both opening and closing sections, Haydn directs attention to the motive that unifies the minuet and to the eccentric manners by which it governs the movement's expansion.

The theme of distraction takes on a particular shade of private absorption in a solo genre such as the keyboard sonata. Where player and auditor are one, "performance" can be a thoroughly self-sufficient amusement, accountable to one's own pleasure alone. If we meet Leander here, it is in his solitary preoccupations, free to digress—in reverie, memory, fantasy—without responsibility to others waiting for a timely and appropriate response. Viewed in this light, Haydn's minuet mirrors an absence of mind from the task at hand that leads to mechanical, even unconscious, repetitions. At the same time, however, the art of seeming distraction becomes a means of alerting the player (and listener) to that very danger. Affecting a freedom to wander over the keys, to linger over a phrase or motive (or to repeat it until it's right), Haydn calls attention to the difference between daydreaming and the absorption of intense concentration. Even in privacy, musical performance requires the latter.

More dramatic in promoting the impression of improvisatory freedoms are the surprising pauses and silences that are frequent and effective accomplices to "superfluous" repetitions. In performance, such seemingly spontaneous delays have an added immediacy as physical gestures, assisting the listener with visual cues to arrested motions and distracted "fancies." In Example 7–13, from the opening movement of Haydn's Sonata in D Major, Hob. XVI:33 (before 1778), repeating gestures in seeming stasis are stopped by silence so as to begin anew—or to resume with alterations that allow proper continuation. Elisions in measure 43 and again in measure 48 mark repeated

EXAMPLE 7-12.   *Piano Sonata in G Major,* Hob. XVI:27/ii,
  mm. 1-14; 29-42

beginnings and progressively lengthened phrases—from the "model" four of
measures 39-42, to five, and then to eleven bars—before a firm cadence is
reached in measure 58.

Conspicuous repetition takes place on several levels here as increasingly
extended pauses act to prolong the approach to resolution, and in each case
the point of delay centers on the pre-dominant harmony of ii^6. The first such
pause (marked with a bracket in mm. 45-46) follows a deflection from the
expected pattern, as the prominent leap up to F sharp in measure 44 is filled
in. Revisited in the next repetition, which begins in measure 48, the F sharp

EXAMPLE 7–13. *Piano Sonata in D Major*, Hob. XVI:33/i,
   mm. 38–58

is approached and reapproached. (Haydn's placement of the *adagio* marking *after* the fermata suggests that an anticipatory ritard will undermine the surprising effect of sudden and extended silence and of the altered repetition that follows.)[22] Within the large-scale delay of repeated moves toward the cadence, local interruptions are carefully modulated to prepare the final ascent through the upper register to a brilliant and hard-won resolution. Framed by fermatas, the *adagio* mock-pathetic statement of the repeating fragment is only the most explicit delay in a series of progressively extended pauses that expand the second key area of the exposition.

The theorist August Kollmann, writing in 1796, remarked on the effect and function of Haydn's "fancy periods of some extended length, in which the composer seems to lose himself in the modulation for the purpose of making the ear attentive to the resolution."[23] In both the minuet of Sonata No. 27 and the opening movement of Sonata No. 33, repeated stops and starts focus attention on wayward pitches and on anomalous repetitions that resist resolution. In keeping with the nature of musical performance, these might remind us of a basic function of repetition, namely, the practice we undertake privately in learning and perfecting the execution of a sonata. What Kollman notes, however, is also a reminder that Haydn's procedures call attention to the ongoing process of listening itself.

Ultimately, it is this nexus of distraction and engagement that animates wit and humor in Haydn's music and that mirrors aesthetic experience in general. Like diversions of the theater, absorption in the life of music's movements necessarily takes one out of the moment. Gestures of comic exaggeration color the affect of that absorption, but the engaged listener is absorbed as well in rehearsing the play of options that artful excess brings to the fore.

Characterizing the Humorous

Comedy's exaggeration of human foibles and eccentricities has many analogues in Haydn's music, but the symphony offered the best "theater of human gestures and actions"[24] in which to characterize the relationship of distracted individual voices to the tutti ensemble as one of dramatic and playful encounter. In the Allegretto movement of Symphony No. 62 (c. 1780), for example, the metric disturbance of a few voices increasingly preoccupies the entire ensemble (Ex. 7–14). The cadential phrase that confirms the dominant in measure 22 begins again in the following measure, but the ambiguity of $\frac{6}{8}$ versus $\frac{3}{4}$ first heard in measure 21 among the strings now suspends progress in more general and extended ambivalence. The first *forte* marking in the movement provokes resolution and continuation in an expansive closing section. Upon return, though, the eccentricity of measures 25–27 is exaggerated in the considerably extended (and compounded) distraction of the strings. Echoing and then diverging from the metrically ambiguous measures, the violins reestablish $\frac{6}{8}$, but stray in sequential repetition of the fragment. In the continuation, which retraces the original approach to the cadence, indecisive meter extends to uncertainty of downbeats and absorption in one last repeating fragment. The ensemble left waiting during this digression seems also to have forgotten its previous resolute conclusion.[25]

A similar displacement in time casts a rather different spell on the ensemble in the musette-like trio of Symphony No. 88 (c. 1787). In evoking rustic drones and scoring, and making repeated reference to the "exotic" raised fourth scale degree, Haydn draws upon folklike associations that recall the trio of Symphony No. 60 and others noted in Chapter 4. But here, as seen in Example 7–15, a trance-like distraction is played out in the repetition of a $\frac{2}{4}$ melodic fragment out of phase with the prevailing meter of the dance. Absorbed in repetition, measures and voices multiply in a confusion of overlapping and layered ostinato patterns. Indeed, the aberrant figure seems capable of infinite repetition, despite changes in the supporting drone harmonies. But open-fifth drones are themselves static elements, grounding melodies without controlling their modal or metric definition; while the *forte* on the downbeat of measure 61 is a reminder of the proper meter, the dominant-seventh harmony is needed to effect resolution. The rustic bearings of the

EXAMPLE 7–14. *Symphony 62/ii, mm. 17–28; 80–91*

EXAMPLE 7–14.   *(Continued)*

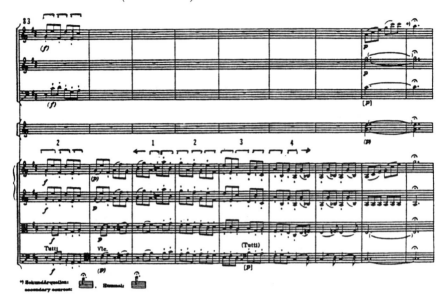

trio promote a sense of flexible time in this curiously static yet graceful rota-
tion, suspending predictable patterns of phrase and meter.

Offering marked contrast to the stiff formality of its framing minuet, the
trio's tendency to digress in repetition is signaled early on. Reiteration generates two extra measures in a six-bar consequent to the opening four-bar
phrase—an irregularity that is exaggerated in the seven-bar phrase at the
trio's close. The influence of repeating $\frac{2}{4}$ fragments is audible in delaying this
closing phrase, in which metric disturbance compounds the conflict of accent
and reiteration of the raised fourth heard in the opening section.

The distracted passages in Symphony No. 88's trio and in the Allegretto
movement of Symphony No. 62 serve again as reminders of the "humorous"
in eighteenth-century terms. Metric irregularities sustained in the repetitions
of both passages provoke a *felt* disturbance—a mild kinesthetic upset. The
paradox of stasis and continuation, and of conflicting metric patterns simultaneously entertained, surprises as a physical double take. Manipulations of
time and pattern in seemingly distracted repetitions have a special potency,
then, in isolating the particulars of the moment and in directing attention to
how their eccentricities are played out in restoring order.

Episodes of eccentric preoccupation in local details provide needed "brakes"
in varying the pacing and scoring of a movement. Effective not only in delaying and dramatizing continuation, distracted passages also motivate compensation for irregularity, that is, passages that reinforce stability. The opening
movement of Symphony No. 100 provides an example. Haydn's frequent procedure of deriving his second-key theme from the opening subject is espe-

EXAMPLE 7-15. *Symphony 88/iii, mm. 57-70*

cially audible in this movement. The Allegro's solo wind beginning, itself striking, remains identical in the transposed version—as far as it goes. Betraying from the start a tendency to reiterate, the theme forgets its ending and breaks off for extended commentary on the incomplete fragment (Ex. 7-16). The tutti is implicated in a digression to the minor before an appropriate setting for the rising E–A can function rhythmically as cadential preparation.

EXAMPLE 7–16. *Symphony 100/i, mm. 72–98*

If the stability of the passage that follows is motivated by a distracted episode, the new theme that it introduces is kin to the first in its disposition for repetition, though now not of afterbeats but of upbeats. In the development section Haydn demonstrates the obsessive repetition that characterizes this new theme, but it is in preparing the recapitulation that manipulation of the figure is exaggerated to the point of a teasing delay (Ex. 7–17). Absorbed in seemingly infinite repetitions, the measure-long fragment deviates in its last reiteration to change a single eighth note just before the return. Both anticipated and unexpected in its timing, the recapitulation resolves an almost hypnotic suspense.

As wayward diversions that seem to waste time, these distractions recall

Samuel Johnson's sense of what it was to amuse: "to draw on from time
to time, to keep in expectation, to divert in order to gain, or waste time."[26]
Haydn's strategies of "gaining time" are not those of the efficiency expert's
shortcuts to *save* time but rather efforts to gain *more* time, to "purchase"
additional time, even while seeming to "waste" it. If Johnson's amusement
diverts attention away from the serious matters at hand, "to entertain with
expectations not to be fulfilled," Haydn directs attention to the agents of
diversion. The paradox of music's humorous distractions is that the listener
is both conscious of heightened expectation and attentive to the details that
sustain it. Elements that conspire in this effect include the stasis of seemingly

EXAMPLE 7–17. *Symphony 100/i, 192–202*

superfluous repetition; fragmentary and distorted recollections of familiar thematic materials; chromatic and rhythmic manipulations that confuse or displace established patterns of harmony, phrasing, and meter; and provocative silences that prolong uncertainty. The interruptions, prolonged anticipations, and reversals heard as theatrical and comic exaggeration in Symphony No. 60 work their effect in a range of contexts in Haydn's instrumental music. As he increasingly addresses listeners in public venues, his musical humor becomes more theatrical in displaying both familiar and eccentric manners.

In London concert halls of the 1790s, Haydn's symphonies—with the composer "presiding at the Pianoforte"—occupied center stage before an admiring public. In that his music had preceded him by some twenty-five years, both in concert performances and in private settings, the English were ready to welcome a familiar original. Haydn produced a series of symphonic works whose direct appeal and surprising turns recreate the festive atmosphere and community of the theater. Yet for all of their theatrical gestures, these works sustain an intimacy of encounter fostered by the play of wit.

Among the late symphonies, the finale of Symphony No. 98 in B-flat Major (1792) is an especially fitting summary example of how intimate and theatrical effects cooperate in the characterization of thematic materials. Displaying the humors of autonomous voices at odds with the communal authority of the full ensemble, Haydn raises playful surprise to the level of dramatic action in this movement, which might be taken as the instrumental equivalent of a comedy of manners. A sonata-form movement with rondo characteristics, this finale is also a case study of the "popular artfulness" that dramatizes classical forms in sustained and ingenious jesting. (While I will quote extensively from this movement, not all references will be included among the musical examples.)

The opening theme, shown in Example 7-18, is reminiscent of the tune that Haydn used in the finale of the "Joke" Quartet. In its marked phrasing, reinforced by an ascending upbeat figure and the underlying harmonic progression, it has the earmarks of a limerick. The repetition of these eight bars, with solo oboe taking over the tune, is consistent with what one might expect will be a rondo finale. But from this point on, Haydn's procedures become less predictable. The *forte* tutti section that follows (mm. 16–40) acts as if it is a transition passage, but its dominant "preparation" remains firmly fixed in the tonic key (Ex. 7-19). Dramatic tutti gestures of repeated dominant chords and silence are weakly echoed in repetitions of the isolated upbeat figure that seem to question the decisive preparation of the preceding bars. The return that is implied here would satisfy the rounded binary scheme of a rondo's refrain section if the theme were brought back in the tonic, B flat. Instead, the anticipatory fragment continues in F major—a return that persuades few members of the ensemble; suspicion that F major has been insufficiently prepared as a stable harmonic goal is confirmed by an abrupt departure for more solid ground. Thus what has been anticipated (according to the norms of rondo form) as a return of the theme in the tonic has been displaced by a dominant pivot to the proper transition section. When a solid cadence in F major does arrive (in m. 86), stability of the second key area has been more than sufficiently established. The stage is set for the entrance of a Leander counterpart, whose presence will dominate much of the ensuing action.

This bustling second-key theme (Ex. 7-20) would seem ideal as "traveling music" for characters on stage in a comic opera finale. Masking as antecedent-consequent pairs, its phrases are anticipatory, little more than a series of extended upbeat figures. Although the accompaniment is perfectly accommodating, the melody seems too preoccupied in repetitive actions to define itself

EXAMPLE 7–18. *Symphony 98/iv, mm. 1–8*

as a proper tune. Tovey likened the effect to that of "the piece of church music in which the choir's main occupation was 'to catch this flee, to catch this flee, to catch this fleeting breath.'"[27] The balancing answer exhales in a leisurely and continuous eight-bar descent. In the varied repeat of this material, the answering period surprises in a detour to the subdominant of the local tonic—a recall of B flat that the full orchestra vehemently questions (mm. 112–24). The momentary disorientation in the continuation of the violins both harks back to the tease of measures 36–42 and prefigures more startling upsets to come.[28]

EXAMPLE 7-19.   *Symphony 98/iv, mm. 34–48*

There is perhaps no more wayward and unpredictable passage in Haydn's
symphonic finales than the lengthy development section of this movement.
Decidedly unlike a conventional symphonic development, it is an entirely
episodic and relaxed excursion, neither linear and cumulative in intensity nor
exploratory of the materials it presents. Rather, it is playful surprise that is
developed here, in the confrontation of solo voice and tutti ensemble. Appro-

EXAMPLE 7-20.   *Symphony 98/iv, mm. 82-102*

priately, the second-key theme is cast as the eccentric protagonist. But the most surprising feature of the development as a whole is the role Haydn creates for his principal violinist and employer in London, J. P. Salomon. (Indeed, the materials and procedures of this finale find many parallels in Mozart's Piano Concerto in E-flat Major, K. 482.) Abrupt stops, shifts, and nonchalant continuations in passages featuring the solo violin isolate the soloist as a whimsical persona in opposition to the full orchestra's heavy-handed interruptions. The authority of these tutti redirections toward new harmonic goals is repeatedly undermined by sudden changes in the soloist's itinerary. Throughout, the ideal of continuous modulation is abandoned in favor of juxtaposed "key patches."

The harmonic plan of the development section (Ex. 7-21) is by no means as random or capricious as it is made to sound, however; its modulatory range

is impressive and retraces on a large scale the tutti's descending triadic motive. After an abrupt beginning in A-flat major, the direction of the next forty-
five measures is plotted through third-related keys back to the dominant, F
major. In the opening sequence, an enharmonic adjustment prevents premature arrival on the tonic—an adjustment pointed up by a sudden halt and
uncertainty of continuation (Ex. 7–22). The device of a repeating upbeat figure, heard previously at the transition junction of measures 39–42 and again
before the closing section (mm. 119–21), here interrupts a key sequence
headed for B-flat minor, and poses the alternative of a deflection to D-flat
minor (!). Instead, the fragment is manipulated to function enharmonically
as a C-sharp minor pivot such that the sequence of third-related keys can be
continued: to A major, A minor, and finally the dominant, F major. Rather
than using this reinterpretation of function as a means to effect a smooth and
unobtrusive drift toward a new harmonic goal, however, Haydn highlights the
play of enharmonic equivalence and exposes its equivocation.

From the *fortissimo* entrance in measure 178 through the fermata in measure 208, the orchestra is increasingly directed toward preparing a recapitulation. The F-major plateau reached in measure 190 would seem the logical

EXAMPLE 7-21. *Symphony 98/iv, development*

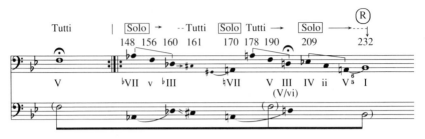

point from which to initiate preparation for such a return. Yet the anticipatory gestures of measures 198–208 are directed toward G minor. The continuation moves abruptly to E-flat major (Ex. 7–23), seemingly disavowing any intentions of recapitulation; the nonchalant beginning in the subdominant becomes tentative, pauses on a prolonged dominant seventh of C minor, and stops. Another beginning is made, in C minor, and immediately deflects to the dominant seventh of B flat. For the next ten measures the solo violin prolongs the (appropriate) dominant preparation while trying out various upbeat approaches to the main theme. With none of the hesitation of previous repeated upbeat fragments, this passage builds tension by means of a quickening pulse and a contraction of phrase length; the delay becomes at once teasing and urgent.

A rejected version of what would become measures 221–31 (Ex. 7–24), crossed out in the autograph copy,[29] lacks the momentum of Haydn's final setting. The revision not only extends the delay by an additional six measures but also makes a subtle transition from the upbeat structure of the second theme to that of the first theme. The effect is one of pantomimic gesturing, as an impatient and ineffectual figure finally makes a slight adjustment and gets the desired response. The now-confident solo voice accelerates into the downbeat without assistance from others.

As might be expected, it is the coda that provides an occasion for additional excursions and surprises. And here the first theme, neglected throughout the development section, is given its due. The beginning of the coda is dramatized by an interrupted cadence (in m. 321) and the now-familiar portentous formula of repeated chords plus extended silence. The listener might well expect a final recall of the first theme at this point, varied perhaps. But the particular transformation that this material undergoes displays the familiar in strikingly novel dress: shifting to *più moderato*, the theme takes on an entirely new aspect of mincing deliberateness, even fussiness (the chromatic variation of m. 330, for example, and the emphasized appoggiaturas). Moreover, this variation reverses the more likely practice of acceleration toward the end of a finale—the wind-up typical of opera buffa, as heard in the fifth movement of "Il distratto." To sustain the energy of renewed closing efforts, Haydn

EXAMPLE 7–22. *Symphony 98/iv, mm. 154–68*

introduces two elements new to the movement thus far: first sixteenth-note motion and then imitative counterpoint (mm. 344–48 and 353–57) create the illusion of accelerated tempo.

That the composer literally had the last word at the work's debut would have been especially amusing to the London audience of Salomon's concerts. For in its final appearance, the theme is accompanied by a cembalo solo—rendered in its first performance by Haydn himself. Here the compositional

EXAMPLE 7-23.   *Symphony 98/iv, mm. 204-33*

persona behind the scenes comes forward as a physical presence in the surprising manners of a continuo player become soloist.[30]

Surveying the various surprises of this movement, one can observe certain
consistencies in the means Haydn uses to set them up: a slowing of harmonic
and rhythmic pace; dramatic tutti gestures that are followed by a sharp reduction in dynamic level and scoring; the stasis of a repeating fragment that
implies yet frustrates continuation; discontinuation (and seeming miscontinuation) and extended silence. In addition, the extensive use of a solo instrument in a symphony and the intrusion of the continuo player isolate conventions incongruous in the genre at hand. All serve to engage and focus the
listener's attention, "making the ear attentive to the resolution," as Kollmann
said.

In revealing their relevance as uniquely appropriate to the work in progress, though, such trespasses against the norms of style and genre are more
than simply eccentric. For the ultimate ingenuity of musical jesting is that it
does obey, in the final analysis, basic syntactic and stylistic conventions—that
a transition will lead to a secondary tonic, that a closing passage will close,
that a development section, however wide-ranging, is charted on a course
toward an anticipated tonic return. In displaying the alternative, even eccentric possibilities that motivate a given resolution as particular and fitting,
Haydn invites attention to the means by which that resolution is suspended
and delayed. Seemingly distracted manners animate this play in gestures that
are familiar and strange, focused and wayward, gestures that the attentive
listener can entertain in a vividly felt suspense.

The "naturally inattentive" Leander doubtless found his counterpart in

190

EXAMPLE 7–23.   (*Continued*)

many a congregation of listeners in Haydn's day. If today's concert halls, darkened and hushed in deference to the ritual of performing works of the Classical masters, hold more than a few wandering minds and somnolent bodies,
reports of late eighteenth-century concertgoers attest to conditions rather less
conducive to attentive listening—to the music, that is. In terms of holding
the attention of an audience, instrumental music was a poor match for theat-

EXAMPLE 7–24.   *Symphony* 98/iv, rejected version of mm. 221ff

rical comedy's attractions. Whereas drama's presence played from the stage, its sounds enhanced by visible cues of gestures, costumes, scenery, and the like, music served as ancillary entertainment brought in to fill the gaps between the acts. (In opera, the role of the instruments was often faulted by those who found the primacy of the singer undermined.) But even if subordinate to the main attraction, instrumental music could assert claims on listeners by calling attention to its own anomalous and engaging distractions.

III

Epilogue: The Implicated Listener

8

"The Great Art of Seeming Familiar"

Wit always assumes an audience. . . . One is never witty for oneself alone.[1]

In his *Essai sur le beau* of 1741, Yves Marie André wrote of music's potential for beauty of genius, beauty of taste, and beauty of caprice, as "sonorous rhetoric which has its grand gestures to inspire the soul, as do words, its charms to move it, and its playfulnesses, its jokes and its games to divert it."[2] Invoking a venerable scholastic tradition of persuasion, André relied upon a hierarchy of styles and effects in which the diversions of music's playfulnesses, jokes, and games occupy a relatively low berth. Noting that diversions of caprice are appropriate for "jocular subjects . . . when, for instance, some bizarre fancy, some comic action or burlesque passion is to be expressed," André begs indulgence for the musician: "every day the most serious minds take pleasure in poetic fantasies. Why should not a similar privilege be accorded to musical caprice, in similar circumstances?"

In that André's essay concerns the beautiful in vocal music—the normal province of eighteenth-century theories of expression—the terms of his "sonorous rhetoric" are set by the poet. Words not only motivate the musician's "fancy" but also make clear for the listener the composer's "response to the matter that is to be expressed." In the matter of instrumental music, on the other hand, debate as to whether comic effects could be compatible with aesthetic values troubled writers a century later, and it continues even today.[3]

Surveying the instrumental works of Haydn and his contemporaries, writers of the late eighteenth century did not find jests, humor, and play incompatible with the beautiful. For these writers, the "humorous composer" was one whose novelty, inventiveness, and bold surprises subverted conventional procedures without breaking faith with the coherence that conventions insured. As Christian Friedrich Michaelis (1770–1834) noted at the turn of the century:

> The humorous composer distinguishes himself through curious fancies that provoke smiles; he disregards the conventional, and without violating the rules of harmony—indeed often with the finest use of contrapuntal art—his imagination sets in motion such an amusing game with the melody and accompaniment that one is astonished at the newness, the uniqueness, the unexpected; and because all the bold modulation and lively variety combine in a beautiful, interesting whole, it is attractive and delightful.[4]

Michaelis brings to the fore the artful play that a humorous composer "sets in motion," and his narrative is alive with details of active engagement in listening: eccentric novelties and unconventional turns move the listener to smiles, astonishment, delight and admiration. By this account, the persuasions of a musical humorist are considerable in range, even in the absence of words. Implicit here is the observation that humor can be recognized and appreciated in instrumental music because the terms of style are sufficiently familiar to become the materials for artful play.

Appreciation of Haydn's humor by contemporary listeners confirms a wide range of perceived norms that sustained the aesthetic validity of "curious fancies that provoke smiles." In exploring the historical aspects of that range, Leonard Ratner invokes "the play of options" as indigenous to late eighteenth-century style: "the spirit of the *Ars combinatoria*, the master game, appeared as valid for music as it did for mathematical speculation."[5] Compositional dice games offered combinations as equivalent options: because the elements of combination were simple and formulaic, chance determined the sequence of melodic and rhythmic permutations over a fixed metric and harmonic grid. The choices of musical jesting differ from such games, however, in contriving to disturb the sequence and pattern of familiar elements on a more broadly based grid of norms and expectations. This "art of combination" issues an explicit challenge to the listener, akin to a riddle, in which incongruous juxtapositions produce a play of seemingly incompatible options; stable meanings and functions of conventions are thus suspended in temporary and paradoxical ambivalence. Although the surprising novelty of the combination may in itself strike the listener as humorous, wit discovers an unsuspected and compensating stability. As Novalis put it: "Wit reveals a balance out of true—It is the consequence of a disturbance, and at the same time the means of restoring it."[6]

The distance of Novalis from Locke is telling in the former's recasting of fancy and judgment: "Where fancy and judgment meet, we have wit—where reason and caprice come together, we have humor."[7] (A radical departure from Locke's concerns is Novalis's delight in "babble"—wordplay that recognizes the futility of stable signification.) Inherent in these definitions is the play of paradox dear to the Romantic's sense of irony. But they also recall a continuous tradition that recognized both playful and serious sides of wit and humor. Even Locke, distrustful of rhetoric's figurative language when stability of meaning was essential to knowledge, recognized "those arts of deceiving wherein men find pleasure to be deceived."[8] Johnson's "amusement" retains something of this ambivalence.

As was typically the case in eighteenth-century writings about music, especially instrumental genres, discussions of musical humor lagged well behind essays on the subject in drama and poetry. Whereas distinctions between wit, humor, the ridiculous, and the ludicrous were repeatedly set forward and debated by men of letters during Haydn's lifetime, it was not until the turn of the century that writers addressed their implications for instrumental music, and then it was German writers who did so. Not surprising, approval of the subjectivity of humor is salient in the two earliest essays, published in Haydn's late years. Each writer focuses on different aspects of the humorous, but like their predecessors, both seek to accommodate a range of departures from the "rules" of stylistic decorum within prevailing tastes and aesthetic categories. These essays suggest a continuum of the "humorous style" and help to locate the roles of both composer and listener in the play of artful jesting.

Early Essays on Musical Wit and Humor

The title of Michaelis's essay "Über das Humoristische oder Launige in der musikalischen Komposition" (1807) suggests a rapprochement of English and German understandings of the term *humorous*. In line with earlier writers, his general sense of musical humor is allied with artistic temperament—those eccentric freedoms that mark a composer's personality as distinctive. Humorous novelties are not simply different from normative procedures, but strikingly so: it is "the peculiar combinations of ideas, the surprising juxtapositions, and the unique turns and nuances of expression . . . that distinguish the humorous style."[9]

Noting a propensity for the "humorous style" among contemporary composers, Michaelis betrays attitudes toward rules and tradition that recall Corbyn Morris's comparison of Jonson and Shakespeare:

> With the old composers the humorous was something very rare, because they willingly adhered to strict regularity, and their imagination did not so easily take the daring flight that goes beyond the traditional. . . . Our newest music, on the other hand, is for the most part humorous, especially since Joseph Haydn as the greatest master in this manner set the tone for it, particularly in his original symphonies and quartets.[10]

Michaelis locates the principal features of the *Humoristische* or *Launige* in the novelties of those works or movements that reveal the greatest originality of an individual composer. Since "music is humorous when the composition reveals more of the temperament [*Laune*] of the composer than the strict practice of a system of composition," Michaelis can accommodate a broad spectrum of musical humor, whether "witty and of a lively, pleasing character," or with "more serious . . . traces of a capricious temperament [*eigensinnigen Laune*]."[11] This latter category, whose exemplar is the capriccio or free fantasia, requires those few like-minded listeners with "enough training and inclination to follow the peculiar paths of the earnest humorist." If a composer wishes "truly to amuse and divert," he exercises more freedom in "jesting-humorous" music—the scherzo being a model here—which is "pleasing almost always to everyone." But in both earnest and jesting humor, the composer "expresses his subjective individuality . . . in his own manner."[12] Among Haydn's contemporaries cited as humorous are Mozart, who "seemed on the whole to be more committed to the serious and the lofty than to the comic and naïve, as well as Pleyel, Viotti, Clementi, and Beethoven. In chamber genres especially, these are composers who "have let flow a rich source of that humor which with some tends more toward the roguish joke [*schalkhaften Scherz*], and with others more toward fanciful earnestness [*schwärmerischen Ernst*]."[13] But it is to Haydn that Michaelis gives pride of place as the first musical humorist to achieve "universal effect."

Michaelis's view of jesting and earnest musical humor, anticipated in Junker's essay, is paralleled by Kant's distinction between humorous and serious wit: the former, in being a source of amusement, is more appropriate for entertainments in the salon; the latter, deserving of admiration, suits more sober propositions.[14] "Humorous wit," as Kant described it, "arises from a propensity for paradoxes" such that "the unexpected animat[es] surprise, but always only as a game."[15] In that aesthetic experience meant for Kant an act of imagination that entertained ideas in an "as if" mode, one might view games of wit as an extension of this fundamental play of ambivalence inherent in all art. Wit's "propensity for paradoxes" brings that ambivalence to the fore as explicitly playful.

While he provides some general notions of where humorous departures might occur, Michaelis is short on specifics: "Melodies, figures, passages, forceful chords appear—one knows not whence they come." The nature of a melody or rhythm might itself be humorous, as might novel harmonic procedures; so too "the unexpected entrances of certain voices or instruments" and the clever interplay between melodic and accompanying voices. A seemingly unpromising beginning—"some accidental notes on paper," as the lexicographer Gerber had noted of Haydn's procedure—might provide an amusing first encounter with an eccentric subject that in time reveals unsuspected possibilities. Such novelties presuppose ingenuity and a certain extravagance of procedure that "cannot be accounted for by the customary practice of musical systems."[16] Like the "comical or humorous narrator who combines the strangest of things, and in his peculiar frame of mind gives to even the most familiar things a new aspect," the humorous composer "gives his ideas free rein" yet does not offend against good taste. The result is an "amusing game" that for all its novel and surprising departures does not violate the beautiful.

If Michaelis seems to have regarded compositional humor as a given in the most original music of his day, the earlier essay of Friedrich August Weber (1753–1806) reveals more of the difficulties in coming to terms with comic effects in instrumental music. In "Über komische Characteristik und Karrikatur in praktischen Musikwerken" (1800), Weber proposed to examine various applications in music of the ancient term *vis comica*.[17] He makes it clear from the outset that he intends an aesthetic sense of the laughable, and he makes a distinction between "excellent comedy"—for which tasteful laughter is appropriate—and the lower form of caricature, perhaps less admirable for its broad strokes and parodistic intent. With primary focus on comic opera and operetta, Weber is only incidentally concerned with purely instrumental music, yet he does allow that instrumental music is capable of comic paradox, wit, and humor. Eighteenth-century distinctions persist in his use of these terms, but paradox emerges as the dominant thread that binds them.

Describing the effect of the comic style as "a feeling of the laughable . . . awakened in the listener whose ear is attuned to it," Weber turns to pictorial analogues in defining its means. A visual artist who seeks to represent something comic indulges "only modest deviations from the rules of eurythmics and symmetry"; the resulting paradox of disproportion impresses the viewer as laughable. Similarly,

> the comic composer who does not wish to stoop to caricature allows himself only moderate deviations from the general rules that govern a composition of the beautiful and serious type as well, and joins sections and phrases in a whole that thereby takes on a shade of paradox and, through a certain joining of ideas, of the comic.[18]

While Weber does not specify the "general rules" of serious composition, nor the particular trespasses of humorous music, his analogy suggests that a judicious departure from symmetry and proportion in music can produce a paradoxical and comic effect. It is not the materials themselves so much as the manner in which they are put together—the particular conjunctions of phrases and sections—that puts things slightly out of joint.

In turning to musical wit, Weber again proceeds by analogy. Now, however, he emphasizes the role of the listener in discovering ingenuity of procedure. If the comic paradox provokes a "ha-ha," the discovery of wit is more akin to an "aha!" Again, ingenious combination is stressed, here of ideas only seemingly unsuited to one another:

> Just as poetic and pictorial wit inheres in the discovery of similarities one would not have thought to find, and just as a skilled joining of two such similarities is required in order that an idea become a witty one, so too musical wit depends on the discovery of unexpected similarities between two musical ideas, and on the surprise of their facile and appropriate combination.[19]

The lingering influence of Locke is apparent in Weber's emphasis on the detection of unsuspected similarities. But he notes that for the majority of listeners, this discovery requires a text of some kind—a "commentary" to the wit, as he puts it—and that "where a text supports singing, nothing further is needed to make it generally clear for everyone." Here a genuine paradox is posed for instrumental music: the composer falls short of his aim if he fails to provide a program to the musical wit, yet in providing such a program, he spoils the surprise that wit intends. As Junker had noted, the recognition of wit without words presupposes an unusually subtle musical intelligence.

Musical humor is apparently less subtle. Regarded by Weber as an eccentric extension of wit, humor supplies an extravagance of manner:

> Musical wit pushed to the highest level of singularity and paradox is called *musical humor*. The motivation for the composer to rave judiciously [*mit Weisheit zu deliriren*] in this manner can lie in previously written words of a text, as well as in the frame of mind [*Gemütsstimmung*] of the composer himself.[20]

Morris's reasonable extravagance finds an echo here, as does the abiding association of an artist's temperament with his style.

Weber's definitions are by no means precise, nor does he offer specific musical examples to clarify them. Nevertheless, his essay invites fresh consideration of humor, wit, and the comic in music—all of which propose the unusual in terms that demand recognition of an artful control of eccentricity. Weber thus promotes a view of ingenious jesting in which wit and judgment are complementary: recognition of paradox sustains the play of tension between the two as artfully intended.

The comic relies on judicious distortion, on the paradoxical juxtaposition of musical elements that appear to be out of balance when measured against the orderly sequence and just proportions expected of "serious" musical discourse. Understood in these terms, overstatement in excessive gestures might be as disproportionate as understatement in elisions that cut short an expected answer or leave something out in a surprising silence. In both categories, Haydn would seem at times to exceed the "moderate deviations" by which Weber meant to distinguish the effects of "excellent comedy" from those of caricature. But like pictorial caricature, comic distortions in music presume familiarity with the undistorted model and rely upon the listener's recognition of the prototype despite exaggerated or suppressed features. Impressions of paradox as comic depend upon the degree of distortion that can be sustained within this double view.

In accord with long-standing conceptions of wit as posing more subtle challenges to the mind (and ear), Weber's concept of musical wit makes additional demands on the listener as an interpreting agent, as one who can detect the *Weisheit* in the *deliriren*. The paradoxical excess in wit lies in its multiplicity of implications and in their seeming contradictions. Here too a double awareness is required, but the surprise started by the mixed messages of incongruous combinations motivates discovery of relationship: seemingly incompatible elements are joined in such a way that their similarities are revealed, the aptness of their association recognized.

Humor is here a general mood or spirit of extravagance, embracing wit and the comic at their extremes. Whether following the suggestion of a text or his own eccentric fantasy, the humorist is not permitted unlimited freedom: while he may "rave," he must do so "judiciously." Seeming to ignore the customary rules, he may stretch but not break them.

Acknowledging the freedoms of wit and humor as novel challenges to compositional norms and expected patterns, the essays of both Michaelis and Weber serve as a fitting reminder that jests lack point where expectation has no grounding in the familiar. Humorous composers, for all their departures from customary procedures, must operate within the framework of a familiar system of reference. Recognition of humor in challenges to the conventional presumes, then, the stability of conventions that a mature style affords.

While retaining connections with eighteenth-century understandings of wit and humor, Weber's essay casts particular light on the notion of humor. Joining earlier notions of a natural and inescapable humor, resident in the personality of the artist, is that of an assumed persona controlling capricious and extravagant manners. An aesthetic of humorous paradox in instrumental music brings forward the rhetor behind the scenes: in the absence of texts and characters that appear to motivate the comedy of songs and actions in opera, the composer-humorist becomes conspicuous in the role of manipulating surprising reverses. But if humor displays an extravagance of manner, wit presumes ingenuity in resolving a seeming contradiction, in the discovery of which both composer and listener play their parts. In this delicate balance of engagement, the humorous "persuader" invites the listener's complicity in the play of "sonorous rhetoric."

The Playful Art of Combinations

August Halm regarded a more explicit game of ambivalence as basic to the business of a musical humorist: "Humor depends on the possibility of working figuratively, of playing hide-and-seek, of dissembling, of fibbing: indeed, in such a way that the listener can detect it, and that it is intended that he shall detect it."[21] By Halm's account the humorous composer is something of a transparent *eiron*, a dissembler who means to reveal his deceptions as such. As I have suggested, Haydn's explicitly playful rhetoric directs attention to its own excess, whether in exaggerated, eccentric gestures or in surprising conjunctions of familiar conventions. The humorist thus displays his means of engaging the listener as salient rather than disguised artfulness.

If the conjunction of rhetoric and play seems a somewhat incompatible match—the one implying a strategy of controlling the listener, the other an invitation to participate in an open-ended, autotelic game—such a combination suits the paradoxical nature of artful jests as both incongruous and appropriate, ludicrous and fitting. Not surprising, phrases used to characterize the comic aspect of incongruity in wit and humor are often themselves paradoxical, whether in eighteenth-century or more contemporary terms: "daz-zling light and agreeable confusion";[22] "relation and want of relation united ... in the same assemblage";[23] "something mechanical encrusted upon the living";[24] "a playful disappointment of the listener's expectations."[25] Such modes of persuasion point up the aesthetic pleasure of a dramatic rhetoric, self-conscious of its pose—its eloquence motivated, as Richard A. Lanham observes, by "pure pleasure in impersonation."[26]

Paradox is a useful trope for "ingenious jesting with art" in suggesting a connection between the persuasions of a humorous rhetor and responsive listeners. A time-honored strategy in classical rhetoric, paradox focuses atten-tion as a seeming violation of sense, a puzzle of self-contradiction. Recog-nized as a temporary and artful departure from the rules of logical argumenta-tion, paradox is one of several tropes that Heinrich Lausberg groups under the rubric of *Verfremdung* (making strange) in his *Elemente der literarischen Rhetorik*.[27] In proposing that the seemingly contradictory can prove strangely fitting, such a rhetorical strategy defies credibility the better to test sound reasoning. Similarly provocative in music, paradox is permissible as wit when seeming contradictions—of syntax and function, sequence and continuity, style and genre, topos and context—are recognized (in time) as being uniquely appropriate to the materials and procedures at hand. Unlike the logician's unyielding paradox, that of the playful rhetor is a seeming contra-diction capable of artful resolution.

In Haydn's music it is often the most familiar of conventions—the rhetori-cal "commonplaces"—that are made strange in paradoxical alterations, com-binations, and contexts. And it was counted as the touchstone of Haydn's genius that he could combine the seemingly artless with the patently artful. Here a propensity for surprise is matched by a simplicity of terms, enhancing recognition of what Triest called Haydn's "popular artfulness," and Gerber his "great art of seeming familiar." Appreciated as humorous in Michaelis's sense, surprising uses of such conventions transform the stereotypical into personalized tokens of an individual style. The relaxed "colloquial cast" of Haydn's late style, remarked by Charles Butler, was promoted by the simple directness of his melodies, yet matched by the rigor of motivic play that ex-tended seemingly artless subjects to "vast complication."[28]

Noting that the comic in music can be "not only the characteristic mood of a work but often, particularly with Haydn, an essential technique," Charles Rosen rightly insists that Haydn's "whimsicality never consisted of empty structural variants."[29] Rather, the particulars of formal procedures proceeded from the musical materials themselves. Rosen's description of musical wit as accomplishing a "surprising change of nonsense into sense" is apt, yet he focuses on the dissonant detail as largely a tonal one. While the centripetal force—as Ratner calls it—of tonal relations is basic to play with formal struc-tures in Classical music, "dissonance" can be more broadly construed in pro-cedures that challenged the sense of associations familiar to Haydn's lis-teners.

Among various categories of the familiar examined extensively by Ratner are those topoi associated with musical functions and genres of court, urban, and country life: the gestures, meters, and patterns of dance; the ceremonial dignity of military fanfares and marches; horn signals of the hunt and drones of the bagpipe; seria and buffa styles of expression in operatic genres; learned counterpoint of the church style and "exoticisms" of the folklike. These and other traditional associations provided musical frames of affective and social reference in instrumental music.[30] Constituting a ready lexicon of the familiar, such topics also provided opportunities for the subversion of traditional categories and hierarchies when used in incongruous combinations and contexts.

A second resource for artful subversion lay in the stability of syntactic and formal conventions that made certain sequences of events highly probable. Treating these as topics for paradoxical manipulation, the composer ensures maximum recognition of both the familiar and the strange as "united in a single assemblage." Normative procedures that defined harmonic function and metric pattern, symmetry of phrase and period, opening and closing gestures, signals of local and large-scale thematic return, and the simple device of repetition—all provided a measure against which the contextually improbable could be recognized.[31] For audiences of his day, Haydn's reputation as a humorous composer might itself have become a measure of the familiar: a known propensity for subverting conventional patterns raises the ante, so to speak, on novel surprises for listeners familiar with a composer's individual manner.

In addition to conventions that confirm general expectations for congruity and continuity, a movement in progress establishes a context of the familiar in its own manner and patterns. The listener's recognition of incongruous reverses depends on the degree to which materials are themselves familiar— easy to take in and remember—and that become familiar by frequent repetition. Here paradoxes arise from subversions specific to chosen materials of the musical discourse.

The means and effects of Haydn's wit and humor are best demonstrated in the specific musical contexts that frame them, and in the foregoing chapters I have suggested some models for that analysis. In proposing artful jesting as a strategy of persuasion, I wish to consider here some of the broader implications for listeners in that play.

Artful Play and the Role of the Listener

In his foundational study of the cultural significance of play, Johan Huizinga emphasizes its "profoundly aesthetic quality" and draws a parallel with music making:

> the activity begins and ends within strict limits of time and place, is repeatable, consists essentially in order, rhythm, alternation, transports audience and per-

formers alike out of "ordinary" life into a sphere of gladness and serenity, which makes even sad music a lofty pleasure. In other words, it "enchants" and "enraptures" them.[32]

In Huizinga's conception, play comprehends not only the experience of art, but its making as well: "in the very idea of 'style' in art, is there not a tacit admission of a certain play-element? Is not the birth of a style itself a playing of the mind in its search for new forms?"[33]

While we might accept Huizinga's notion that musical style admits an essential element of exploratory play, and that musical experience is "playful" in the broad sense he intends, jesting in music implies a more sportive transport, one in which play is self-consciously engaged as interactive. Using the language of game and play, Oliver Strunk proposed a specific application of play to musical style and to Haydn's strategy of surprise. Quoting Eduard Hanslick's statement that the "secret of music's effect" is that "everything comes as it must come, but otherwise than we expect," Strunk noted:

> Only when the rules of the game are well established is it feasible for the composer to play on the expectation of his listener. And even then, to play on expectation he must first arouse it. To secure emphasis he must first exercise self-control. He cannot afford to be continually surprising his listener. He must be straightforward before he is startling.[34]

Strunk's comments address the importance of a mature style for the effective use of surprise as an artistic technique. While Haydn's personal stamp in artful play depends upon timing and restraint, the effect of surprise presupposes a certain stability of the familiar if listeners are to recognize ingenuity in its use as a compositional strategy.[35]

While some who have explored the relationship of humor to art have stressed the exploratory behavior that characterizes aesthetic play,[36] and others the game strategies involving rule systems and deviance from logical thinking,[37] Wolfgang Iser's phenomenological orientation in examining literary texts seems to me a promising one in considering the listener's role in musical jesting. Iser, a leading exponent of reception theory, regards readers as fundamental to the production of meaning in literary works. Indeed, readers produce the work, in Iser's view, in the process of reading: "As the reader passes through the various perspectives offered by the text and relates the different views and patterns to one another he sets the work in motion, and so sets himself in motion too."[38] Imagining the text-reader relationship as a two-way interaction, Iser construes literary texts as structurally patterned to guide the reader, but also as fundamentally incomplete: strategic points of indeterminacy—"gaps," "blanks," "negations of the familiar"—prod the reader's imaginative participation. Filling in what is left out or only partially revealed, the reader brings the work to life in acts of interpretation.[39]

Iser's analyses of Fielding's *Joseph Andrews* (1742) and *Tom Jones* (1749), in particular, yield insights into the self-conscious interplay of author and reader. Noting that Fielding "often speaks of the offer of participation that must be made to the reader, if he is to fulfill the promise of the novel," Iser considers the larger aim of the novelist as one of "arousing a sense of discernment":

> This is to be regarded as a pleasure, because in this way the reader will be able to test his own faculties. It also promises to be profitable, because the need for discernment stimulates a process of learning in the course of which one's own sense of judgment may come under scrutiny.[40]

While the issue of critical authority remains itself indeterminate in Iser's formulation, suspended somewhere between text and reader, his attention to reading as a process of active engagement is a useful reminder of the listener's task in music, the more so as Iser takes seriously the historical and social contexts in which texts are made and experienced. His remarks on the effects of Fielding's surprising "reversals" apply equally well to Haydn's strategies of jesting: "an idea, a norm, or an event can only take on its full shape in the reader if it is accompanied more or less simultaneously by its negative form."[41] In the recall of "those memories which are contradicted by the surprising facts and unexpected actions," the reader seeks "a point of convergence that will provide a motivation for the surprises and contradictions."[42]

In musical analysis such points are most often made in reference to "the work itself," the listener's role in realizing it being taken for granted. The phenomenon of musical jesting, however, makes the case for a more listener-oriented approach. Iser's concept of a testing of discernment relies upon what he terms a "repertoire of the familiar." The Classical style proved an ideal vehicle for the musical humorist in providing that repertoire for incongruous combinations. Haydn's gambit in a musical jest is to make the simplest stock-in-trade convention opaque, its expected function indecisive, and to subvert the most familiar topic, rendering it ambiguous. In such manipulations of expression and syntax, he relies on the listener's response to their stable meanings and functions, even as he proposes to undermine that stability. However plausible the new frame of reference that liberates a convention from its habitual context, the ordinary, normative associations of that convention continue to exert an influence on its new and uncommon context. Indeed, it is in this persistence of the familiar that one recognizes paradox itself. In addition to forcing attention to the immediate, such a strategy invites predictions about potential options brought into play. By extension, incongruous and unconventional means also affirm the essential value of conventions themselves.

The active role of the reader asserted by Iser, and by Ted Cohen as inherent in the persuasion of jokes, helps to frame the mechanism and effect of an artful jest as an alliance of rhetoric and play. Governed by mixed (and incomplete) messages that breach conventional "rules" of language and logic, the persuasion of jests is both manipulative and complicit. Certain procedures can be inherently paradoxical as disturbances of music's temporality, and others as more local contradictions of patterns that have been established within a given work. In any case, when paradox is displayed as an explicit gambit, it becomes a provocative gesture, a signal of intentional play with the normative, ordinary meanings of conventions.

Central to the heightened awareness that ingenious jesting provokes is a focusing of attention on the particulars not only of paradox itself but of its implications for the work in progress. In arts governed by temporal patterns of pacing, duration, and sequence, the timing and placement of such signals will be critical to "felt" recognition. Depending on when, where, and the degree to which ongoing patterns are disturbed, the effect may be visceral as well as conceptual in its humor. Such an effect is most likely at the end of a piece, when expectations are informed by all that has come before. An example is the paradox of an ending that is also a beginning, heard most emphatically in the finale of Haydn's "Joke" Quartet. In that work, the joke becomes manifest as implicating beginning and ending patterns only in the last section of the movement. Earlier paradoxes also contribute to the final effect: continuation where none is expected; a superfluity of closing remarks, none of which is needed and all of which prove unsatisfactory in function; the stasis of indecision; and the suggestion of infinite continuation.

In displaying the ingenuity of wit, Haydn engages both the materials of his art and the attention of his listener in this kind of aesthetic play, dramatizing not only the role of conventions and the ingenuity of the unconventional but also the interplay of composer and listener. He invites the listener to become self-conscious about his predictions, to participate, in a sense, in the creative "play of options" of the compositional process. Although fun and often funny, this game of wits is as earnest as it is playful—one that fully satisfies what we expect of aesthetic experience at the same time that it makes us highly conscious of those expectations. For here apparent paradoxes of dysfunction, distortion, disruption, and discontinuity (and miscontinuation), along with other transgressions of decorum, are taken not in earnest but as temporary stand-ins for their opposites. Thus a musical joke doesn't displace aesthetic values, but rather invites a temporary suspension of the prevailing norms by which they are measured.

That Haydn's particular humor was recognized in his own day suggests the accomplishments of listeners who were responsive to the challenges of his art of combinations. The implications for today's listeners are no less dependent on discerning engagement. Even though darkened and hushed concert halls might discourage overt expressions of amusement, knowledgeable listeners do at times chuckle and even laugh outright in performances of Haydn's and others' instrumental works. Whether audible as laughter or silent in a "smile of surprise and wonder," recognition of musical wit signals a cooperative achievement of compositional and interpretive strategies. In this sense, the play of ingenious jesting affirms both continuity and community in the pleasures of musical experience.

List of Abbreviations

AfMw	*Archiv für Musikwissenschaft*
AMZ	*Allgemeine musikalische Zeitung.* Leipzig, 1798–1848.
CCLN	*Collected Correspondence and London Notebooks of Joseph Haydn.* Edited by H. C. Robbins Landon. Fair Lawn, N.J.: Essential Books, 1959.
CECS	*Joseph Haydn. Critical Edition of the Complete Symphonies.* Edited by H. C. Robbins Landon. 12 vols. 2d ed., Vienna: Universal Edition, 1981.
CM	*Current Musicology*
ECS	*Eighteenth-Century Studies*
EM	*Early Music*
HS 1975	*Haydn Studies: Proceedings of the International Conference, Washington, D.C., 1975.* Edited by Jens Peter Larsen, Howard Serwer, and James Webster. New York: Norton, 1981.
H-St	*Haydn-Studien*
HYb	*The Haydn Yearbook*
IRASM	*International Review of the Aesthetics and Sociology of Music*
JAAC	*Journal of Aesthetics and Art Criticism*
JAMS	*Journal of the American Musicological Society*
JbMP	*Jahrbuch der Musikbibliothek Peters*
JHI	*Journal of the History of Ideas*
JHK 1982	*Bericht über den Internationalen Joseph Haydn Kongreß, Wien Hofburg, 5.–12. September 1982.* Edited by Eva Badura-Skoda. Munich: Henle, 1986.

JHW	*Joseph Haydn Werke.* Edited by the Joseph Haydn-Institut, Cologne, under the direction of Jens Peter Larsen and Georg Feder. Munich: Henle, 1958–.
JM	*The Journal of Musicology*
JMT	*Journal of Music Theory*
Mf	*Die Musikforschung*
ML	*Music and Letters*
MN	*Musical Newsletter*
MQ	*The Musical Quarterly*
MR	*The Music Review*
NGD	*The New Grove Dictionary of Music and Musicians.* Edited by Stanley Sadie. 20 vols. London: Macmillan, 1980.
OED	*Oxford English Dictionary.* 13 vols. New York: Oxford University Press, 1933.
ÖMz	*Österreichische Musikzeitschrift*
PMLA	*Publications of the Modern Language Association*
PRMA	*Proceedings of the Royal Musical Association*
StM	*Studia musicologica*

Notes

Preface

1. The most recent discussion of this issue has appeared as this book goes to press, in James Webster, *Haydn's "Farewell" Symphony and the Idea of Classical Style* (Cambridge: Cambridge University Press, 1991). Webster consistently uses the word Classical in quotation marks—indeed, his study is an extended call for reexamination of our assumptions about the so-called Classical style and era and of Haydn's own compositional development.

1. The Musical Joke: A Laughing Matter?

1. W. Jackson Bate, *Samuel Johnson* (New York: Harcourt Brace Jovanovich, 1977), p. 481.
2. Tim Appelo, review of *Laughing Matters: A Serious Look at Humor*, ed. John Durant and Jonathan Miller, in *The Sciences*, September/October 1989, pp. 45–48. The subjects of laughter and humor have engaged broad theoretical and experimental attention across many disciplines, the range of which can be only suggested here. For a comprehensive overview and discussion of theories of laughter and play, see Daniel E. Berlyne, "Laughter, Humor, and Play," in *The Handbook of Social Psychology*, ed. Gardner Lindzey and Elliot Aronson, vol. 3, *The Individual in a Social Context* (Reading, Mass.: Addison-Wesley, 1969), pp. 795–852. Extensive bibliographies of humor studies are provided in Antony J. Chapman and Hugh C. Foot, eds., *It's a Funny Thing, Humour: International Conference on Humour and Laughter, 1976* (New York: Pergamon Press, 1977) and in the more recent *Handbook of Humour Research*, ed. Jeffrey H. Goldstein and Paul E. McGhee (New York: Springer-Verlag, 1983). A recent collection of philosophical essays on laughter and humor, from Plato to the present, may be found in John Morreall, ed., *The Philosophy of Laughter and Humor* (Albany, N.Y.: State University of New York Press, 1987); see also Morreall's earlier study, *Taking Laughter Seriously* (Albany, N.Y.: State University of New York Press, 1983). Critical studies of the aesthetic contexts of laughter are relatively few in comparison with psychological and sociological essays. G. B. Milner offers a concise and thoughtful review of theories of laughter in his "Homo Ridens: Towards a Semiotic Theory of Humour and Laughter," *Semiotica* 5 (1972): 1–30. Addressing various aspects of humor and the comic in literature, Paul Lewis makes a case for the importance of humor research to literary criticism in *Comic Effects:*

Interdisciplinary Approaches to Humor in Literature (Albany, N.Y.: State University of New York Press, 1989).

3. D. H. Monro, *Argument of Laughter* (Melbourne, Australia: Melbourne University Press, 1951), p. 92.

4. William Shakespeare, *Love's Labour's Lost* 5.2.851–52.

5. Although analytical approaches to wit, humor, and the comic in instrumental music have ranged widely, the tendency to isolate the particular features noted here is often uncritical and typically ahistorical. I discuss these issues with reference to several general studies in "Wit, Humor, and the Instrumental Music of Joseph Haydn" (Ph.D. diss., Yale University, 1979), chap. 1. General considerations of the subject extend from the early essays of Anton Penkert (1914), August Halm (1916), Richard Hohenemser (1917), and Henry Gilbert (1926) to more recent articles by Zofia Lissa (1969), Siegfried Borris (1973), and Wilfried Gruhn (1983). With two exceptions, Victor Ravizza (1974) on Brahms and Susan Wollenberg (1988) on C. P. E. Bach, composer-oriented studies have focused on the works of Beethoven and Haydn. On the former, see Theodor Veidl (1929), Ernst Laaf (1962–63), and Ludwig Misch (1967). An early study particular to Haydn is Alfred Heuss's "Der Humor im letzten Satz von Haydns Oxford-Sinfonie," *Die Musik* 12 (1912): 270–86. The single published monograph (in Swedish) is C.-G. Stellan Mörner's *Joseph Haydn, musikens Humorist* (Stockholm: Lindfors, 1945). Stephen E. Paul's "Wit, Comedy, and Humour in the Instrumental Music of Franz Joseph Haydn" (Ph.D. diss., Cambridge University, 1980) can be consulted on microfilm at Isham Library, Harvard University. See also note 36, Chapter 8.

6. In this connection, see especially Richard Hohenemser, "Über Komik und Humor in der Musik," *JbMP 1917* (1918): 65–83, and Zofia Lissa, "Über das Komische in der Musik," in *Aufsätze zur Musikaesthetik* (Berlin: Henschel, 1969), pp. 91–136.

7. James F. English emphasizes this point in "The Laughing Reader: A New Direction for Studies of the Comic," *Genre* 19 (1986): 129–54, where he urges a "trans-generic" approach to the study of humor in literary criticism.

8. Exceptional in this regard are Susan Wollenberg, "A New Look at C. P. E. Bach's Musical Jokes," in *C. P. E. Bach Studies*, ed. Stephen L. Clark (Oxford: Clarendon Press, 1988), pp. 295–314, and Jane Perry-Camp, "A Laugh a Minuet: Humor in Late Eighteenth-Century Music," *College Music Symposium* 19 (1979): 19–29.

9. The same instrumentation is found among Mozart's works in the Salzburg divertimenti K. 247, 287, and 334 of the late 1770s. Alan Tyson's study of the autograph materials of K. 522 indicates that Mozart composed much of the work long before 14 June 1787, the date he entered it in his register of works (see "Notes on the Genesis of Mozart's 'Ein musikalischer Spass,' KV 522," in *Festschrift Rudolf Elvers zum 60. Geburtstag*, ed. Ernst Herttrich and Hans Schneider [Tutzing: Hans Schneider Verlag, 1985], pp. 505–18; reprinted in Alan Tyson, *Mozart: Studies of the Autograph Scores* [Cambridge: Harvard University Press, 1987], pp. 234–45). Tyson's findings challenge the view held by Wolfgang Hildesheimer, among others, that Mozart wrote the work in response to his father's death.

10. Hermann Abert, *W. A. Mozart: Neubearbeitete und erweiterte Ausgabe von Otto Jahns "Mozart"* (Leipzig: Breitkopf und Härtel, 1923–24), 2:394; see pp. 394–98 for an engaging and perceptive discussion of K. 522.

11. The title page of J. André's first (1802) edition is reproduced in Tyson, "Notes," p. 506.

12. See the exhibit catalogue *Mozart en France*, (Paris: Bibliothèque Nationale, 1956), p. 49 and Plate XVI, p. 46.

13. John Barth's collection of stories *Lost in the Funhouse* (New York: Bantam, 1969) was accompanied by a Möbius strip to be assembled by the reader, upon which was written this infinite loop of beginning and repeating. A counterpart, recited with infinite delight by children, is the patience-trying dialogue: "Pete and Repeat were sitting on the fence. Pete fell off. Who was left?" "Repeat.". . . Susan Stewart's *Nonsense: Aspects of Intertextuality in Folklore and Literature* (Baltimore: Johns Hopkins University Press, 1979) is a provocative anthropological study of ways in which the seemingly nonsensical makes sense in play.

14. Sigmund Freud, *Jokes and Their Relation to the Unconscious*, trans. and ed. James Strachey (New York: Norton, 1963), pp. 199–202.

15. Heinrich Koch, *Kurzgefaßtes Handwörterbuch der Musik* (Leipzig, 1807; facsimile reprint, Hildesheim: Georg Olms, 1981), s.v. "Scherz," "Scherzo, scherzando, scherzhaft."

16. Hans Robert Jauss, *Aesthetic Experience and Literary Hermeneutics*, trans. Michael Shaw. Theory and History of Literature, vol. 3 (Minneapolis: University of Minnesota Press, 1982), p. 191.

17. Edward T. Cone, *The Composer's Voice* (Berkeley and Los Angeles: University of California Press, 1974), p. 1. For a collection of recent essays on Cone's theories of persona and agency, see "Edward T. Cone's *The Composer's Voice*: Elaborations and Departures," *College Music Symposium* 29 (1989): 1–80.

18. Cone, *Voice*, p. 5.

19. Ibid., p. 57.

20. Ibid., p. 157.

21. Jauss, *Aesthetic Experience*, p. 191.

22. For a recent discussion of the multiple species of musical time in relation to absolute, or "ordinary" time, see Jonathan D. Kramer, *The Time of Music: New Meanings, New Temporalities, New Listening Strategies* (New York: Schirmer Books, 1988). In discussing beginnings and endings, Kramer notes: "The purpose of simplification and convention rather than contextual reference at the end is to avoid any implications toward a future which cannot be. . . . the ending does not succeed as a process if we have to experience the post-composition framing silence before we realize that the piece has ended" (pp. 139–40). Although Kramer discusses the "Joke" finale (pp. 140, 143), he does not engage the issues of time that its ending suggests.

23. Stephen Paul, "Comedy, Wit, and Humor in Haydn's Instrumental Music," *HS 1975*, p. 452.

24. Hans Lukas Teuber, discussant in Gregory Bateson, "The Position of Humor in Human Communication," in *Transactions of the Ninth Conference on Cybernetics* (New York: Josiah Macy, Jr., Foundation, 1953), p. 16.

25. Leonard B. Meyer, *Style and Music: Theory, History, and Ideology* (Philadelphia: University of Pennsylvania Press, 1989); on the concept of constraints, see especially pp. 8–23.

26. Mary Douglas, "Jokes," in *Implicit Meanings: Essays in Anthropology* (London: Routledge & Kegan Paul, 1975), p. 96. In her attention to the larger social structures that jokes mirror, Douglas's model seems to me more useful here than Arthur Koestler's concept of "bisociation," as elaborated in *The Act of Creation: A Study of the Conscious and Unconscious in Science and Art* (New York: Dell, 1964). Koestler uses this term to identify the feature that jokes and creative discovery have in common: the perception of "two self-consistent but habitually incompatible frames of reference" (p. 35) generates a third term—laughter, in the case of jokes, and the "aha" insight of aesthetic and scientific invention.

27. Douglas, "Jokes," pp. 96, 106–7. Douglas's observations recall Carl Dahlhaus's comment on the paradoxical relationship of individual expression to stylistic norms in music: "Expression, then, is paradoxically yoked to convention, the particular to the general. . . . But, precisely in its dialectic, the principle of expression has become definitive for a historical consciousness and activity in which progressive and conservative traits mutually condition each other" (*Esthetics of Music*, trans. William Austin [Cambridge: Cambridge University Press, 1982], p. 23).

28. Johann Friedrich Reichardt, *Musikalisches Kunstmagazin* (Berlin, 1782), p. 205; the full review is translated in H. C. Robbins Landon, *Haydn: Chronicle and Works*, vol. 2, *Haydn at Eszterháza, 1766–1790* (Bloomington: Indiana University Press, 1978), pp. 466–67. Translations here are my own unless otherwise noted. See Chapter 5 for an extended discussion of the Op. 33 quartets in the context of Haydn's changing style and audience.

29. Leonard Meyer addresses the seeming conundrum that a theory based on music's dynamic process is compatible with the pleasure of repeated hearings of a work in "On Rehearing Music," in *Music, the Arts, and Ideas* (Chicago: University of Chicago Press, 1967), pp. 42–53. Meyer's well known theories of expectation and affect, first elaborated in *Emotion and Meaning in Music* (Chicago: University of Chicago Press, 1960), have informed much of my thinking about the issues addressed in this study.

30. Edward T. Cone, *Musical Form and Musical Performance* (New York: Norton, 1968), p. 54.

Here, as in *The Composer's Voice* (pp. 126–28), Cone puts particular emphasis on the role of the performer: in conveying the immediacy of a surprising gesture, the player is convincing "only if he succeeds in being startled himself" (*Voice*, p. 127).

31. Giuseppe Carpani, *Le Haydine ovvero lettere su la vita e le opere del celebre maestro Giuseppe Haydn* (Milan, 1812; 2d ed., Padua, 1823), pp. 120–21, unpub. trans. Phillip Keppler and Vernon Gotwals.

32. Quoted in Landon, *Chronicle*, vol. 3, *Haydn in England, 1791–1795* (Bloomington: Indiana University Press, 1976), p. 150. Landon includes several accounts of the Andante's effect and Haydn's motivation for composing the surprise (pp. 149–51).

33. Georg August Griesinger, *Biographische Notizen über Joseph Haydn* (Leipzig, 1810), ed. Franz Grasberger (Vienna: Paul Kaltschmid, 1954), p. 32. Griesinger's biography is translated, with introduction and notes, by Vernon Gotwals in *Haydn: Two Contemporary Portraits* (Madison: University of Wisconsin Press, 1963); the passage cited here is his translation, p. 33.

34. Landon, *Chronicle* 3:528–29. See also Georg Feder, "Haydns Paukenschlag und andere Überraschungen," *ÖMz* 21 (1966): 5–6.

35. Facsimile reprint of the Naples, 1730 ed. (Farnborough, England: 1967); translation by Ralph Kirkpatrick in his *Domenico Scarlatti*, rev. ed. (Princeton, N.J.: Princeton University Press, 1983), p. 102. Kirkpatrick notes that this preface is a rare instance of recorded "verbal utterances" by Scarlatti, and "the only occasion on which he addresses us directly in the whimsical and flowery language his music has led us to expect."

2. The Decorum of Wit and the Nature of Humor in Eighteenth-Century Essays

1. Carpani, *Le Haydine*, p. 107, unpub. trans. Philip Keppler and Vernon Gotwals.

2. *Poems of Jonathan Swift*, ed. Harold Williams (Oxford: Clarendon Press, 1937), 1:215–16.

3. Corbyn Morris, *An Essay towards Fixing the True Standards of Wit, Humour, Raillery, Satire, and Ridicule* (London, 1744), Essays on Wit, no. 4 ([Los Angeles]: Augustan Reprint Society, 1947), pp. 23–24. In his introduction to this volume, James L. Clifford notes that Morris (1710–79) was a friend of Hume and Boswell, and he cites Edward Hooker's estimate of the *Essay* as "probably the best and clearest treatment of the subject in the first half of the eighteenth century." (See also 2d facsimile reprint [New York: Garland, 1970].)

4. Ibid., p. 25.

5. William Hazlitt, *Lectures on the English Comic Writers* (1818), 3d ed. (London: John Templeman, 1841), pp. 24–25. In *The Triumph of Wit: A Study of Victorian Comic Theory* (Oxford: Clarendon Press, 1974), Robert Bernard Martin traces the return to favor of intellectual comedy associated with wit and the declining fortunes of sentimental humor. He notes that in comparison to their immediate predecessors, writers at the end of the nineteenth century had reinstated many of the values associated with wit in the eighteenth century.

6. Dugald Stewart, *Elements of the Philosophy of the Human Mind* (Edinburgh, 1792; 2d ed. Boston, 1814), 1:256.

7. For Addison, wit demands "Delight and Surprise" (*Freeholder* no. 45 [London, 1716]); for George Campbell, "an agreeable Surprise" (*The Philosophy of Rhetoric* [Edinburgh, 1757; "new edition," New York, 1885], p. 30). According to James Beattie, a witticism must be "new and surprising" (*On Laughter and Ludicrous Composition*, 3d ed. [London, 1779], p. 389); and for Georg Friedrich Meier, "A sprightly jest, in order to have a due novelty and liveliness, must . . . be entirely unexpected" (*Gedanken von Scherzen*, anonymous trans. of the 2d ed. of 1754: *Thoughts on Jesting* [London, 1764]; modern ed. by Joseph Jones [Austin: University of Texas Press, 1947], p. 82).

8. John Locke, *An Essay Concerning Human Understanding* (London, 1690), 2.9.2. Although wit assumes more positive values among later writers, in both German and English theories Locke's formulation has an abiding influence. In two recent articles on *Witz* among the early Romantics (in connection with Schumann's Piano Fantasy in C Major, Op. 17), Locke's

definition is clearly traceable. See John Daverio, "Schumann's 'Im Legendenton' and Fried-rich Schlegel's *Arabeske*," *19th-Century Music* 11 (1987): 150–63, and, in the same issue, An-thony Newcomb, "Schumann and Late Eighteenth-Century Narrative Strategies," pp. 164–74.

9. William Jackson, "On Wit," in *The Four Ages, Together with Essays on Various Subjects* (Lon-don, 1798; facsimile reprint, New York: Garland, 1970), p. 122.

10. In *Leviathan* (1651), Thomas Hobbes had allowed that speech might be used to "please and delight ourselves and others, by playing with our words, for pleasure or ornament, inno-cently,"cited in M. H. Abrams, *The Mirror and the Lamp*, p. 286. Monroe C. Beardsley, *Aesthetics from Classical Greece to the Present* (Tuscaloosa: University of Alabama Press, 1982), notes that although Locke seems to have had a low opinion of wit and fancy, Hobbes had granted the privilege of fancy over judgment in the ornaments of poetic expressions. Here "fancy must be more eminent; because they please for the extravagancy; but ought not to displease by indiscretion" (*Leviathan* 1:58; Beardsley, p. 172). Overall, though, the figurative language of rhetoric occupies a relatively low position on Hobbes's scale of the uses that speech might serve. That he was no less wary than Locke of language's potential to deceive is clear in his allowances for "metaphors and tropes of speech: these are the less dangerous, because they profess their inconstancy." Unlike concealed (or even unwitting) deceptions, the "lie" of a metaphor could be readily recognized as deliberately inconstant, safe because meaning is openly displayed as figuratively intended.

11. For German counterparts, see, for example, Charles Gottlob Küttner and William Nicholson, *New and Complete Dictionary of the German Language for Englishmen According to the German Dictionary of Mr. J. C. Adelung* (Leipzig, 1805): "Witz: wit, the power of the mind; sentiments produced by the quickness of the fancy, and raising pleasure in the mind; genius, sense, reason, wits, judgment, brains, cunning, craft, subtlety, the faculty of imagination, conception, thought or notion." For a collection of philological essays tracing the usage of *wit, humor,* and related words in English and German sources through the nineteenth cen-tury, see *Europäische Schlüßelwörter,* vol. 1, *Humor und Witz,* ed. Wolfgang Schmidt-Hidding (Munich: Max Hueber, 1963).

12. Samuel Johnson, "Life of Cowley," in *The Lives of the English Poets,* ed. George B. Hill (Oxford: Clarendon Press, 1905), 1:20; excerpts in *Johnson as Critic,* ed. John Wain (London: Routledge & Kegan Paul, 1973), pp. 253–68.

13. Sir Richard Blackmore, *Essay upon Wit* (1716), Essays on Wit, no. 1 ([Los Angeles]: Augustan Reprint Society, 1946), p. 193.

14. Henry Home [Lord Kames], *Elements of Criticism* (Edinburgh, 1762), ed. Abraham Mills (New York: Sheldon, 1883), p. 132.

15. Adam Smith, *Essays on Philosophical Subjects* (London, 1795), p. 13.

16. Morris, *Essay,* p. 25.

17. Francis Hutcheson, *Dublin Journal* no. 11 (12 June 1725), reprinted in Scott Elledge, ed., *Eighteenth-Century Critical Essays* (Ithaca, N.Y.: Cornell University Press, 1961), 1:383.

18. Johnson, "Cowley," p. 20.

19. Henry Home, Lord Kames, for example, regards the "play of words" as a "low species of wit" that finds favor in earlier stages of a society's "progress toward refinement of taste and manners, and has gradually gone into disrepute" (*Elements,* p. 189). William Duff asserts that puns are the lowest of the low, the "petulant sallies of a rambling and undisciplined fancy" (*An Essay on Original Genius* [London, 1767], facsimile reprint, [Gainesville, Fla.: Scholars' Facsimiles and Reprints, 1964], p. 51).

20. Johnson, "Cowley," p. 21.

21. Morris, *Essay,* p. 1.

22. William Richardson, *Essays on Shakespeare's Dramatic Character of Sir John Falstaff* (1788), quoted in *Monthly Review* 81 (1789): 55. Richardson asserts that the effect produced by wit is "laughter, or a tendency to laughter."

23. Kames, *Elements,* p. 185.

24. James Beattie, *On Laughter,* p. 340.

25. Hester [Thrale] Piozzi, *British Synonymy* (Dublin, 1794), pp. 488–91.

26. Samuel Johnson, A *Dictionary of the English Language* (London, 1755), s.v. "Humour." See the comparable definitions in German sources listed in note 11.

27. "An Essay on Humour" (London, 1741), in *The Repository: A Select Collection of Fugitive Pieces of Wit and Humour in Prose and Verse by the Most Eminent Writers*, ed. Isaac Reed (London, 1777; 2d ed., 1789), 1:21.

28. Henry Fielding, "Essay on Humour," *The Covent Garden Journal* no. 19 (17 March 1752); reprinted in *Edinburgh Magazine, or Literary Miscellany* 18 (1801): 411–13; modern ed. by Gerard Edward Jensen (New Haven, Conn.: Yale University Press, 1915), 2:250.

29. John Trusler, *The Difference Between Words Esteemed Synonymous*, rev. ed. (London, 1783, repr. Menston, Engl.: Scholar Press, 1970), p. 7. The Earl of Chesterfield's strictures against laughter as common and ungentlemanly were considered a bit extreme by the time the *Letters* to his son (begun in 1737 and continuing to 1768) were published in 1774. Nonetheless, the status of laughter in polite society was somewhat uncertain. James Beattie, writing in 1764, finds it unfortunate that laughter is considered unfashionable, and he urges its natural expression, free from "the control of affectation or delicacy" (*On Laughter*, p. 401).

30. Stuart M. Tave, *The Amiable Humorist: A Study in the Comic Theory and Criticism of the Eighteenth and Early Nineteenth Centuries* (Chicago: University of Chicago Press, 1960), p. viii. See also Joyce M. S. Tompkins, *The Popular Novel in England, 1770–1800* (Westport, Conn.: Greenwood Press, 1976), p. 113: "In England the brand of humour most acceptable was that which has a strong substratum of sentiment. Human foibles are noted in a mood drenched in benevolence, and promptly offset by some notable virtue."

31. Johnson, *Dictionary*, s.v. "Humour."

32. Nathan Bailey, "Humour," *New Universal Etymological English Dictionary* (London, 1755).

33. Edward Niles Hooker, "Humour in the Age of Pope," *Huntington Library Quarterly* 11 (1947–48): 361.

34. Tave, *Amiable Humorist*, p. 166.

35. Richard Cumberland, *Henry* (1795), book 8, chap. 1; cited in Tompkins, *Popular Novel*, p. 112, n. 3.

36. Tompkins, *Popular Novel*, p. 112.

37. Oliver Goldsmith, "A Comparison between Laughing and Sentimental Comedy," *The Westminster Magazine* (1773); reprinted in *European Magazine and Monthly Review*, February 1786, pp. 97–98.

38. Morris, *Essay*, pp. 33–34, 36.

39. Johnson, preface to *The Plays of William Shakespeare* (1765), reprinted in Elledge, *Critical Essays* 2:646–86. For a discussion of Johnson's own "sense" of humor, see Bate, *Samuel Johnson*, pp. 480–99.

40. See, for example the *Morning Chronicle* reviewer, reporting on the first Salomon concert of the 1791 season: "It is not wonderful that to souls capable of being touched by music, HAYDN should be an object of homage, and even of idolatry; for like our SHAKSPEARE, he moves and governs the passions at his will" (Landon, *Chronicle* 3:49). A correspondent for the *European Magazine*, at Oxford on the occasion of Haydn's receiving an honorary doctorate, writes of the "modest Haydn": "this musical Shakespeare—this musical Drawcansir, who can equal the strains of a Cherub, and enchant in all the gradations between those and a ballad—a genius whose versatility comprehends all the powers of harmony, and all the energy, pathos, and passion of melody! who can stun with thunder, or warble with a bird!" (*European Magazine and London Review*, 15 July 1791, quoted in Landon, *Chronicle* 3:93). According to the *OED*, Drawcansir (incorrectly "Drawcausir" in Landon) is a swashbuckling, impetuous character in a Villiers play of 1672 modeled after Dryden.

41. *The Times*, 20 February 1792, quoted in Landon, *Chronicle* 3:134. Landon has thoroughly documented the critical reception of the "London" Symphonies in this volume of his monumental biography, and in his earlier *The Symphonies of Joseph Haydn* (New York: Macmillan, 1956) and its *Supplement* (London: Barrie & Rockliff, 1961).

42. Compare the comments of biographers Griesinger and Dies, pp. 31–32.

43. Rev. Sydney Smith, "Lectures on Wit and Humor," in *Elementary Sketches of Moral Philosophy delivered at the Royal Institution . . . 1804–1806*; reprint in *Wit and Wisdom of the Rev. Sydney Smith*, ed. Evert A. Duyckinck (New York: Redfield, 1856), p. 217.

44. For a thorough discussion of Germany's debt to English theories of comedy, see Betsy Aiken-Sneath, *Comedy in Germany in the First Half of the Eighteenth Century* (Oxford: Clarendon Press, 1936). Regarding the popularity of English literary models in Vienna, see especially Roswitha Strommer, "Die Rezeption der englischen Literatur im Lebensumkreis und zur Zeit Joseph Haydns," in *Joseph Haydn und die Literatur seiner Zeit*, ed. Herbert Zeman, Jahrbuch für österreichische Kulturgeschichte 6 (Eisenstadt, 1976): 123–55. Strommer notes that Viennese periodicals of the 1780s attest to the popularity of English language and literature, challenging the long hegemony of French literature. The works of Richardson, Fielding, and Sterne were particularly favored in the last decades of the century. In "The Delayed Reflex: Journalism in Josephinian Vienna," Joyce S. Routledge examines the growth of the periodic press after 1760 in Vienna and such phenomena as the twice-removed imitation of German models, themselves patterned on English sources (in *Studies in Eighteenth-Century Culture* 9 [1979]: 79–92). On the reception of English ideas in Germany generally, see Bernhard Fabian, "English Books and Their German Readers," in *The Widening Circle: Essays on the Circulation of Literature in 18th-Century Europe*, ed. Paul Korshin (Philadelphia: University of Pennsylvania Press, 1976), pp. 117–96. See also Lawrence Marsden Price, *The Reception of English Literature in Germany in the 18th Century* (Berkeley and Los Angeles: University of California Press, 1932), and Marjorie B. Price and Lawrence M. Price, *Publications of English Literature in Germany in the 18th Century*, University of California Publications in Modern Philology, vol. 17 (Berkeley and Los Angeles: University of California Press, 1934).
45. Johann Georg Sulzer, *Allgemeine Theorie der schönen Künste*, (Leipzig, 1771–74), 2d ed. (1792–97; reprint, Hildesheim: Georg Olms, 1967–70), s.v. "Lächerlich."
46. Ibid., s.v. "Witz."
47. Meier, *Thoughts on Jesting*, p. 39.
48. Sulzer, *Allgemeine Theorie*, s.v. "Laune."
49. Ibid.
50. Christian Wilhelm Kindleben, *Student-Lexikon* (Halle, 1781).
51. Immanuel Kant, "Anthropologie," par. 55, in *Gesammelte Schriften*, ed. Königlich Preussischen Akademie der Wissenschaften (Berlin: G. Reimer, 1910), 7:221. See also Chapter 8.
52. Sulzer, *Allgemeine Theorie*, s.v. "Lächerlich." Compare the anonymous "An Essay on Humour" (1741) in Reed, *Repository*, p. 12: "Humour consists in picturing objects to the imagination, under the appearance of shifting off their own nature or character, to assume a direct contrary one; hanging, as it were, dubious between both."
53. Sulzer, *Allgemeine Theorie*, s.v. "Witz." Meier, *Thoughts on Jesting*, pp. 47–48, is similarly inclined toward the moral function of jests.
54. Sulzer, s.v. "Komisch." Heinrich Koch condenses Sulzer's description in his *Musikalisches Lexikon* (Frankfurt a/Main, 1802; facsimile reprint, Hildesheim: Georg Olms, 1964), s.v. "Komisch": "One sometimes divides the comic into the high, middle, and low, or at other times into the high and low only, whose difference consists in the greater or lesser remoteness of the style from the lofty and elegant manner of writing." On the hierarchy of serious and comic styles in eighteenth-century music, see Leonard G. Ratner, *Classic Music: Expression, Form, and Style* (New York: Schirmer Books, 1980), chap. 21. I discuss these distinctions in Chapter 3.
55. *Literary Magazine and British Review* 2 (June 1789): 433–37 (misprinted 453–57).
56. Ibid., p. 456.
57. I use the word *personality* advisedly; the modern sense of those collective personal or individual characteristics that make a person distinct from others is a late eighteenth-century notion. (The earliest citation of this meaning found in the OED dates from 1795.) While Richardson's use of the word in *Clarissa* has been cited as the first usage in its modern sense, his meaning appears to be that of an individual trait; i.e., one has many "personalities," or personal qualities.
58. Sulzer, *Allgemeine Theorie* (1771), s.v. "Ausdruck in der Musik"; the full entry from the 1792 edition is translated in Peter Le Huray and James Day, *Music and Aesthetics in the Eighteenth and Early-Nineteenth Centuries* (Cambridge: Cambridge University Press, 1981), p. 125.

59. The Reverend Robert Burrowes, *On Style in Writing, Considered with Respect to Thoughts and Sentiments As Well As Words, and Indicating the Writer's Peculiar and Characteristic Disposition, Habits and Powers of Mind* (London, 1793-94), quoted in M. H. Abrams, *The Mirror and the Lamp: Romantic Theory and the Critical Tradition* (London: Oxford University Press, 1974), pp. 234-35. Similarly: "The choice of [his subject] is an act directed by the habits and dispositions of the author, and therefore indicative of these" (p. 235).

60. Ernst Ludwig Gerber, "Eine freundliche Vorstellung über gearbeitete Instrumentalmusik, besonders über Symphonien," *AMZ* 15, no. 28 (14 July 1813), col. 462.

61. As Griesinger noted, "In Haydn there was complete confirmation of Kant's observation 'that the author of a product which he owed to his genius did not himself know how he found within himself the ideas for it, nor did he have it in his power to think out such at will or methodically and to instruct others how they might produce similar works.' His theoretical *raisonnements* were very simple: namely, a piece of music ought to have a fluent melody, coherent ideas, no superfluous ornaments, nothing overdone, no confusing accompaniment, and so forth. How to satisfy these requirements? That, he confessed himself, cannot be learned by rules, and simply depends on natural talent and on the inspiration of inborn genius" (Gotwals, *Haydn*, p. 60).

62. Griesinger, *Biographische Notizen*, p. 57; Gotwals, *Haydn*, p. 57 (translation slightly modified). Elsewhere in his biography Griesinger reports the special characteristics of Haydn's nationality, including his broad dialect, and "that comic and naïve manner of speaking peculiar to the Austrians." (Perceptions of an Austrian "humor" are examined in Chapter 3.) Griesinger was first acquainted with Haydn in 1799 as a go-between for the publishers Breitkopf & Härtel. His biography first appeared in nos. 41-49 of the *AMZ*, 12 July-6 September 1809, and was published as a book in Leipzig in July 1810.

63. Albert Christoph Dies, *Biographische Nachrichten von Joseph Haydn* (Vienna, 1810), modern ed. by Horst Seeger (Berlin: Henschelverlag, 1962), pp. 116-117; 208; Gotwals, *Haydn*, pp. 145 and 203 (translation slightly modified).

64. Dies continues (Gotwals, *Haydn*, p. 145): "I ventured to question Haydn on the subject of teasing in his musical output. He admitted to me that it was a characteristic of his that used to be due to an abundance of good health. 'Perhaps,' I said, 'like merry boys who from sheer soundness of health don't know what to do with themselves and romp about in innocent mischief, now rolling around in the grass, now teasing one another in all sorts of ways.' 'Exactly!' Haydn replied. 'One is seized by a certain humor that will not be tamed.'" Koch quotes from Platner's *Philosophische Aphorismen* a similar notion of the excess-energy theory of *scherzend*: "When either cheerfulness or gaiety achieves the highest level, then the excess of energy becomes a kind of tickling, the stimulus of which wants to be appeased. That is the concept of mischievousness" (*Kurzgefaßtes Handwörterbuch*, p. 309).

3. "A Question of Taste"? Early Views of Haydn as Humorist

1. *Gentleman's Magazine* 37 (1767): 75.

2. Sir John Hawkins, *A General History of the Science and Practice of Music* (London, 1776), preface, vol. 1, n.p.

3. Charles Burney, *A General History of Music from the Earliest Ages to the Present Period*, 2d ed. (London, 1789; reprint, New York: Dover, 1957), 1:xvii.

4. Ibid., xiv.

5. John Gilbert Cooper, *Letters Concerning Taste*, 3d ed. (London, 1757), letter 1.

6. Alexander Gerard, *An Essay on Taste* (1759), 3d ed. (1780; facsimile reprint, Gainesville, Fla.: Scholars' Facsimiles and Reprints, 1963), pp. 88-89, 139-40.

7. David Hume, "Of the Standard of Taste," in *Four Dissertations* (London, 1757; facsimile reprint, New York: Garland, 1970), p. 229.

8. Jean-Jacques Rousseau, *Dictionnaire de musique* 2d ed. (Paris, 1768), s.v. "Le goût"; trans. in Le Huray and Day, *Music and Aesthetics*, pp. 113-14. Rousseau's dictionary was translated into English by William Waring (London, 1779).

9. James Webster, "Prospects for Haydn Biography After Landon," *MQ* 68 (1982): 476-95, here p. 490. On the relation of Haydn's Op. 33 string quartets to this change, see Chapter 5.

10. Burney, *General History* 2:958-59. For later writers who refer to Haydn's early detractors, see, among others, the anonymous "An Account of Joseph Haydn, a Celebrated Composer of Music," in *European Magazine, and London Review for October, 1784*, reprinted with corrections and notes in A. Peter Brown, "The Earliest English Biography of Haydn," *MQ* 59 (1973): 341-47; Ernst Ludwig Gerber, *Historisch-biographisches Lexikon der Tonkünstler*, vol. 1 (Leipzig, 1790), col. 611; and Griesinger in Gotwals, *Haydn*, p. 13.

11. See Landon, *Chronicle* 3:191. Extant evidence does not support Landon's assertion that many "scurrilous pamphlets" criticizing Haydn's music circulated in Germany throughout his lifetime. Unfavorable reviews appear to have emanated largely from North German writers in the 1770s. Haydn himself refers to his Berlin critics in his "autobiographical sketch," where he accuses them of being unable to perform his works and "too conceited to take the trouble to understand them properly" (see Landon, *CCLN*, p. 20). The genesis and publication history of Haydn's autobiographical sketch are briefly reviewed in A. P. Brown, "Earliest English Biography," p. 340.

12. Gotwals, *Haydn*, p. 13; Griesinger, *Biographische Notizen*, p. 13. Here one might compare Gerber's retrospective view: Haydn's "first quartets, which became known around 1760, made a great sensation. On the one hand, the extraordinary naïveté and gaiety that prevail in them were smiled at and delighted in, while on the other, the degradation of music to comic trifles and unheard-of octaves was deplored" (*Historisch-biographisches Lexikon*, vol. 1, col. 611).

13. Johann Adam Hiller, ed., *Wöchentliche Nachrichten und Anmerkungen die Musik betreffend*, vol. 2 (Leipzig, 1767), p. 14. See also Christian Friedrich Daniel Schubart, *Ideen zu einer Aesthetik der Tonkunst*, ed. Ludwig Schubart (written c. 1784-85; publ. Vienna, 1806), p. 274; and Heinrich Koch, *Journal der Tonkunst* 1 (Erfurt, 1795): 99.

14. *Gelehrter Nachrichten des Wiener Diarium* no. 26 (18 October 1766); trans. in Landon, *Chronicle* 2:128-31. Following the suggestion of Norbert Tschulik, Daniel Heartz argues that the author of this article was likely Dittersdorf, whose own music was most directly attacked by North German writers for displaying trite wit and low humor. See Heartz, "Ditters, Gluck und der Artikel 'Von dem Wienerischen Geschmack in der Musik' (1766)," in *Kongreßbericht; Gluck in Wien: Wien, 12-16 November 1987*, ed. Gerhard Croll and Monika Woitas (Kassel: Bärenreiter, 1989), pp. 78-80.

15. Johann Christoph Stockhausen, *Critischer Entwurf einer auserlesenen Bibliothek für die Liebhaber der Philosophie und schönen Wissenschaft* (4th ed., Berlin, 1771), quoted in Klaus Winkler, "Alter und neuer Musikstil im Streit zwischen den Berlinern und Wienern zur Zeit der Frühklassik," *Mf* 33 (1980): 40. Winkler surveys the North German critical stance toward Viennese instrumental composers in various reviews of the late 1760s and early 1770s. See also Thomas Bauman, "The Music Reviews in the *Allgemeine deutsche Bibliothek*," *Acta musicologica* 49 (1977): 69-85.

16. *Unterhaltungen* 2 (Hamburg, 1766): 226; quoted in Winkler, "Alter und neuer Musikstil," pp. 38-39.

17. A reviewer for the *AMZ*, on hearing an unspecified Haydn symphony, remarks: "it does have many instances of the laughable and the teasing that are, strictly speaking, more suitable for a solo, or possibly a quartet" (*AMZ* 10, no. 31 [27 April 1808], col. 495). See also Gerber, "Eine freundliche Vorstellung," col. 461, and Koch's remarks cited on p. 38.

18. See J. G. K. Spazier's review of an unidentified Haydn symphony in *Musikalisches Wochenblatt* 1, no. 10 (1791): 79, and an article explaining his position, "Über Menuetten in Sinfonien," *Musikalisches Wochenblatt* 2, no. 12 (1792): 91-92; most of this latter is translated in Neal Zaslaw, *Mozart's Symphonies: Context, Performance Practice, Reception* (Oxford: Oxford University Press, 1989), pp. 415-16.

19. Ratner's *Classic Music* offers the most comprehensive survey of the various understandings of style in late eighteenth-century sources; see especially chap. 20, on national styles, and chap. 21, on categories of the serious and comic.

20. The comments of Johann Forkel in Cramer's *Magazin der Musik* of 1783 are telling: "With the undeniable decline of church and theater music, the concert remains the only means by which taste can be developed and the ideals of music achieved. . . . The union of poetry

and music, touching both mind and heart, is so advantageous that undeniably herein do we have the full power of expression. . . . only such compositions, among them especially the oratorios with sacred or moralistic content, deserve the first and most important place in our concerts" (translated in Ratner, *Classic Music*, p. 366).

21. Johann Joachim Quantz, *On Playing the Flute*, ed. Edward Reilley (London: Faber & Faber, 1966), pp. 311, 315.

22. Quoted in Wye Jamison Allanbrook, *Rhythmic Gesture in Mozart: "Le nozze di Figaro" and "Don Giovanni"* (Chicago: University of Chicago Press, 1983), p. 17. Allanbrook's study demonstrates the powerful expressive role of meter and associated dance topics in eighteenth-century music. In her analysis of Mozart's operas, this association and others have broad explanatory application.

23. Koch, *Musikalisches Lexikon*, s.v. "Scherzo, scherzando."

24. Ibid., s.v. "Styl, Schreibart."

25. Ibid.

26. Ibid. This passage is discussed in Chapter 6 in connection with chamber and theater symphonies.

27. Hiller, *Wöchentliche Nachrichten*, vol. 1 (1766), p. 67. On the status of the symphony among other late eighteenth-century genres, see Zaslaw, *Mozart's Symphonies*, pp. 511-25.

28. See Schubart, *Ideen*, p. 234; and Hiller, *Wöchentliche Nachrichten*, vol. 3 (1768), p. 107.

29. Karl Ditters von Dittersdorf, "Über die Grenzen des Komischen und des Heroischen in der Musik," AMZ 1, no. 9 (1798): col. 141.

30. Wolfgang Amadeus Mozart, Letter to Leopold Mozart, 28 December 1782; widely quoted, here from Stanley Sadie, *The New Grove Mozart* (New York: Norton, 1984), p. 103.

31. Ratner, *Classic Music*, p. 364.

32. Hiller, *Wöchentliche Nachrichten* 3:107. Examining the criticism of such writers as Hiller, Koch, Schubart, and others, Hans Eggebrecht concludes that a decided bias against "new-fashioned" South German (especially Viennese and Mannheim) composers motivated North German theorists in their use of the term *comic* as a catchall pejorative. A term that accompanied others, such as *base, silly, frivolous, wanton*, and especially *plebeian*, it denoted Italian opera's influence on the one hand and folk influence on the other. See Eggebrecht, "Der Begriff des Komischen in der Musikaesthetik des 18. Jahrhunderts," *Mf* 4 (1951): 144-52.

33. Hiller (1728-1804), whose compositional focus was on vocal music, was active primarily in Leipzig as writer, composer of *Singspiele*, conductor of the Gewandhaus concerts, and promoter of improved singing in Germany. He authored nearly all the articles and reviews in the *Wöchentliche Nachrichten*, which he edited in the 1760s. In her entry on Hiller in NGD, Anna Amalie Abert quotes his self-professed aim of scrupulous impartiality that "'always looked for good qualities rather than faults.' Thus his reviews were invariably sympathetic" (p. 566). Either Hiller was out of sorts on the day he wrote the review under discussion here, or the review was written by another contributor. Although it cannot be proved that Hiller is the author, the grounds of these criticisms are consistent with his earlier comments on Haydn and other Viennese composers.

34. Johann Adam Hiller, *Musikalische Nachrichten und Anmerkungen auf das Jahr 1770*, pp. 37-38. Landon (*Chronicle* 2:169) quotes an excerpt from this review; for discussion of the individual symphonies in the Bailleux print see *Chronicle* 1:288-89, 295-96, 559-60, 570-73.

35. Hiller, *Musikalische Nachrichten*, p. 37. Symphonies Nos. 28 and 29, the only ones of the group extant in autograph, are dated 1765. On the authenticity of symphonies in the Hummel print, see the work-list prepared by Georg Feder in Jens Peter Larsen, *The New Grove Haydn* (New York: Norton, 1983), and Landon, *Chronicle* 1:570, 2:169 (Landon is inconsistent on the ordering of the symphonies in the print).

36. Landon (*Chronicle* 2:169) suggests that the reviewer simply tosses this off as an exaggerated demonstration of the technique he deplores. The same kind of melodic scoring is found in the Andante of Symphony No. 3 (cf. esp. mm. 17-20 and 75-79), but the reviewer's excerpt does not match this movement either. He also complains of the finale, entitled Presto fuga, that "whoever wants to take the thing for a fugue can have it." In fact, though, the Presto of Symphony No. 29 is not labeled as a fugue, nor does it even resemble one. The author

does concede that the formidable double fugue, marked *alla breve*, that concludes Symphony No. 3 of this collection is "more deserving of the title 'fugue.'"

37. Junker, Reichardt, Burney, and Gerber all report octave doublings in Haydn's string quartets as the target of criticisms by other (nameless, but presumably "pedantic") commentators. Perhaps the earliest reference to this feature is found in the *Wiener Diarium* notice of 1766. For others, see Winkler, "Alter und neuer Musikstil," pp. 40, 43.

38. Hiller, *Musikalische Nachrichten*, p. 37.

39. Landon, *CECS*, vol. 3, p. xiv. Landon also notes that Haydn uses this tune again in the last movement of the Baryton Trio Hob. XII:5 (*Chronicle* 1:573).

40. W. H. Hadow, *A Croatian Composer: Notes toward the Study of Joseph Haydn* (London: Seeley, 1892), p. 47.

41. Hiller, *Wöchentliche Nachrichten* 3:107.

42. Ibid.

43. Symphony No. 23 was published in Paris in 1766-67 in a set that included Symphonies Nos. 3, 5, and 14; the slow movement of the last of these appears in a keyboard arrangement in Hiller's *Wöchentliche Nachrichten* of 1766 (1:248-50). Tilden Russell discusses canonic techniques in the minuet as related to contrapuntal play that had a long history in the scherzo; see his "Minuet, Scherzando, and Scherzo: The Dance Movement in Transition, 1781-1825" (Ph.D. diss., University of North Carolina, 1983), pp. 76-97.

44. I discuss this and other canonic minuets in Chapter 4.

45. See the Quartets in C Major, F Minor, and A Major (Nos. 2, 5, and 6) in this set. Here Haydn's purpose appears to be to give a new intensity and weight to the finale. He abandons thoroughgoing fugal technique for closing movements in both symphony and quartet, however, reverting to the idea only in Symphony No. 70 (?1778/79) and String Quartet Op. 50, No. 4 of 1787.

46. Hiller, *Wöchentliche Nachrichten* 1:243. These remarks are made in the context of a review of six symphonies by one Giovanni Gabriel Meder, published by Hummel in Amsterdam.

47. Spazier, "Über Menuetten," p. 92.

48. Karl Ludwig Junker, *Zwanzig Componisten: Eine Skizze* (Bern, 1776), pp. 55-67. The *Skizze* were included in Junker's later *Portfeuille für Musikliebhaber* (Leipzig, 1792); selected passages are translated in Landon, *Chronicle* 3:189-91. Roye D. Wates, "Karl Ludwig Junker (1748-1797), Sentimental Music Critic" (Ph.D. diss., Yale University, 1965) makes the case for Junker's progressive attitudes toward new instrumental music of his day. In this, his first book, however, Junker adopts a somewhat hostile tone toward the music of Haydn. Bellamy Hosler's valuable study, *Changing Aesthetic Views of Instrumental Music in 18th-Century Germany* (Ann Arbor, Mich.: UMI Research Press, 1981) provides a useful framework for estimating both Junker's aesthetic bearings and the general ambivalence with respect to the symphony betrayed by several German critics of the 1770s.

49. Jauss traces this distinction between ridicule and the comic in *Aesthetic Experience*, pp. 123-34.

50. Junker, *Skizze*, p. 64. An obvious difficulty for anyone trying to comprehend Junker's response to Haydn's music is in understanding his meaning of *musikalische Laune*. He uses *Laune* and *Humor* interchangeably throughout his essay, the former more often. In a brief excerpt from Junker, Landon (*Chronicle* 2:401) translates *Laune* as "caprice." I have preferred to retain the word's ambiguity, translating *Laune* as "humor" in the eighteenth-century sense of temperament. Junker's *Laune* suggests this broader conception of a dominant mood, or temper, in Haydn's music; implicit in this conception are the capricious and eccentric—traits that the humorist cannot suppress.

51. Junker, *Skizze*, p. 63.

52. Junker, "Ditters," in *Skizze*, pp. 28-29. Schubart's report of a visit to Salzburg in the 1770s echoes Junker's impression of Austrian humor: "In recent times the ecclesiastical musical style began to deteriorate into the theatrical—an epidemic that has already affected more than one church! ... The Salzburger's spirit is exceedingly inclined to low humor. Their folk songs are so comical and burlesque that one cannot listen to them without side-splitting laughter" (*Ideen*, p. 158, as translated in Zaslaw, *Mozart's Symphonies*, p. 203).

53. On the complexities of this ambivalence and the larger aesthetic issues at stake, see Hosler, *Changing Aesthetic Views*, and Zaslaw, *Mozart's Symphonies*, pp. 510–13; 517–21. For a concise discussion of trends in German composition during this period, see Thomas Bauman, "Courts and Municipalities in North Germany," in *The Classical Era: From the 1740s to the End of the 18th Century*, ed. Neal Zaslaw (Englewood Cliffs, N.J.: Prentice-Hall, 1989), pp. 240–67.

54. Friedrich Nicolai, *Beschreibung einer Reise durch Deutschland und die Schweiz, im Jahre 1781 . . .* , vol. 4 (Berlin and Stettin, 1784), p. 526. Quoted in Herbert Zeman, "Joseph Haydns Begegnungen mit der Literatur seiner Zeit—zur Einleitung," in *Joseph Haydn und die Literatur seiner Zeit*, ed. Herbert Zeman. *Jahrbuch für österreichische Kulturgeschichte 6* (Eisenstadt, 1976), p. 23.

55. *Musikalischer Almanach auf das Jahr 1782* ("Alethinopel" [Leipzig]), p. 19. Roye Wates ("Karl Junker," pp. 39–44) believes that Junker is the author of the *Almanach* (see also her entry on Junker in *NGD*). If so, his view of Haydn here indicates something of a turnaround in the space of six years since his *Skizze*. In a recent study, Mark Evan Bonds traces the reference to Sterne in later accounts of Haydn; he explores this comparison as evidence of a perception among Haydn's contemporaries of "ironic distance between the work and the listener." See his "Haydn, Laurence Sterne, and the Origins of Musical Irony," *JAMS* 44 (1991): 57–91, and his "Haydn's False Racapitulations and the Perception of Sonata Form in the Eighteenth Century" (Ph.D. diss., Harvard University, 1988), esp. chap. 7, "Ironic Distance and the Destruction of Aesthetic Illusion."

56. Hummel issued the symphonies as Oeuvre XVIII, and the quartets as Oeuvre XIX. Printed in three *libri*, the symphonies included were Nos. 75, 63, 70, 71, 62, and 74. The Op. 33 quartets are considered closely in Chapter 5 in connection with Haydn's contract of 1779 and its implications for works addressed to a broader public.

57. Reichardt, *Musikalisches Kunstmagazin* (Berlin, 1782), p. 205. Carl F. Cramer, in his review of the same collections, shares (borrows?) the same sentiments (see *Magazin der Musik* 1 [Hamburg, 1783]: 259 and Chapter 5, p. 114).

58. See Lionel de la Laurencie, "L'apparition des oeuvres d'Haydn à Paris," *Revue de musicologie* 16 (1932): 191–204.

59. For recent documentation of sales and performances of Haydn's works in London through 1780, see David Wyn Jones, "Haydn's Music in London in the Period 1760–1790," part 1, *HYb* 14 (1983): 144–72. Landon summarizes information bearing on Haydn's reputation in England in the 1780s in *Chronicle* 2:595–602.

60. Burney, *General History* 2:958; Burney's italics.

61. *Musikalische Real-Zeitung* no. 36 (1789): 280. From Carl F. Pohl, *Joseph Haydn*, vol. 2 (Leipzig: Breitkopf & Härtel, 1882; reprint, 1928), p. 320; see also Landon, *Chronicle* 2:723.

62. Gerber, *Lexikon*, col. 611.

63. A correspondent to the *AMZ* (7, no. 13 [26 December 1804], col. 197) uses this phrase in reporting on a "well-known, but one of the most excellent of Haydn's symphonies," in B-flat major (the description fits No. 102), which opened a subscription concert in Berlin. Later references to "Papa Haydn," though fond, are more condescending than reverent. Witness Robert Schumann's comment that "Father Haydn" was like a familiar houseguest, whom one is glad to have around, but who "has no deeper interest anymore for our age" (quoted in Landon, *Chronicle*, vol. 5, *Haydn: The Late Years, 1801–1809* [London: Thames and Hudson, 1977], p. 421). In the closing chapter of this final volume of his biography, Landon reviews the decline of Haydn's popularity in the nineteenth century.

64. Johann Reichardt, *Vertraute Briefe geschrieben auf einer Reise nach Wien . . . 1808/9* (Amsterdam, 1810), 14th letter (16 December 1808), 1:231–32; also quoted in Landon, *Chronicle* 5:409. One would like to know which quartets Reichardt heard, but as is usual in such reports, specific works are not identified. Other writers comparing these composers were not as favorably disposed to Mozart and Beethoven. See, for example, William Crotch, *Substance of Several Courses of Lectures on Music, Read in the University of Oxford and in the Metropolis* (London, 1831), pp. 143, 145, and Carpani, *Le Haydine*, pp. 40–41, 256–57. On contemporary estimations of Beethoven, see Robin Wallace, *Beethoven's Critics: Aesthetic*

Dilemmas and Resolutions During the Composer's Lifetime (Cambridge: Cambridge University Press, 1986).

65. *Reminiscences of Charles Butler, Esq. of Lincoln Inn: With a Letter to a Lady on Ancient and Modern Music*, 4th ed. (New York, 1825), p. 337. The "Letter to a Lady," from which the quote is drawn, is dated 4 November 1818.

4. Humorous Manners and the "Really *New* Minuet"

1. Lionel de la Laurencie, "L'apparition," p. 197; *Musikalischer Almanach auf das Jahr 1782* (Leipzig), p. 21. The often-noted originality of Haydn's minuets is reported as fact by Dies: "Haydn is the inventor of the so-called Haydn minuets, which are stamped with the mark of the rarest originality" (Gotwals, *Haydn*, p. 201).

2. Burney, *General History* 2:960.

3. Gerber, "Etwas über den sogennanten musikalischen Styl," AMZ 1, no. 20 (13 February 1799): col. 310.

4. Griesinger, *Biographische Notizen*, in Gotwals, *Haydn*, p. 61.

5. The long-standing performance tradition of omitting repeats in the da capo of the minuet—and of notated repeats generally—has been challenged in recent literature on performance practice. In the absence of documentary evidence to the contrary, recent conductors have observed repeats in the return of the minuet (Christopher Hogwood, Roger Norrington, Ton Koopman, and John Eliot Gardiner, among others). Vexed by nineteenth-century performance traditions and tastes (and twentieth-century constraints on recording time?), the question of repeats in works of the Classical era is examined from a variety of perspectives in Nicholas Temperley, "Tempo and Repeats in the Early Nineteenth Century," ML 47 (1966): 323–38; Bernard Jacobson, "Once More with Feeling: A Polemic on Repeats," *Musical Newsletter* 7, no. 2 (1977): 3–7; Hugh Macdonald, "To Repeat or Not to Repeat?" PRMA 111 (1984/85): 121–38; and Michael Broyles, "Organic Form and the Binary Repeat," MQ 66 (1980): 339–60. See also Zaslaw, *Mozart's Symphonies*, pp. 502–4; Max Rudolf, "Inner Repeats in the Da Capo of Classical Minuets and Scherzos," *Journal of the Conductor's Guild* 3 (1982): 145–50 and Frederick Neumann, "How Fast Should Classical Minuets be Played?" Historical Performance 4 (1991): 3–13.

6. Georg Joseph Vogler, *Betrachtungen der Mannheimer Tonschule* (Mannheim, 1778–79; facsimile reprint, Hildesheim: Georg Olms, 1974), 1:380–81 (original pagination), 4:118. For further on Vogler, see Floyd K. Grave and Margaret G. Grave, *In Praise of Harmony: The Teachings of Abbé Georg Joseph Vogler* (Lincoln: University of Nebraska Press, 1987).

7. Among composers who contributed to the genre of combinatorial composition were C. P. E. Bach, Mozart, and Haydn himself. Leonard Ratner surveys this literature and its implications in "*Ars combinatoria*: Chance and Choice in Eighteenth-Century Music," in *Studies in Eighteenth-Century Music: A Tribute to Karl Geiringer on his Seventieth Birthday*, ed. H. C. Robbins Landon and Roger E. Chapman (New York: Oxford University Press, 1970), pp. 343–63. See also Thomas H. O'Bierne, "940, 369, 969, 152: Dice-Music Trios," MT 109 (1968): 911–13, and Stephen Hedges, "Dice Music in the Eighteenth Century," ML 59 (1978): 180–87. Tilden Russell notes that in such games the minuet becomes "a protean plaything, a kind of musical Silly Putty" ("Minuet," p. 90).

8. The fashion for the *volkstümlich* in German *Lieder* of the middle to late eighteenth century makes the question of what genuine folk dances and songs of Haydn's day were really like a highly problematic one. Compilers and composers undoubtedly refashioned folk melodies to conform to more regular harmonic, metric, and phrase patterns of the Classical style, and "rude" texts were replaced by polite ones. The history of the melody that Haydn used in his early keyboard Capriccio in G Major, Hob. XVII:1, is instructive in this regard (see A. Peter Brown, *Joseph Haydn's Keyboard Music: Sources and Style* [Bloomington: Indiana University Press, 1986], pp. 13–14, and Landon, *Chronicle* 1:549–50). For a more general discussion of the complex relationship of folk sources and art music, see Bence Szabolsci, "Folk Music—Art Music—History of Music," StM 7 (1965): 171–79.

9. Rousseau, *Dictionnaire*, cited in Shirley Wynn, "The Minuet," in *Institute of Court Dances of the Rennaissance and Baroque Periods*, ed. Juana de Laban (New York: Dance Notation Bureau, 1972), p. 44. Tempo is suggested in other characterizations of the minuet: Giovanni Andrea Gallini equates the minuet with "dancing in the serious style" in his *Treatise on the Art of Dancing* (London, 1762; facsimile reprint, New York: Broude Brothers, 1967), pp. 173–74; and Charles Pauli, *Elémens de la danse* (Leipzig, 1756), notes that "L'action du menuet est toujours serieuse . . . et grave" (pp. 62–63). Dance historian Wendy Hilton offers suggestive observations on the relationship of tempo and execution in courtly dances, all of which presume a degree of both "nobility" and "liveliness." See her *Dance of the Court and Theater: The French Noble Style, 1690–1725* (n.p., Princeton Book Co., 1981), pp. 262–66. On the history of the minuet as a dance see also Russell, "Minuet," pp. 43–72.

10. Allanbrook, *Rhythmic Gesture*, pp. 33–34. The relationship of metric signature and tempo is somewhat confusing in Allanbrook's examples, however. Citing Figaro's "Se vuol ballare" (in $\frac{3}{8}$) as a "prototypical quick minuet," and the "slower type" as that represented in the ballroom scene of *Don Giovanni*, she maintains that both of these are moderate in tempo, sharing features of slower minuets that "habitually begin on the downbeat." Comparison with Mozart's dance minuets of this period, e.g., K. 568 (1788), shows a preponderance of the "slower" type: dotted rhythms, upbeats, even quarter-note stress of a "walking" bass, etc. (See nos. 1, 2, 3, 10, 12; no. 6 in this collection is similar to the *Don Giovanni* type.) For further discussion of tempo in Mozart's symphonic minuets, see Zaslaw, *Mozart's Symphonies*, pp. 496–97.

11. Among many who have discussed the musical and social implications of this scene, see especially Allanbrook, *Rhythmic Gesture*, pp. 276–87; Stefan Kunze, "Mozarts *Don Giovanni* und die Tanzszene im ersten Finale," *Analecta musica* 18 (1974): 172–77; and Justus Mahr, "Tanzmusik auf Don Giovannis Schloss: Anmerkungen zum Ballfinale des ersten 'Don Giovanni'-Aktes," *Neue Zeitschrift für Musik* 127, no. 12 (1966): 473–78. Gottfried Scholz notes the acoustic reality captured in Mozart's collage: the masked balls in Vienna's Redoutensaal featured minuets and German dances heard simultaneously from orchestras in two rooms. See his "Zu Haydns Menuetten," in *JHK 1982*, p. 466.

12. Johann Wolfgang von Goethe, *Italienische Reise: Zweiter Aufenthalt in Rom* (1788), quoted in Curt Sachs, *World History of the Dance*, trans. Bessie Schönberg (New York: Norton, 1937), p. 399. On the decorum of the minuet as a representation of courtly etiquette extending to moral education, see Josef Gmeiner, *Menuet und Scherzo: Ein Beitrag zur Entwicklungsgeschichte und Soziologie des Tanzsatzes in der Wiener Klassik* (Tutzing: Hans Schneider, 1979), pp. 19–22. Gmeiner investigates idioms of courtly and folk styles as a kind of sociological encoding in the minuets of Haydn and his contemporaries. He finds various stages of integration of these idioms in both danced minuets and instrumental movements, and he attributes the changes to increasing participation by the middle classes in courtly society.

13. See Hilton, *Dance of Court and Theater*, pp. 291–308; Shirley Wynn, "The Minuet"; and Meredith Ellis Little, "Minuet," NGD.

14. Hilton, *Dance of Court and Theater*, p. 191.

15. The following are some of the variations suggested in eighteenth-century descriptions of the *pas de menuet*:
♩♩ | ♩♩ : Kellom Tomlinson, *The Art of Dancing Explained* (London, 1735), and Gottfried Taubert, *Rechtschaffener Tanzmeister* (Leipzig, 1717)
♩♩ | ♩♩ : Pierre Rameau, *Le maître à danser* (Paris, 1725)
♩. | ♩♩♩ : C. J. von Feldtenstein, *Erweiterung der Kunst nach der Choreographie zu Tänzen* (Braunschweig, 1772), and Tomlinson, *Art of Dancing*
♩♩ | ♩♩♩ : Pierre Rameau, *Le maître à danser*, and Charles Compan, *Dictionnaire de la danse* (Paris, 1787)
See Russell, "Minuet," pp. 69–70, and Wheelock, "Wit and Humor," pp. 148–49.

16. C. J. von Feldtenstein, *Die Kunst nach der Choreographie zu tanzen und Tänze zu schreiben* (Braunschweig, 1767), pp. 21–22; translated in Allanbrook, *Rhythmic Gesture*, p. 33. It should be noted that in this passage von Feldtenstein is quoting a letter from the Grand Chancellor of France to his son. The relation of French courtly traditions of dance to those in Germany and Austria is problematic, especially in an era when dependence on French manners was

being criticized, and things German promoted. The passage suggests, in any event, that the courtly bearing of the minuet is at risk in being danced by the nonconnoisseur.

17. Although Joseph II's mother, the Empress Maria Theresa, had opened the imperial ballroom to others than the royal family in a decree of 1748, Joseph's more expansive gesture extended the privilege to a much broader population. See Gmeiner, *Menuet und Scherzo*, pp. 34–35.

18. Quoted in Eva Campianu, "Die Tänze der Haydn-Zeit," in *JHK 1982*, pp. 470–75. See also Günther Thomas, "Studien zu Haydns Tanzmusik," *H-St* 3 (1973): 7–8.

19. Concepts of tempo and character, obviously embedded in a complex web of cultural practices and local habits, are most difficult to assess in contexts remote from one's own—an issue I take up later in this chapter.

20. Two minuet collections dating from the 1790s are available in modern editions: Joseph Haydn, *24 Menuetti, Hob. IX:16*, edited by H. C. Robbins Landon (Vienna: Doblinger, 1974), composed in 1796 or 1797; and Joseph Haydn, *Wiener Hofball-Menuette* [Hob. IX:11], edited by Franz Burkhart (Mainz: B. Schott's Sohne, [1936]). An additional fourteen minuets from the 1780s are found in *Raccolta de menuetti ballabili*, edited by H. C. Robbins Landon (Vienna: Doblinger, 1970; Diletto Musicale no. 301). On Haydn's dance music see Thomas, "Studien"; and idem, "Haydns Tanzmusik—zeitgebunden oder persönlich geprägt?" *Musica* 36, no. 2 (1982): 140–47.

21. Many of Haydn's dance minuets feature a lengthened second section in which an excursion away from the tonic and preparation for its return may occupy from four to sixteen measures; a complete and often literal reprise of the first section is heard in most of these expanded minuets. Wolfram Steinbeck, *Das Menuett in der Instrumentalmusik Joseph Haydns* (Munich: Emil Katzbichler, 1973) offers a Riemannian analysis of phrase structure in several minuets from Haydn's instrumental works.

22. Johann Mattheson, *Der vollkommene Capellmeister* (Hamburg, 1739), trans. and ed. Ernest C. Harriss (Ann Arbor, Mich.: UMI Research Press, 1981). See esp. chap. 9.

23. Haydn wrote only one such musical palindrome, but he reused it in his keyboard Sonata in A Major, Hob. XVI:26 (1773). The principal difference between the two versions is that the sonata, probably intended for harpsichord, has no dynamic markings. The player who wishes to perform it on the piano might consult the symphonic version, since here the dynamic and scoring contrasts ensure that the retrograde procedure will be discovered by the listener.

24. R. Larry Todd discusses this movement in "Joseph Haydn and the *Sturm und Drang*: A Revaluation," *MR* 41 (1980): 172–96. Todd points out the minuet's relationship to another Haydn probably knew, from *Der curiose musikalische Instrumentalkalendar* by Gregor Joseph Werner, the man who was Haydn's immediate superior in his early years with Prince Anton Eszterházy. I have found only one other retrograde minuet among Haydn's Viennese contemporaries. A divertimento for string quartet by the Viennese composer Josef Starzer (1727–87) contains a minuet whose second half is a retrograde of the first (printed in *Denkmäler der Tonkunst in Österreich* 15/2: *Wiener Instrumentalmusik vor und um 1750*, ed. Karl Horwitz and Karl Riedel, 1:97–98). If the editors noted this peculiarity, they make no mention of it—nor does Starzer display his artifice, and does not label the minuet as a canon. Starzer's connection with Haydn is noted by Griesinger, who reports that he was a violinist who performed Haydn's pieces at Baron von Swieten's (Gotwals, *Haydn*, p. 38). Burney notes that Starzer played Haydn's quartets at the private concerts of Sir l'Angier, physician to Maria Theresa (see the editors' preface to DTÖ 15/2, 1:xxiii–xxiv).

25. Gerber, *Historisch-biographisches Lexikon*, vol. 1 (1790), col. 610.

26. J. K. F. Triest, "Bemerkungen über die Ausbildung der Tonkunst in Deutschland im achtzehnten Jahrhundert," *AMZ* 3, no. 24 (11 March 1801), col. 407; Gotwals translates the portion of Triest's article on Haydn in his *Haydn*, pp. 197–200. On Butler's remark, see Chapter 3, p. 51.

27. See, for example, Landon's rather deprecating estimate of Haydn's works of the late 1770s and early 1780s as a fall from the elevated *Sturm und Drang* of the previous decade (*Chronicle* 2:341, 561–64, 582, and *CECS* 5:xiv). Here Landon seems to follow Robert Sondheimer's *Haydn: A Historical and Psychological Study Based on his Quartets* (London: Bernoulli, 1951) in judging the popular style as something of a fatal attraction. Charles Rosen discusses

Haydn's mastery of "a deliberately popular style" as an absorption of folklike simplicity in
his late works (*The Classical Style: Haydn, Mozart, Beethoven* [New York: Viking, 1971],
pp. 329–50).

28. The *Menuet alla Zingarese* of Haydn's String Quartet in D Major, Op. 20, No. 4, is perhaps
the most extreme example of this syncopated pattern. Here, however, overlapping displaced
accents thoroughly confuse the $\frac{3}{4}$ meter. In *Playing with Signs: A Semiotic Interpretation of
Classic Music* (Princeton, N.J.: Princeton University Press, 1991) V. Kofi Agawu examines
this movement as a "'trimetric' structure involving two dance topics, gavotte and minuet,
overseen by an umbrella Gypsy style" (p. 42). For another Haydn movement on the "Gypsy"
topos, see the *Rondo all'Ongarese* finale of the Piano Trio in G Major, Hob. XV:25. Michael
Dittrich has reconstructed a plausible instrumentation from the only extant copy (for harpsichord) of Haydn's *Zingarese*, Hob. IX:28, recorded under his direction by Ensemble Bella
Musica de Vienne (Harmonia Mundi HM 1057, 1981).

29. These melodies are transcribed by Eugene L. Beenk in "Ländler Elements in the Symphonic
Minuets of Joseph Haydn" (Ph.D. diss., University of Iowa, 1969), pp. 155–56, 158. They
are contained in "Ländler im Klavierbuche einer preussischen Prinzessin," *Klavier Noten*,
Österreichischen Nationalbibliothek, Sig. S.M.29.273, a collection that was owned by Prin-
cess Friedericke Louise Wilhemine Amalia of Prussia and copied c. 1815–20.

30. Strong metric displacement, relatively rare in symphonic minuets before 1785, is frequent
in the "London" Symphonies. Examples are found in Symphonies Nos. 65, 69, 86, 88, 92,
98–102, and 104. This technique is rather more common in the minuets of Haydn's string
quartets. Salient examples can be found in the following: Op. 9, No. 1; Op. 17, No. 5; Op.
33, No. 5; Op. 50, No. 5; Op. 64, Nos. 3, 5, 6; Op. 74, No. 1; Op. 76, Nos. 4, 5, 6; and most
prominently, in Op. 77, No. 2.

31. For a late description of the dance as featuring a hopping step on the third beat of the
measure, see Rudolf Flotzinger's entry "Ländler" (1974) in *Handwörterbuch der musikalischen Terminologie*, ed. Hans Heinrich Eggebrecht (Wiesbaden: Franz Steiner Verlag, 1972-).

32. The peculiar "exoticism" here recalls earlier trios in Symphonies Nos. 28 and 29 (see also
the trios of Symphonies Nos. 58 and 49). Modal instability is heard as well in the trios of
Symphonies Nos. 36, 43, 46, 60, 64, and 63.

33. Koch, *Musikalisches Lexikon*, s.v. "Ländler," "Walzer," "Menuet." See Flotzinger, "Ländler,"
on the various meanings of the term.

34. In "Toward a 'New' (Old) Minuet," *Opus* 1 (1985): 14–21, for example, William Malloch bases
his argument for faster minuet tempos in Haydn and Mozart symphonies on transcriptions
made for (extant) mechanical organ clocks, as well as on metronome markings in early nineteenth-century piano arrangements. In "Carl Czerny's Metronome Marks for Haydn and
Mozart Symphonies," *EM* 16 (1988): 72–81, he again considers tempo markings indicated
for piano four-hand arrangements. Whether or not these "reduced" settings faithfully repro-
duce the tempos appropriate in symphonic minuets is open to question. Neal Zaslaw treats
the question of eighteenth-century minuet tempos in *Mozart's Symphonies*, pp. 496–97. Documentation of specific tempos, nearly all from French sources before 1775, suggests much
faster minuets than one normally hears in performance today.

35. Zaslaw, *Mozart's Symphonies*, p. 497.

36. A thorough study of Haydn's tempo markings is needed, and the minuet offers a good starting point. Two trends are evident in the symphonies and string quartets: over time, a decreas-
ing number of minuets lack a tempo indication and an increasing number are indicated as
fast movements. Although *allegretto* remains the most frequent marking, faster minuets are
indicated for five of the last twelve symphonies (*allegro*: Nos. 93, 98, 102, 104; *allegro molto*:
No. 94); and those of the last nine quartets all fall in the *allegro* to *presto* range. As with many
other features of his notation in works prepared for public circulation, Haydn becomes more
attentive to tempo markings in works of the 1780s and 1790s; one can safely assume that in
his latest symphonies he means to mark differences between moderate and fast minuets. In
minuets and trios that fall outside the *allegretto* range, attention to chronology and genre,
and to specific features of harmonic rhythm, phrase structure, melodic profile, articulation,

and scoring, can inform decisions about what that range might be and about the pacing of minuets lacking any tempo marking.

37. Thomas Robertson, *An Inquiry into the Fine Arts*, vol. 1, *Of Music* (London, 1784; facsimile reprint, New York: Garland, 1971), p. 434.

38. Landon (*Chronicle* 2:595) identifies this work as one that gave Haydn's reputation in England a "marked impetus." It was also one of the most frequently arranged of Haydn's symphonies, cited in advertisements as "The Celebrated Overture" known from its performances at the Bach and Abel concerts. For an account of the wide circulation in London of Symphony No. 53, among other works, in arrangements of the late 1780s, see my "Marriage à la Mode: Haydn's Instrumental Works 'Englished' for Voice and Piano," *JM* 8 (1990): 356–96.

39. A perfect "model of regularity" is hard to find among Haydn's minuets. While the opening section of this minuet is thoroughly symmetrical, the section after the first double bar is not. A slight irregularity of phrasing is felt in the expansion of phrase at m. 11 and the elision of m. 14. Even so, the two-measure extension that follows the exact return of the opening section is a surprising afterword, the more so as its deflection to the submediant motivates further expansion. And here the phrase lengths become most unpredictable: the grand pause extends two bars to three, followed by a five-bar cadential phrase. Complete stablity is regained only with the addition of four measures of cadential confirmation.

40. The playful preparation for return in this minuet is anticipated in the opening movement of Symphony No. 66 (see mm. 97–102); its finale is discussed in Chapter 6.

41. I discuss the comic effect of distraction in Chapter 7.

42. *The Autobiography of Karl von Dittersdorf Dictated to his Son* (Vienna, 1810), trans. A. D. Coleridge (London: Richard Bentley, 1896), p. 233.

43. Gerber, "Eine freundliche Vorstellung," col. 462.

44. The influence of the minuet is heard in continued play with upbeat figures in the trio section of this movement, and the manner in which it begins signals the role of anticipatory (and ambiguous) repetition throughout. But here, relaxing into the remote key of B-flat major, a Ländler-like grace prevails.

5. Engaging Wit in the Chamber: Opus 33 Revisited

1. Reverend William Jones, *Treatise on the Art of Music* (1784), p. 49; cited in Ratner, *Classic Music*, p. 27.

2. Alexandre Choron and F. J. Fayolle, *Dictionnaire historique des musiciens, artistes et amateurs, morts ou vivans* (Paris, 1810–11), s.v. "Joseph Haydn."

3. Rosen, *Classical Style*, p. 142. In summarizing his discussion of the Haydn quartets, Rosen suggests a parallel between verbal and musical discourse in this period: "Eighteenth-century prose in England, Germany, and France had become, in comparison with the previous age, much more syntactic, relying more exclusively on balance, proportion, shape, and the order of words than did the heavier cumulative technique of the Renaissance." His attention to the specifics of conversation in the quartets is brief, however, and confined largely to matters of texture (see pp. 141–42). The French in particular cultivated manners of spirited conversation that were detailed in contemporary manuals of conversational etiquette. The relationship of such manuals to the fashion of the *quatuor dialogué* (or *quatuor concertant*) in Paris is discussed in Barbara R. Hanning, "Conversation and Musical Style in the Late Eighteenth-Century Parisian Salon," *ECS* 22 (1989): 512–28. Hanning notes that "the sense of well-being that derived from participating in a company of congenial conversants was likened by several writers to the pleasures of making music" (p. 514). A fundamental study of the musical style and context of the *concertant* genre is Janet M. Levy's "*Quatuor concertant* in Paris in the Latter Half of the Eighteenth Century" (Ph.D. diss., Stanford University, 1971).

4. Theodor Adorno, *Introduction to the Sociology of Music* (original ed. *Einleitung in die Musiksoziologie*, 1962), translated by E. B. Ashton (New York: Seabury Press, 1976), p. 85. Adopting the conversational metaphor for chamber music generally, Adorno characterized its mode as competitive. With no product but the process of production itself, the contest of chamber

music differed from that of the marketplace, however; indeed, its very premise offered a critique of bourgeois competition: "The first step in playing chamber music is to learn not to thrust oneself forward but to step back . . . chamber music—as the corrective of the bumptious bourgeois who stands on what is his—practices courtesy" (pp. 86–87).

5. In her thoroughly documented *Concert Life in Haydn's Vienna* (Stuyvesant, N.Y.: Pendragon Press, 1989), Mary Sue Morrow finds no evidence of string quartets having been performed in public in Vienna during these years. Although it can be assumed that private gatherings featured string quartets, precise documentation is rare. The first performance of one or more of the Op. 33 quartets may have taken place in Vienna on Christmas Day in 1781: a concert of Haydn's works given in the apartments of the visiting Russian Grand Duke Paul and his consort featured a string quartet "received with gracious applause by the illustrious audience" (Landon, *Chronicle* 2:456). Ludwig Finscher, in the most thorough study of Haydn's string quartets through Op. 33, is able to document only one public performance of the Op. 33 quartets, at Hamburg in 1782. He postulates that there may have been several, however, during the 1782–83 concert tour of violinist Ernst Schick and cellist Jean Balthasar Trickler. See his *Studien zur Geschichte des Streichquartetts*, vol. 1, *Die Entstehung des klassischen Streichquartetts: Von den Vorformen zur Grundlegung durch Joseph Haydn*. Saarbrücker Studien zur Musikwissenschaft, ed. Walter Wiora, 3 (Kassel: Bärenreiter, 1974), p. 268.

6. Adorno, *Sociology*, p. 90. László Somfai notes a distinctly public feature in "noise killer" chords that open several of the Opp. 71 and 74 quartets of 1793. (See "Haydn's London String Quartets," *HS 1975*, pp. 389–92.) He suggests that conditions of performance in London's concert halls motivated a more public style in these works in comparison with earlier quartets. The "performative" elements that I wish to discuss in the Op. 33 quartets do not exceed the private chamber but rather the exclusivity of conversation among players.

7. Finscher, *Studien*, pp. 283–90, quotes from many contemporary accounts that document the growing distinction of the quartet as conversation among serious and learned equals.

8. Carpani, *Le Haydine*, pp. 96–97. I am grateful to Patrick Macey for help with the translation of this passage.

9. Koch, *Musikalisches Lexikon*, s.v. "Quatuor"; cited in Finscher, *Studien*, p. 291. See also Koch's *Versuch einer Anleitung zur Composition*, vol. 3 (Leipzig, 1793), trans. Nancy Kovaleff Baker as *Introductory Essay on Composition* (New Haven, Conn.: Yale University Press, 1983), p. 207.

10. Ted Cohen, "Jokes," in *Pleasure, Preference and Value: Studies in Philosophical Aesthetics*, ed. Eva Schaper (Cambridge: Cambridge University Press, 1987), pp. 120–36.

11. Ibid., p. 132, 123.

12. Ibid., p. 132. In "Metaphor and the Cultivation of Intimacy," in *On Metaphor*, ed. Sheldon Sacks (Chicago: University of Chicago Press, 1981), pp. 1–10, Cohen urges attention beyond the truth values of metaphors—long the issue of interest to many literary critics—to the meaning *in* what they accomplish in the "contexts of their use." In departing from everyday communications and literal meanings, jokes and metaphors "initiate explicitly the cooperative act of comprehension" (p. 7). Cohen's emphasis on process in collaborative construction of meaning is shared by literary critics such as Stanley Fish and others of the school of "affective stylistics." Anthony Newcomb has examined the relevance of this approach for the analysis of affective values in music in "Sound and Feeling," *Critical Inquiry* 10 (1984): 614–43.

13. Haydn to Griesinger, in Gotwals, *Haydn*, p. 17. If Haydn implies that the originality of his musical experiments was the inevitable consequence of isolation from the musical mainstream—that he was an original composing in a vacuum—he overstates the case. He was by no means cut off from current music making in Vienna, and that at Eisenstadt and Eszterháza was far from provincial, as documented in archives of these liberaries. (Numerous archival inventories are reported in *H-St* and *HYb*; Landon, *Chronicle*, also contains much of this data.) Haydn did, however, regret the long absences from Vienna that grew longer as Prince Nicolaus became more devoted to his summer estate at Eszterháza.

14. Trans. in Landon, *Chronicle* 2:399.

15. The full contract of 1761 is translated in Landon, *Chronicle* 1:350–52; portions of the 1779 contract are reported in 2:42–3. Landon regards Haydn's new contract as a "dead letter" issue for the composer, whose music was already in wide circulation. Webster, "Prospects for Haydn Biography," notes a general lack of attention to the importance of this change in the new contract, however, and stresses a need to view it against the backdrop of changing patterns of patronage in the late eighteenth century.

16. The set of six keyboard sonatas, Hob. XVI:21–26, dedicated to Prince Nicolaus, was published in 1774 by Kurzböck in Vienna. On the general circulation of Haydn's works in manuscript copies and unauthorized prints in the 1760s and 1770s, see the critical reports for respective volumes in *JHW*, gen. ed., Georg Feder (Munich: 1958–); Landon, *Chronicle*, passim; and Anthony van Hoboken, *Joseph Haydn: Thematisch-bibliographisches Werkverzeichnis* (Mainz: B. Schotts Söhne, 1957–78).

17. Letter of 25 February 1780, in Dénes Bartha, ed., *Gesammelte Briefe und Aufzeichungen* (Kassel: Bärenreiter, 1965), no. 27, pp. 90–91; translation from Landon, *CCLN*, pp. 24–25. The sonatas in question (Hob. XVI:35–39, 20) were published by Artaria as Op. 30 in 1780 and dedicated to Caterina and Marianna von Auenbrugger, daughters of a well-known physician in Graz. The dedicatees were gifted, in Leopold Mozart's opinion: "Both of them, and in particular the elder, play extraordinarily well and are thoroughly musical." See A. P. Brown, *Keyboard Music*, p. 25.

18. A. P. Brown (*Keyboard Music*, pp. 23–24, 121) surmises from Haydn's "Avvertissement" that others in this set (for example, Hob. XVI:36 in C-sharp Minor) may have been earlier works. Landon comes to the same conclusion based on the style of the works (*Chronicle* 2:584). Brown also notes that Haydn's letters to Artaria demonstrate the composer's sharp business tactics, characteristic of his dealings with publishers eager for new works.

19. Of the perhaps sixteen letters that Haydn sent, three survive: to Johann Caspar Lavater, a prominent Swiss physiologist active in the *Sturm und Drang* movement; Prince Krafft Ernst Öttingen-Wallerstein of Bavaria; and Robert Schlecht, abbot of Salmannsweiler in Baden, Germany. (See Bartha, *Briefe*, nos. 39–40, pp. 106–7, and Landon, *Chronicle* 2:454–55; the Schlecht letter is reprinted in Georg Feder, "Ein vergessener Haydn-Brief," *H-St* 1, no. 2 [1966]: 115.) The famous phrase "auf eine gantz neue besondere art, denn zeit 10 Jahren habe Keine geschrieben" is slightly varied in each letter. (See also note 22 below.)

20. Finscher, *Studien*, pp. 237–44; Rosen, *Classical Style*, p. 116. Karl Geiringer, *Haydn: A Creative Life in Music*, 2d ed. (Garden City, N.Y.: Doubleday, 1968), p. 303, asserts that "with the year 1781 Haydn entered upon his classical period of composition." He and some others subscribe to the notion that the intensely serious quartets of Op. 20 represented a cul de sac, and that Haydn's phrase signals the resolution in Op. 33 of a "romantic crisis" (p. 309). Orin Moe, Jr. ("The Significance of Haydn's Opus 33," in *HS 1975*, p. 445) asserts the candidacy of the Op. 50 quartets as "The first set to contain all the essential elements of [Haydn's] mature style." James Webster acknowledges Op. 50 as the set in which "we see all the essential features of the Classical quartet style (as we conceive it) united for the first time." He regards as misbegotten, however, the attempts to mark a precise "arrival" of Haydn's mature style within a particular set of quartets. Maintaining that such an effort obscures the individual merits of each opus, Webster exhorts us to "let each *opus* speak for itself" ("The Chronology of Haydn's String Quartets," *MQ* 61 [1975]: 45, 46).

21. Jens Peter Larsen, *Die Haydn-Überlieferung* (Copenhagen: Einer Munksgaard, 1939; reprint, Munich: Kraus International, 1980), p. 83, n. 59.

22. If Haydn hoped for such a list, it was not to be, for Artaria rushed to print. Haydn's letter of 4 January 1782 is revealing, both of his shrewd business sense and of the number of patrons he may have solicited. Angered by Artaria's premature announcement of the printed issue of Op. 33, he threatens to break off all future relations with his new publisher. At issue is the financial loss he will suffer if his subscribers realize that cheaper printed copies are soon to be had: "[B]y God! you have damaged me to the extent of more than 50 ducats, since I have not yet satisfied many of the subscribers, and cannot possibly send copies to many of those living abroad" (Landon, *Chronicle* 2:461–62). Feder, "Haydn-Briefe," p. 115, points out that if Haydn's claim is not exaggerated, at least eight subscribers were still await-

ing their manuscript copies—at the price of six ducats, in comparison with the printed cost of four gulden. Haydn mentions in a later (5 April 1784) letter to Artaria that he has received one hundred ducats from subscribers. Feder deduces from this that Haydn sold more than sixteen manuscript copies of Op. 33 by private subscription.

23. Among many who have written on the Op. 33 quartets, Finscher, whose treatment is the most extensive, is clearly partial to this group as decisive in Haydn's development. (See also the sources listed in note 20.) On the shifting placement of middle movements in Opp. 20 and 33, see László Somfai, "Vom Barock zur Klassik: Umgestaltung der Proportionen und des Gleichgewichts in zyklischen Werken Joseph Haydns," in *Joseph Haydn und seine Zeit*, ed. Gerda Mraz, Jahrbuch für Österreichische Kulturgeschichte 2 (Eisenstadt, 1972): 64–72 and Tables, pp. 160–64. Landon summarizes this material in *Chronicle* 2:326–28, 577–79.

24. The familiar numbering of the quartets does not correspond to their order in the Artaria print (nor in other early editions, which offered various orderings), but originated with Pleyel's edition of the complete quartets in 1801–2; Hoboken's ordering conforms to Pleyel's. No autograph survives, nor does any complete manuscript copy that originated with a copyist in the Eszterházy orbit, but it seems likely that Artaria's order was Haydn's own:

Artaria	Pleyel (Hob. III:37–42)
1. G Major	1. B Minor
2. E-flat Major	2. E-flat Major
3. B Minor	3. C Major
4. C Major	4. B-flat Major
5. D Major	5. G Major
6. B-flat Major	6. D Major

(See foreword to *JHW*, ser. XII, vol. 3, ed. Georg Feder and Sonja Gerlach.)

25. Rosen quotes the opening two measures (without the double bar) of this movement as "the simplest, wittiest, and most superficial form" of displacing a conventional phrase from its normative context. Without further discussion, he describes it as one example among many in Haydn's works of "an opening phrase which becomes a closing phrase" (*Classical Style*, p. 78). Even though in earlier quartets Haydn recycles opening material at the close of the movement (in the minuets of Op. 9, No. 1, and of Op. 17, Nos. 4 and 5, and in the finale of Op. 9, No. 3), he does not "confuse" the functions of opening and closure. Similarly, in several early quartets of Mozart (e.g., the finales of K. 158, 160, 171, 172) opening phrases are manipulated to serve as closing phrases; in his later quartets this procedure initiates extended codas (e.g., K. 464/i, K. 465/i and iv, K. 499/iv). For a probing analysis of Haydn's play with the implications of an incomplete cadential gesture in the opening movement of Haydn's Op. 50, No. 1, see Janet M. Levy, "Gesture, Form, and Syntax in Haydn's Music," in *HS 1975*, pp. 355–62. In this movement the "improper" continuation of an opening that implies closure becomes itself thematic.

26. In Gregory Bateson's terms, this self-referential use of convention is one in which "a message about the message is contained in the message itself," thus enabling interpretation as play. See "The Position of Humor," p. 4. While Bateson's formulation seems close to that of Mary Douglas (discussed in Chapter 1), his point of departure is in Gestalt psychology. For Bateson, the phenomenon of laughter itself suggests the oscillation of perception in figure-ground reversal.

27. Finscher, *Studien*, p. 247.

28. Janet Schmalfeldt, "Cadential Processes: The Evaded Cadence and the 'One More Time' Technique," *Journal of Musicological Research* 12, nos. 1–2 (1992): 1–51.

29. Rosen notes the comic effect of the stubborn three-note motive that effects the move to the dominant (*Classical Style*, pp. 97–98).

30. See Rosen, *Classical Style*, pp. 115–18, for an excellent discussion of the opening movement of the B Minor Quartet. Although he does not consider the Op. 33 set in the context of Haydn's new independence, Rosen is a clear champion of these works as "new and special" in style.

31. Hoboken notes that in one early manuscript source the ambivalence of B minor and D major was "resolved" in favor of the latter by editorial alterations of m. 2. (See *Joseph Haydn*, 1:395. Tovey and Rosen both point to the parallel case of D major/B minor ambiguity in the opening of Haydn's only other B minor quartet, Op. 64, No. 2 (1790); Rosen disputes Tovey's claim that Haydn "got" the idea from C. P. E. Bach's Sonata in B Minor, published in 1779 in *Sechs Clavier-Sonaten für Kenner und Liebhaber*, Wq. 55/3 (Helm 245) (see Donald Francis Tovey, "Haydn, Franz Joseph, 1732–1809," in *Cobbett's Cyclopedic Survey of Chamber Music*, ed. Walter W. Cobbett, 2d ed. [London: Oxford University Press, 1963], p. 538; Rosen, *Classical Style*, pp. 114–15). For a convincing evaluation of the "question of influence" of C. P. E. Bach on Haydn, see A. P. Brown, *Keyboard Music*, pp. 203–29. Susan Wollenberg, in "A New Look at C. P. E. Bach's Musical Jokes," rightly takes issue with Stephen Paul's assertion that Haydn was "the 'inventor' of pure, intrinsic musical humour" ("Wit, Comedy and Humour," p. 359), as also with those who evaluate the eccentricities of Bach's works with a sonata-form agenda. "Expectational defeat" is much more audible in its play in Haydn's Op. 33 quartets, however, than in the subtle details that Wollenberg examines as evidence of Bach's wit.

32. Landon regards the B Minor Quartet as "the most conservative one in the set and the only one in which the serious style precludes comical touches" (*Chronicle* 2:579). While tonic keys in the minor mode are relatively rare in the works of Haydn and his contemporaries, and often associated with the dramatic intensity of the "serious style," Haydn's use of minor keys does not in my view "preclude" playful effects. The G Minor Quartet of Haydn's Op. 20 (Hob. III:33) seems a good candidate for second thoughts on this question, as does the Piano Sonata in E Minor (Hob. XVI:34). On characterizations of the various keys, major and minor, in commentaries by listeners of Haydn's day, see Rita Steblin, *A History of Key Characteristics in the Eighteenth and Early Nineteenth Centuries* (Ann Arbor, Mich.: UMI Research Press, 1983).

33. Somfai, "Vom Barock zur Klassik," pp. 71–72.

34. See the finales of Op. 20, No. 1 (E-flat Major), No. 3 (G Minor) and No. 4 (D Major). In earlier sets, the finale of Opus 17, No. 5, is emphatic in its final cadence.

35. Tovey, "Haydn," p. 539.

36. If m. 39 of the opening movement is an audible parallel of the repeated sixteenth notes in mm. 153–55 of the finale, an equally audible difference is its success in moving to the intended cadence.

37. The influence of such a disturbance is audible in the repetition of mm. 13–16 at mm. 17–20, where harmonic deflection is heightened by a fermata. At the second return of the opening section (mm. 155ff), where the tune is treated to its most extreme distortions, the harmonic progression that seemed to elude the voices in mm. 5–6 is found.

38. Not until the 1790s does Haydn return to *allegro* and even *presto* minuets in the quartets (see Hob. III:70, 72–73, and 77–79—all *allegro*—and the *presto* minuets of Hob. III:75, 79, and 82 [*ma non troppo*]). Along with the fast tempos of these late works, one finds increasingly irregular manners of the sort demonstrated in the Scherzo of Op. 33's G Major Quartet. On tempo in Haydn's symphonic Minuets, see Chapter 4, pp. 75–76.

39. Also known as the "Russian" and the "Jungfern" Quartets, Op. 33 acquired the former nickname in reference to a dedication to the Grand Duke Paul of Russia, as inscribed in the Artaria issue of the *Collection complette des quatuors* of 1810. The picture of a young woman on the Hummel print of 1782 accounts for the latter title (though one might wonder if the choice of such an engraving might itself advertise a characterization of these quartets as engaging a female audience in the chamber).

40. Jánós Harich, "Das Repertoire des Opernkapellmeisters Joseph Haydn in Eszterháza (1780–1790)," *HYb* 1, no. 1 (1962): 9–107, provides year-by-year accounts of a decade of opera performances at Eszterháza under Haydn's direction, including information about works premiered and repeated (the figures for 1780 are tabulated on p. 33). Harich's access to newly available archival material permits corrections to figures given in the monumental study of Haydn's opera activities by Dénes Bartha and László Somfai, *Haydn als Opernkapellmeister* (Budapest: Verlag der ungarischen Akademie der Wissenschaften, 1960). Aside from docu-

menting the incredible burden that Haydn assumed in satisfying his patron's growing appetite for opera from 1776 on, figures in this letter indicate Prince Nicolaus's overwhelming preference: seventy-six of eighty-eight operas performed from 1776–90 were comic operas.

41. Rosen, whose discussion of opera in *The Classical Style* focuses on Mozart, asserts that the Classical style is essentially that of comic opera. Stephen Paul, "Wit and Humour," pp. 386–402, discusses instances of instrumental *Tonmalerei* (literal illustrations of the text) and parody in Haydn's operas, asserting parallels in the Op. 33 quartets and other works.

42. Webster, "Chronology," pp. 45–46.

43. Orin Moe ("Significance," p. 449), in promoting the quartets of Op. 50 as the "first set to contain all the essential elements of [Haydn's] mature style," is somewhat dismissive of the "mannerisms" of Op. 33's irregularities. But Landon is more outspoken in regarding the Op. 33 quartets as a regrettable departure from the intense and serious mood that characterizes Haydn's quartets of the early 1770s. He finds a similar falling off in symphonies of the late 1770s, attributable to the seduction of "that fatally popular style" (*Chronicle* 2:341; Op. 33 is discussed on pp. 576–82). In his summary remarks about Op. 33, Landon appears to subscribe to the view of Robert Sondheimer that their "intellectual naivety" was the sign of Haydn's "quest for the applause of the multitude" (*Chronicle*, 2:582).

44. Arrangements, even if often considerable abridgements of the original, extended Haydn's works and reputation in the 1780s and 1790s to a much broader public. Scored for various combinations of instruments as well as for piano, and even set for piano and voice, the Op. 33 quartets circulated well beyond patrician chambers, promoting participation in that music by amateurs in domestic settings among family and friends. Among complete quartets arranged from Op. 33, those most frequently issued were the G Major, the E-flat Major, the B-flat Major, and the C Major (in that order). Favored movements separately issued were the finales of the G Major (also the only one arranged by Haydn himself) and B-flat Major Quartets and the minuets of the B-flat and C Major Quartets. Hoboken lists many of the arrangements of these movements; I discuss these sources and their relevance to Haydn's popularity in England in "Marriage à la Mode," pp. 356–96.

45. Cramer, *Magazin der Musik* 1 (Hamburg, 1783): 259. The full text of Reichardt's review (in Landon, *Chronicle* 2:466–67), excerpts of which are quoted in Chapter 3, p. 49, suggests that Cramer might have borrowed from it.

46. Sadie, *The New Grove Mozart*, p. 94.

47. In its rhythmic patterning and *più allegro* closing variation, the finale of K. 421 recalls the variation finale of Haydn's G Major Quartet; the rondo finale of K. 428 exploits playful anticipation and delay of thematic return; the sonata-form finale of K. 458 is particularly reminiscent of the opening movement of Haydn's B-flat Major Quartet in its reiteration of a wayward descending third (in the second theme of this movement there is also a perhaps coincidental "reference" to mm. 9–16 of Haydn's Op. 2, No. 2/i); and in the finale of K. 465, Mozart's use of silence and written-out ritards in the exposition and at the recapitulation recalls Haydn's technique; the relationship of the coda of this movement to Haydn's C Major Quartet is audible in the four-voice "laughing" sixteenths.

48. Gerber, "Eine freundliche Vorstellung," cols. 460–61.

49. In distinguishing between connoisseur and amateur, *Kenner* and *Liebhaber*, writers throughout the second half of the eighteenth century traditionally assigned a spontaneous response of the heart to the music lover, and a more studied (and discriminating) taste to the music knower. Both might be moved by an excellent work, but the connoisseur could explain the reasons for a work's excellence. (See also Chapter 3.)

50. Gerber, "Ein freundliche Vorstellung," cols. 461, 463.

6. Extended Play in Eccentric Finales

1. For a recent evaluation of the symphony's status in eighteenth-century musical life as compared with our own, see Zaslaw, *Mozart's Symphonies*, pp. 511–25.

2. Bathia Churgin, "The Symphony as Described by J. A. P. Schulz (1774): A Commentary and Translation," *CM* 29 (1980): 7-16; here pp. 11-12.
3. Spazier would advocate similar standards for the symphony some twenty years later (*Musikalisches Wochenblatt* 2 [1792]: 91-92; see Chapter 3, p. 45). Imagining the three movements of the symphony as something of an emotional da capo, Spazier claims that such affective symmetry "accords with the laws of psychology": the dominant sentiment of the first movement is varied by a slower and more peaceful movement, so that in the finale "the former mood, with which the symphony began, is all the more powerfully roused again." As noted in Chapter 3, Spazier was opposed to the inclusion of minuets in symphonies, both because of their functional associations with dance and, as here, because they were "contrary to the unity of the symphony."
4. Symphony No. 63's opening movement was originally the overture to *Il mondo della luna* (before 1777). Landon remarks that the adaptable use of such movements "interchangeably as a first and final movement shows that [Haydn] had not yet solved the question of the finale as a genre" (*Chronicle* 2:562). Despite the dubious implication that Haydn was conscious of a problem to be "solved"—let alone a genre to be created—Landon's remark does point up the absence of defining differences that mark a clear stylistic distinction between opening and closing movements. That distinction, which becomes much clearer in later symphonies, might be viewed as functional in works destined for performance in public concerts.
5. The obverse might also apply: Haydn's symphonic style had become sufficiently dramatic by the late 1770s that symphonies themselves might be written with an eye to their utility in theatrical contexts. Elaine Sisman explores this question in "Haydn's Theater Symphonies," *JAMS* 43 (1990): 292-352.
6. See Landon, *CECS* 5:147.
7. See the second movements of Symphonies Nos. 35, 49, 65, and 82 and the finale of Symphony No. 25. I do not include here the many instances in which a tonic is established and soon undermined.
8. "Off-tonic" openings are found almost equally distributed among opening, closing, and minuet movements of the string quartets, and with nearly the same frequency in works of the 1770s, 1780s, and 1790s. Some of these pose very brief uncertainties, and none is as prolonged as the finale of Symphony No. 62. See:

Movement 1	Movement 4	Minuet
Op. 17, No. 4 (c)	Op. 20, No. 2 (C; fugue)	Op. 9, No. 1 (Trio: c)
Op. 33, No. 1 (b)	Op. 50, No. 4 (f sharp; fugue)	Op. 17, No. 3 (Minuet: E flat)
Op. 50, No. 6 (D)	Op. 55, No. 1 (A)	Op. 50, No. 5 (Minuet and trio: F)
Op. 55, No. 3 (B flat)	Op. 77, No. 1 (G)	Op. 71, No. 3 (Minuet: E flat)
Op. 64, No. 2 (b)		Op. 74, No. 3 (Minuet: G)

9. See Koch, *Musikalisches Lexikon*, s.v. "Styl, Schreibart."
10. Landon (*Chronicle* 2:266-393) favors the *crise romantique* view of Austrian musical style in the late 1760s and early 1770s. On the mixed messages of the so-called *Sturm und Drang*, see Todd, "Joseph Haydn and the *Sturm und Drang*," 172-96, and William Youngren, "Haydn Recovered," *The Hudson Review* 27 (1974): 69-81. See also Paul F. Marks, "Aesthetics of Music in the Philosophy of *Sturm und Drang*: Gerstenberg, Hamann and Herder," *MR* 35 (1974): 247-59. Sisman's "Haydn's Theater Symphonies" sheds new light on the whole question of a dramatically charged style in consideration of the use of symphonies in theatrical contexts.
11. The remaining five *scherzando* movements are more various in tempo and placement within their respective works; all of these, listed below, are in duple meters, four of the five in A major.
   1. String Quartet in D Major, Op. 20, No. 4 (1772), finale, *Presto e scherzando*
   2. String Quartet in A Major, Op. 20, No. 6 (1772), mvt. 1, *Allegro di molto e scherzando*
   3. String Quartet in A Major, Op. 64, No. 1 (1790), mvt. 3, *Allegretto scherzando* (variations)

4. Piano Sonata in C-sharp Minor, Hob. XVI:36 (before 1780), mvt. 2 (A major), *Scherzando, allegro con brio*
5. Baryton Trio in A Major, Hob. XI:103 (before 1778), finale, *Scherzando*
The Six Scherzandi, Hob. II:33–38 (before 1765) were so named in the Breitkopf catalogue of 1765; elsewhere they were known as Divertimenti and Sinfonie (see Landon, *Chronicle* 1, 554).
12. See Elaine R. Sisman, "Haydn's Variations" (Ph.D. diss., Princeton University, 1978).
13. The issue of eighteenth-century associations of keys with specific affects and character is fascinating and complex, and well beyond the scope of this study. Steblin's *Key Characteristics* provides ample documentation of such associations and a variety of perspectives on their origins. According to her data (Appendix A, p. 303), B major—a key whose many sharps guaranteed uncertain intonation—attracted polarized descriptions: "wild passions" and "glaring colours" of "anger, rage, jealousy, fury, despair" (Schubart, *Ideen*) versus "brilliant and playful" (Grétry, *Mémoires*). The character of Haydn's Presto e scherzando finale is clearly more in line with Grétry's description. The first movement, on the other hand, has more of the earmarks of intensity associated with the so-called *Sturm und Drang* style. Mark Evan Bonds discusses the relationship of the outer movements of Symphony No. 46 in "Haydn, Laurence Sterne" (pp. 72–76).
14. Landon, *Chronicle* 2:304.
15. Triest, "Bemerkungen," col. 407; Gotwals, *Haydn*, p. 199.
16. Cramer, *Magazin* 2 (1787): 1310. The first two movements of the Piano Trio Hob. XV:2 are arranged after an earlier work of c. 1772, the Baryton Trio No. 103 (see Landon, *Chronicle* 2:583).
17. Samuel Johnson ["Papilius"], *The Rambler* no. 141 (23 July 1751).
18. "Bescheidene Anfrage an die modernsten Komponisten und Virtuosen," AMZ 1, no. 10 (5 December 1798), cols. 153–54.
19. Additional long-range effects are the major-minor alternation in the second theme's presentation of "A" material in the dominant (mm. 53–65); the preparation for return of the A refrain before the development section (mm. 80–84); and the long canonic episode that constitutes this development (mm. 109–31).
20. Gotwals, *Haydn*, p. 57. See above, Chapter 2, pp. 31–32.

7. The Paradox of Distraction

1. Stephen Fisher examines closely the overture-symphony connection in "Haydn's Overtures and their Adaptations as Concert Orchestral Works," (Ph.D. diss., University of Pennsylvania, 1985). I discuss one such case in Chapter 6, pp. 117–24.
2. Rudolph Angermüller presents the evidence for Symphony No. 60's origins, noting the locations of various midcentury German translations of the Regnard play, and prints the full Salzburg review in "Haydns 'Der Zerstreute' in Salzburg (1776)," *H-St* 4, no. 2 (1978): 85–93. Robert A. Green examines programmatic aspects of the work in " 'Il Distratto' of Regnard and Haydn: a re-examination," *HYb* 11 (1980): 183–95. Apparently unaware of Angermüller's article, Green's analysis of the relationship of movements to incidents in the acts of the play proceeds from his assumption that movements 1 and 2 of the symphony were both heard before Act I. The Salzburg review clarifies the order as that of the symphony, one movement before each act, the sixth coming after the play's fifth act. Arnold Schering, "Bemerkungen zu J. Haydns Programmsinfonien," *JbMP* 46 (1939): 9–27, investigated Symphony No. 60, among several others, for programmatic elements. Sisman's "Haydn's Theater Symphonies" provides a much-needed fresh perspective on *Sturm und Drang* symphonies and their possible connections with spoken plays in Vienna. She examines the question of theatrical connections in a number of Haydn's symphonies, including Symphony No. 60.
3. *Preßburger Zeitung*, 23 July 1774, as quoted in Angermüller, "Haydns 'Der Zerstreute'," p. 88, from Marianne Pandi and Franz Schmidt, "Musik zur Zeit Haydns und Beethovens in der Preßburger Zeitung," *HYb* 8 (1971): 171.

4. The Salzburg review, from *Theaterwochenblatte für Salzburg* no. 21 (27 January 1776), is printed in full in Angermüller, "Haydns 'Der Zerstreute'," pp. 90–92.

5. The subdominant is also implicated in a wavering of F natural and F sharp in the passage immediately preceding this one (see mm. 56–66). A conspicuous passage that exploits both raised and natural $\hat{4}$ is found in the development section preceding the retransition (see esp. mm. 123–28). Haydn's self-quotation (in mm. 109ff) from the "Farewell" Symphony has been noted by many. In the earlier work the raised fourth is prominent as an alteration of the original theme's progress when it is stated in the dominant minor (mm. 38ff), and, as here, provides a forceful diminished-seventh chord above a prolonged pedal.

6. Angermüller, "Haydns 'Der Zerstreute'," p. 91.

7. Landon identified this melody after a manuscript in the archives of the Metten Monastery, a facsimile of which is reproduced in his *Supplement*, facing p. 32; commentary on pp. 46–47. Many uses of the tune in works of Haydn's contemporaries are traced in Geoffrey Chew, "The Night-Watchman's Song Quoted by Haydn and its Implications," *H-St* 3, no. 2, (1974): 106–24. Chew also explores the relationship of the tune and its theme of keeping watch to the Advent tradition of the *pastorella*.

8. Angermüller, "Haydns 'Der Zerstreute'," p. 91.

9. See Chapter 3, pp. 43–44.

10. Schering was of the opinion that Haydn's tune was used for the song in this scene ("Bemerkungen," p. 18). Angermüller ("Haydns 'Der Zerstreute'," p. 93, n. 24) notes several German translations of the French original, suggesting that Wahr used Bergopzoomer's text (printed in Vienna in 1775) rather than the Reuling translation that Schering assumes. In both versions, Chevalier interrupts his song to make pointed reference to B minor, a connection with the music that neither Schering nor Angermüller notes. In the Reuling translation, however, the reference is played to the audience: "Isn't the B minor sure to win applause?" Perhaps Haydn, too, takes this opportunity to recall the striking shift toward B minor in the first movement (see mm. 120ff).

11. The instability of minor versus major thirds in this movement affects the dominant in m. 38 (and the tonic in the parallel spot at m. 114) and is played out in a G minor digression that follows the ill-prepared recapitulation. This episode in the minor (mm. 85ff) is additional confirmation of the theme's relationship to the French song.

12. Our reviewer may have found his "Turkish" melody in the last of these, although in Haydn's terms this resembles most closely the Hungarian topos in the *Rondo all'Ongarese* finale of his late G Major Piano Trio, Hob. XV:25. See Bence Szabolsci, "Joseph Haydn und die ungarische Musik," in *Bericht über die Internationale Konferenz zum Andenken Joseph Haydns, Budapest, 17.-22. September 1959*, ed. Bence Szabolsci and Dénes Bartha (Budapest: Akadémiai Kiadó, 1961), pp. 159–75. In view of the uncertain origin of such melodies and the problematic relationship of art music to the *Volk*, Landon argues for the more inclusive "Slavonic" and "Balkan" as terms of reference for Haydn's use of scales and rhythmic patterns that suggest eastern European influence. (See his remarks on Symphony No. 103/ii in *Supplement*, pp. 44–45.) Oskar Elschek examines the influence of western European tradition on folk melodies of this region in "Problem of Variation in 18th-Century Slovak Folk Music Manuscripts," *StM* 7 (1965): 47–59; see also Szabolsci's "Folk Musik," pp. 171–79 in this same volume.

13. Angermüller, "Haydns 'Der Zerstreute'," p. 91.

14. The *Lamentatione* in the movement's title has not been identified as liturgical, although the irregular phrasing and contour of the melodic line in mm. 13–21 is suggestive of chant, especially in mm. 17–21.

15. *Preßburger Zeitung*, 30 June 1774, in Pandi and Schmidt, "Musik zur Zeit Haydns," p. 170.

16. Haydn wrote in 1803 to his copyist Elssler to ask for "the old Symphony (entitled *die* [sic] *Zerstreute*), for Her Majesty the Empress expressed a desire to hear the old pancake" (Landon, *Chronicle* 5:262). At the remove of nearly thirty years since its composition, Haydn was perhaps less enthusiastic about the work than his empress was.

17. Symphonies noted by Landon as possible candidates for origins in incidental music for the stage include Nos. 64 and 65, which he dates from around 1771–73. See his *CECS* 6:xiv–xv.

Sisman, "Haydn's Theater Symphonies," suggests others Haydn might have composed with the possibility of a theatrical use in mind. In addition to Symphonies Nos. 64 and 65—the slow movements of which may have figured as entr'actes for Viennese performances of *Hamlet*—she notes that Symphonies Nos. 22, 34, and 49 may have had similar use in other dramas. Her findings suggest the rich possibilities of further research in informing our estimate of Haydn's dramatic style, both comic and serious, in works of the 1770s.

18. Henri Bergson, *Laughter* (orig. *Le rire*, 1900), in *Comedy*, ed. Wylie Sypher (Baltimore: Johns Hopkins University Press, 1980), p. 84; on absentmindedness and the mechanical, see pp. 67–69.

19. Ibid., pp. 72–73.

20. Aristotle, *The Poetics*, trans. Hamilton Fyfe (London: Heinemann, 1927), pp. 19–21: "Comedy . . . is a representation of inferior people, not indeed in the full sense of the word bad, but the laughable is a species of the base or ugly. It consists in some blunder or ugliness that does not cause pain or disaster, an obvious example being the comic mask which is ugly and distorted but not painful."

21. A. P. Brown, *Haydn's Keyboard Music*, p. 121, suggests that this sonata may have been written considerably earlier than the others in the "1776" collection (Hob. XVI:27–32).

22. I consider performance practice issues in this and other sonatas of Haydn in "What's Going On When the Music 'Stops'?," in *Proceedings of the Westfield Center for Early Keyboard Studies Conference on Haydn's Piano Sonatas*, ed. Elaine Sisman (forthcoming).

23. August F. Kollmann, *An Essay on Musical Harmony. . . .* (London, 1796), p. 84.

24. I borrow this phrase from Allanbrook, *Rhythmic Gesture*, p. 6.

25. The opening material of the movement signals a disposition for repetition, and the development section one for unexpected continuations. The reiterated B flat–A at the end of the quoted excerpt is perhaps a recollection of the extended F major passage in the development, which is framed by these pitches in the bass (see mm. 47–63).

26. See Chapter 1, p. 13.

27. Tovey, *Essays in Musical Analysis*, vol. 1, *Symphonies*, 3d ed. (London: Oxford University Press, 1938), p. 155.

28. The remainder of the exposition is only relatively uneventful: the extended closing section of mm. 124–47 flirts briefly with a possible detour (mm. 130–33) before coming to an emphatic cadence in F major. A measure's rest with fermata dramatizes the repeat of the exposition and the beginning of the development.

29. Landon gives the first version along with the final version entered elsewhere in the manuscript (see *CECS*, vol. 2, Appendix IV, p. 365).

30. For documentation of the keyboard solo, see Landon, *Chronicle* 3:534–36.

8. "The Great Art of Seeming Familiar"

1. *Goethes Gespräche*, ed. F. von Biedermann, 2d ed. (Leipzig, 1909), 2:20; quoted in *Europäische Schlüßelwörter*, 1:171, n. 1.

2. Yves Marie André, *L'Essai sur le beau* (1741; rev. ed., 1763); text in Le Huray and Day, *Music and Aesthetics*, pp. 27–35, translated from *Oeuvres philosophiques du Père André*, ed. Victor Cousin (Paris, 1843), part 2, pp. 77–96.

3. Tilden Russell, in "'Über das Komische in der Musik': The Schütze-Stein Controversy," *JM* 4 (1985/86): 70–90, examines essays of the 1830s for their conservative and progressive attitudes toward instrumental music's capacity for the comic. At considerable remove from Stein and Schütze are two recent writers who contend that music cannot produce a comic effect in the absence of a text, a specific program, or parodistic devices. See Siegfried Borris, "Das Lächeln der Melpomene: Betrachtungen über das Komische in der Musik," in *Festschrift für einen Verleger: Ludwig Strecker zum 90. Geburtstag*, ed. Carl Dahlhaus (Mainz: B. Schott's Sohne, 1973): 111–18, and Wilfried Gruhn, "Wie heiter ist die Kunst? Semiologische Aspeckte musikalischer Komik," *ÖMz* 38 (1983): 677–88.

4. Christian Friedrich Michaelis, "Über das Humoristische oder Launige in der musikalischen

Komposition," *AMZ* 9, no. 46 (12 August 1807), col. 726. An association of play and the aesthetic in philosophic thought comes to the fore in the late eighteenth century in the writings of Kant, whose student Michaelis was, and most notably in Friedrich Schiller's *On the Aesthetic Education of Man* (1795). For Schiller, aesthetic contemplation deserved elevated status among other rational endeavors. Acknowledged as nonpurposive in being detached from the world, aesthetic play was nonetheless subject to inner rules of consistency and coherence. As such, it offered the ideal model of freedom and restraint, and an essential exercise in education for full moral responsibility in the world.

5. Ratner, *Classic Music*, p. 436.
6. Novalis, *Vermischte Bemerkungen* (1797), no. 30; translated in Kathleen M. Wheeler, ed., *German Aesthetic and Literary Criticism: The Romantic Ironists and Goethe* (Cambridge: Cambridge University Press, 1984), p. 88.
7. Ibid.
8. Locke, *Essay*, book 3, chap. 10. On Locke's distinction of wit and judgment, see Chapter 2, p. 21.
9. Michaelis, "Über das Humoristische," col. 725.
10. Ibid., cols. 725–29. In his *Über den Geist der Tonkunst mit Rücksicht auf Kants Kritik der aesthetischen Urteilskraft* (Leipzig, 1795–1800), Michaelis opposed Kant's claims regarding music's ontological status. Kant assigned music and wit to the category of "agreeable" rather than fine arts, in that their appeal was to pleasures of sensation; engaging the activity of the body, both could "enliven the mind," but were "unproductive of any thought conveying an interest" (*Critique of Aesthetic Judgement* [1790], trans. James Creed Meredith [Oxford: Clarendon Press, 1911], pp. 197–99). Michaelis argued that while "charm and sense stimuli have a larger share in music than in any of the other arts," to assert that music "can aim at and achieve nothing more than a physical enjoyment, nothing but a mere sensual pleasure or feeling of well-being, seems to me entirely false" (*Über den Geist*, p. 65).
11. Michaelis, "Über das Humoristische," cols. 725, 729.
12. Ibid., cols. 727–28.
13. Ibid., col. 729.
14. Kant, "Anthropologie," par. 55; quoted in *Europäische Schlüßelwörter*, p. 172.
15. Ibid., p. 171.
16. Michaelis, "Über das Humoristische," col. 727. Gerber's remark is found in his entry on Haydn in the *Historisch-biographisches Lexikon der Tonkünstler*, vol. 1 (1790), cols. 610–11.
17. Friedrich August Weber, "Über komische Charakteristik und Karrikatur in praktischen Musikwerken," *AMZ* 3, no. 9 (26 November 1800), cols. 137–43; no. 10 (3 December 1800), cols. 157–62. Koch notes (*Musikalisches Lexikon*, col. 873) that an earlier version of Weber's essay was published in the form of a letter for the forty-sixth and forty-seventh issues of the *Musikalische Korrespondez der teutschen Filarmonischen Gesellschaft* of 1792. Gerber, *Lexikon*, vol. 2 (Leipzig, 1792), lists the numerous and varied accomplishments of F. A. Weber (b. 1753), Doctor of Medical Arts and City Physician in Heilbronn. Devoting six and a half columns to the man (Haydn is given four), Gerber cites him as "among the most learned of dilettantes and most insightful and enlightened writers on music" and lists a number of his essays, which range from pedagogical studies to musical aesthetics. An obituary notice in *AMZ* 8, no. 27 (2 April 1806) gives Weber's full name. The *AMZ* essay of 1800, signed simply "D. Weber," is discussed by Ratner, who identifies the author as Daniel Weber without comment (*Classic Music*, pp. 387–89). In light of the evidence favoring Friedrich, "D." perhaps an abbreviation for "Doktor"—or a typographical error.
18. Weber, "Über komische Charakteristik," cols. 139–140. Koch (*Musikalisches Lexikon*) offers a similar definition of *Komisch*: "The comic in music consists in a particular use of melodic and harmonic artfulness whereby the feeling of the laughable is raised. This feeling can arise as much from an easy perception of an actual as from an only seeming misfit that exists between the presented object and the artistic means by which it is represented, as much from an intentional disregard of custom as—even more—from a transference of the same [customs] to contradictory situations." Koch cites an example from comic opera to illustrate this last, in which the characterization and style of singing appropriate to a man of culture

are given over to a young farmer (in Hiller's *Die Liebe auf dem Lande*). In his *Handwörterbuch*, Koch cites Eberhard's definition of the laughable as "that in which we perceive with gay aspects a surprising contradiction of the rules, from which arises a slight imperfection" (p. 208).

19. Weber, "Über komische Charakteristik," col. 141.
20. Ibid.
21. August Halm, "Humor und Musik," in *Von Grenzen und Ländern der Musik: Gesammelte Aufsätze* (Munich: Georg Muller, 1916), p. 103. Theodor Veidl refers to Beethoven's humor in similar terms in his *Der musikalische Humor bei Beethoven* (Leipzig: Breitkopf & Härtel, 1929). The comic in music "arises when the composer seduces the listener into taking seriously a musical event that he himself does not mean to be serious at all—this, however, such that the listener can see through to the intention of the composer" (p. 19). Veidl does not pursue the question of how the composer signals such intentions, except to say that the "prepared ground of a gay mood" is important. Anton Penkert also provided that recognition of comic intent in music is "much facilitated if the underlying mood, rather than being one of unremitting gloom, has in some way betrayed from the beginning an inclination for jest and cheerfulness." (See "Die musikalische Formung von Witz and Humor," *Kongreß für Aesthetik und allgemeine Kunstwissenschaft, Berlin, 7.–9. Oktober 1913* [Stuttgart: F. Enke, 1914], p. 483.) Like Veidl, Penkert does not enlighten us as to how such a mood is created and recognized.
22. Meier, *Thoughts on Jesting* p. 66.
23. Beattie, *On Laughter*, p. 320.
24. Bergson, *Laughter*, p. 84.
25. Max Eastman, "Humor," in *Dictionary of World Literary Terms, Forms, Technique, Criticism*, ed. Joseph T. Shipley (rev. ed. Boston: Writer, 1970), p. 150; see also his *Enjoyment of Laughter* (New York: Simon & Schuster, 1936).
26. Richard A. Lanham, *The Motives of Eloquence: Literary Rhetoric in the Renaissance* (New Haven, Conn.: Yale University Press, 1976), p. 13. Lanham takes a radical view of rhetoric as play in viewing man as inherently double in his private and public selves: "At least half the time his living is play, his motive dramatic and self-contrived, his self a role. It is to sustain this second man and second reality that rhetoric exists" (p. 210).
27. Heinrich Lausberg, *Elemente der literarischen Rhetorik*, rev. ed. (Munich: Max Hueber, 1963), pp. 41–84 and passim. Related to this concept in the realm of poetics is the theory of "defamiliarization" promoted by Russian formalist Victor Shklovsky. See "Art as Technique," in *Russian Formalist Criticism: Four Essays*, trans. Lee T. Lemon and Marion Reis (Lincoln: University of Nebraska Press, 1965), pp. 3–24. For Shklovsky, "art is a way of experiencing the artfulness of an object," and the artist's task is "to make objects 'unfamiliar,' to make forms difficult, to increase the difficulty and length of perception because the process of perception is an aesthetic end in itself and must be prolonged" (p. 12).
28. *Morning Herald*, 24 March 1792; quoted in Landon, *Chronicle* 3:149.
29. Rosen, *Classical Style*, p. 98.
30. See Ratner, *Classic Music*, pp. 3–30, for further topoi.
31. In discussing the formal anomalies in the finale of Haydn's String Quartet in C Major, Op. 54, No. 2, Edward T. Cone puts the case for today's listener: "comparison between the unique pattern and the normal one leads to an awareness of the tension between them that sharpen's one perception of the extent to which Haydn ... widened the boundaries of his own style." See "The Uses of Convention: Stravinsky and His Models," *MQ* 48 (1962): 284, reprinted in *Music: A View from Delft: Selected Essays*, ed. Robert P. Morgan (Chicago: University of Chicago Press, 1989), pp. 281–92.
32. Johan Huizinga, *Homo ludens: A Study of the Play Element in Culture*. Anon. trans. from the 1st German ed. of 1944 in conjunction with Huizinga's own English trans. (Boston: Beacon Press, 1955), p. 42.
33. Ibid., p. 186.
34. W. Oliver Strunk, "Haydn," in *From Bach to Stravinsky: The History of Music by Its Foremost*

Critics, ed. David Ewen (New York: Norton, 1933); reprint in *Essays on Music in the Western World* (New York: Norton, 1974), p. 116.

35. Agawu's *Playing with Signs* demonstrates the complex interplay of rhetorical conventions in the instrumental works of Mozart, Haydn, and Beethoven. In an ingenious overlay of eighteenth-century paradigms of musical rhetoric's expression (a "Universe of Topics," based on Ratner) and of its syntactic and structural order ("Beginnings-Middles-Ends"), Agawu makes a persuasive case for their integration with Schenkerian models of voice leading and harmonic unfolding. His analysis of the listener's interpretive strategies is thus admirably responsive to historical and contemporary theories of Classical music's coherence and dynamic. Implicit in this system of signs (and signaled in the title of Agawu's book) is the composer's role in playing with the stability of conventional reference—and, by extension, upon the expectations of his audience—and a shared responsibility in the interpretations of adept listeners. That the original humors of Mozart, Haydn, Beethoven, and others were distinguished by various contemporaries attests to recognition of a range of compositional strategies in such play. The particular profile of Haydn's humor in this company is salient, I have argued, in his surprising inversions of the familiar in paradoxical combinations. Agawu's semiotic approach can provide the analytical tools for a comprehensive and rigorous testing of such manifestations of the playful.

36. Among behavioral psychologists who have investigated the motivational aspects of play, Daniel E. Berlyne is notable in considering its implications for aesthetic experience. Regarding his subjects in stages of aroused curiosity, exploratory behavior aimed at reducing tension, and pleasure at mastering perceptual challenges, he locates play "in the class of 'intrinsically motivated' and 'intrinsically reinforced' behavior, a class that includes much exploratory and esthetic behavior" ("Laughter, Humor, and Play," p. 814). Berlyne includes among "collative variables" that motivate such behavior novelty, surprise, incongruity, and ambiguity—factors that figure in many theories of humor. See also Susanna Millar, *The Psychology of Play* (Baltimore: Penguin Books, 1969), p. 21: "a certain degree of choice, lack of constraint from conventional ways of handling objects, materials and ideas, is inherent in the concept of play. This is its main connexion with art and other forms of invention."

 Among recent literary studies of game and play, see the special issue *Yale French Studies* 41 (1968): *Game, Play, Literature*, ed. Jacques Ehrmann (reprint, Boston: Beacon Press, 1971); Peter Hutchinson, *Games Authors Play* (London: Methuen, 1983); Richard A. Lanham, *Tristram Shandy: The Games of Pleasure* (Berkeley and Los Angeles: University of California Press, 1973). On the intertextual connections of language play in folklore and literature, see Susan Stewart's *Nonsense* (1979).

37. Marie Swabey, *Comic Laughter: A Philosophical Essay* (New Haven, Conn.: Yale University Press, 1961), for example, locates agonistic aspects of comic experience within a controlling framework of the rules of logic: "Admittedly the discovery and creation of the comical is like inventing and taking part in a game. Participation in it involves a kind of sport, a contest of skill, acceptance of a set of rules or what is called today more abstractly a postulational system. Success with such a system involves committing oneself both to a freely chosen, local set of conventions and to the necessary, inclusive principles of rationality" (pp. 17–18).

38. Wolfgang Iser, *The Act of Reading: A Theory of Aesthetic Response* (Baltimore: Johns Hopkins University Press, 1978), p. 21.

39. In *The Implied Reader: Patterns of Communication in Prose Fiction from Bunyan to Beckett* (Baltimore: Johns Hopkins University Press, 1974), Iser performs something of a theoretical balancing act between an objective text and an infinite multiplicity of subjective responses. His Implied Reader is a construct of the virtual life of the text, which "incorporates both the prestructuring of the potential meaning by the text, and the reader's actualization of this potential through the reading process" (p. xii). The project of criticism, apparently, is to divine the Implied Reader's reading.

40. Ibid., pp. 30–31.

41. Ibid., p. 48.

42. Ibid., p. 52.

Bibliography

Primary Sources (before 1850)

"An Account of Joseph Haydn, a Celebrated Composer of Music." *European Magazine, and London Review for October, 1784*, 252–54. German translation in *Magazin der Musik*, ed. Carl Friedrich Cramer, 2 (7 April 1785): 585–94.

ADDISON, JOSEPH. *Freeholder*, no. 45. London, 1716. Essays on Wit, no. 1. [Los Angeles]: Augustan Reprint Society, 1946.

ALISON, ARCHIBALD. *Essays on the Nature and Principles of Taste*. Dublin, 1790.

Allgemeine deutsche Bibliothek. Edited by Christoph Friedrich Nicolai. Berlin-Stettin, 1766–96.

Allgemeine musikalische Zeitung. Leipzig, 1798–1848.

Almanach der deutschen Musen. Leipzig, 1770–81.

Almanach des muses. Paris, 1765–1833.

ANDRÉ, YVES MARIE. *L'essai sur le beau*. Paris, 1741; rev. ed., 1763. In *Oeuvres philosophiques du Père André*, edited by Victor Cousin, 77–96. Paris, 1843.

ARISTOTLE. *The Poetics*. Translated by Hamilton Fyfe. London: Heinemann, 1927.

[ARNOLD, IGNAZ FERDINAND CAJETAN.] *Gallerie der berühmtesten Tonkünstler des 18. und 19. Jahrhunderts*. Erfurt, 1810; 2d ed. 1816.

———. *Joseph Haydn, seine kurze Biographie und aesthetische Darstellung seiner Werke: Bildungsbuch für junge Tonkünstler*. Erfurt, 1810; 2d ed. 1825.

ASH, JOHN. *The New and Complete Dictionary of the English Language*. 2d ed. 2 vols. London, 1795.

BAILEY, NATHAN. *New Universal Etymological English Dictionary*. 2d ed. London, 1755.

BEATTIE, JAMES. *Essays on Poetry and Music as They Affect the Mind; On Laughter and Ludicrous Composition; On the Usefulness of Classical Learning*. Edinburgh, 1776. 3d ed. London, 1779.

Berlinische musikalische Zeitung. Edited by Johann Gottlieb Karl Spazier. Berlin, 1793–94.

"Bescheidene Anfrage an die modernsten Komponisten und Virtuosen." *AMZ* 1, no. 10 (5 December 1798), cols. 141–44; 152–55.

BLACKMORE, SIR RICHARD. *Essay Upon Wit* (1716). Augustan Reprint Society, Series 1: Essays on Wit, no. 1 (May, 1946).

BROWN, JOHN. *Dissertation on the Rise, Union, and Power, the Progressions, Separations, and Corruptions of Poetry and Music.* London, 1763. Reprint. New York: Garland, 1971.

BURGH, ALLATSON. *Anecdotes of Music, Historical and Biographical, in a Series of Letters from a Gentleman to his Daughter.* 3 vols. London, 1814. Translated into German by C. F. Michaelis as *Anekdoten und Bemerkungen, Musik betreffend.* Leipzig, 1820.

BURNEY, CHARLES. *A General History of Music from the Earliest Ages to the Present Period.* 4 vols. 1776–89. 2d ed. London, 1789. Edited by Frank Mercer. 2 vols. New York: Harcourt, Brace, 1935. Reprint. New York: Dover, 1957.

BURROWES, REV. ROBERT. *On Style in Writing, Considered with Respect to Thoughts and Sentiments as Well as Words, and Indicating the Writer's Peculiar and Characteristic Disposition, Habits and Powers of Mind.* London, 1793–94.

[BUTLER, CHARLES.] *Reminiscences of Charles Butler, Esq. of Lincoln Inn: With a Letter to a Lady on Ancient and Modern Music.* 4th ed. New York, 1825.

CAMPBELL, GEORGE. *The Philosophy of Rhetoric.* Edinburgh, 1757. Reprint. Carbondale, Ill.: Southern Illinois University Press, 1988.

CARPANI, GIUSEPPE. *Le Haydine ovvero lettere su la vita e le opere del celebre maestro Giuseppe Haydn.* Milan, 1812. 2d ed. Padua, 1823.

[CHESTERFIELD] STANHOPE, PHILIP DORMER, 4th Earl of Chesterfield. *The Letters of Philip Dormer Stanhope, 4th Earl of Chesterfield.* Edited by Bonamy Dobrée. London: Eyre & Spottiswoode, 1932.

CHORON, ALEXANDRE, and F. J. FAYOLLE. "Joseph Haydn." In *Dictionnaire historique des musiciens, artistes et amateurs, morts ou vivans. . . .* 2 vols. Paris, 1810–11.

COMPAN, CHARLES. *Dictionnaire de la danse.* Paris, 1787.

COOPER, JOHN GILBERT. *Letters Concerning Taste.* 3d ed. London, 1757.

CRAMER, CARL FRIEDRICH, ed. *Magazin der Musik.* Hamburg, 1783–86. Reprint. Hildesheim: Georg Olms, 1971.

CROTCH, WILLIAM. *Substance of Several Courses of Lectures on Music, Read in the University of Oxford and in the Metropolis.* London, 1831.

DIES, ALBERT CHRISTOPH. *Biographische Nachrichten von Joseph Haydn.* Vienna, 1810. Edited by Horst Seeger. Kassel: Bärenreiter, 1964. Translated by Vernon Gotwals in *Haydn: Two Contemporary Portraits.* Madison: University of Wisconsin Press, 1968.

DITTERSDORF, KARL DITTERS VON. *Lebensbeschreibung, seinem Sohn in die Feder diktiert, 1801.* Vienna, 1810. Translated by A. D. Coleridge as *The Autobiography of Karl von Dittersdorf Dictated to his Son.* London: Richard Bentley, 1896.

———. "Über die Grenzen des Komischen und des Heroischen in der Musik." *AMZ* 1, no. 9 (28 November 1798): cols. 139–41.

[———?] "Von dem Wienerischen Geschmack in der Musik," *Wiener Diarium,* no. 26 (18 October 1766).

DUFF, WILLIAM. *An Essay on Original Genius.* London, 1767. Reprint. Gainesville, Fla.: Scholars' Facsimiles and Reprints, 1964.

Edinburgh Magazine, or Literary Miscellany. Edinburgh, 1783–91; n.s. 1793+.

"An Essay on Humour." London, 1741. In *The Repository: A Select Collection of Fugitive Pieces of Wit and Humour in Prose and Verse by the Most Eminent Writers,* edited by Isaac Reed. 2 vols. London, 1777. 2d ed. 1789.

"An Essay on Humour, Translated from the German." *Literary Magazine and British Review* 2 (June 1789): 433–37 (misprinted 453–57).

An Essay on Laughter, Wherein are Displayed, Its Natural and Moral Causes, with the Arts of Exciting It. London, 1769.

Essay on Wit. London, 1748. Essays on Wit, no. 2. [Los Angeles]: Augustan Reprint Society, 1946.

European Magazine and London Review. London, 1782+.

FELDTENSTEIN, C. J. VON. *Die Kunst nach der Choreographie zu tänzen und Tänze zu schreiben.* Braunschweig, 1767.

———. *Erweiterung der Kunst nach der Choreographie zu Tänzen....* Braunschweig, 1772.

FIELDING, HENRY. "Essay on Humour." *The Covent Garden Journal* no. 19 (17 March 1752). Reprint in *Edinburgh Magazine, or Literary Miscellany* 18 (1801): 411–13.

———. *The History of the Adventures of Joseph Andrews, and of His Friend Mr. Abraham Adams.* London, 1742. Edited by Irvin Ehrenpreis. New York: New American Library, 1960.

FORKEL, JOHANN NIKOLAUS, ed. *Musikalischer Almanach für Deutschland.* 4 vols. Leipzig, 1782–84, 1789.

———. *Musikalisch-kritische Bibliothek.* Gotha, 1778–79.

FRAMERY, NICHOLAS ETIENNE, ed. *Journal de musique.* Paris, 1770–74, 1777.

GALLINI, GIOVANNI ANDREA. *A Treatise on the Art of Dancing.* London, 1762. Reprint. New York: Broude Brothers, 1967.

Gentleman's Magazine, and Historical Chronicle. London, 1731+.

GERARD, ALEXANDER. *An Essay on Genius.* London, 1774. Reprint. New York, Garland, 1970.

———. *An Essay on Taste.* London, 1759. 3d ed. 1780. Reprint. Gainesville, Fla.: Scholars' Facsimiles and Reprints, 1963.

GERBER, ERNST LUDWIG. "Eine freundliche Vorstellung über gearbeitete Instrumentalmusik, besonders über Symphonien." AMZ 15, no. 28 (14 July 1813): cols. 457–63.

———. "Etwas über den sogennanten Musikalischen Styl." AMZ 1, no. 20 (13 February 1799): cols. 305–12.

———. *Historisch-biographisches Lexikon der Tonkünstler.* 2 vols. Leipzig, 1790–92.

———. *Neues historisch-biographisches Lexikon der Tonkünstler.* 4 vols. Leipzig, 1812–14.

GOETHE, JOHANN WOLFGANG VON. *Italienische Reise, Zweiter Aufenthalt in Rom.* 1788. Translated as *Italian Journey* by Robert R. Heitner, and edited by Thomas P. Saine and Jeffrey L. Sammons. New York: Suhrkamp, 1989.

GOLDSMITH, OLIVER. "A Comparison between Laughing and Sentimental Comedy." *The Westminster Magazine,* 1773. Reprint. *European Magazine and Monthly Review,* February 1786, 97–98.

GRIESINGER, GEORG AUGUST. *Biographische Notizen über Joseph Haydn.* Leipzig, 1810. Edited by Franz Grasberger (Vienna: Paul Kaltschmid, 1954). Translated by

Vernon Gotwals in *Haydn: Two Contemporary Portraits*. Madison: University of Wisconsin Press, 1963.

HAWKINS, SIR JOHN. *A General History of the Science and Practice of Music*. 5 vols. London, 1776.

HAZLITT, WILLIAM. *Lectures on the English Comic Writers*. London, 1818. 3d. ed. London: John Templeman, 1841.

HILLER, JOHANN ADAM. *Lebensbeschreibungen berühmter Musikgelehrten und Tonkünstler neuerer Zeit*. Part 1. Leipzig, 1784.

———, ed. *Wöchentliche Nachrichten und Anmerkungen die Musik betreffend*. 4 vols. Leipzig, 1766–1770. Vol. 4: *Musikalische Nachrichten und Anmerkungen auf das Jahr 1770*. Reprint. Hildesheim: Georg Olms, 1970.

HOME, HENRY, LORD KAMES. *Elements of Criticism*. Edinburgh, 1762. "New edition" by Abraham Mills. New York: Sheldon, 1883.

HUME, DAVID. "Of the Standard of Taste." *Four Dissertations*. London, 1757. Reprint. New York: Garland, 1970.

HUTCHESON, FRANCIS. "Reflections upon Laughter." *Dublin Journal*, no. 11 (12 June 1725). In *Eighteenth-Century Critical Essays*, edited by Scott Elledge, 1:382–86. Ithaca, N.Y.: Cornell University Press, 1961.

JACKSON, WILLIAM. "On Wit." In *The Four Ages, Together with Essays on Various Subjects*. London, 1798. Reprint. New York: Garland, 1970.

———. *Observations on the Present State of Music in London*. Dublin, 1791.

JOHNSON, SAMUEL. *A Dictionary of the English Language*. 2 vols. London, 1755.

———. *The Lives of the English Poets*. London, 1779–81. Edited by George B. Hill. 3 vols. Oxford: Clarendon Press, 1905.

———, ed. *The Rambler*. London, 1750–52. London: Jones, 1825.

JONES, REV. WILLIAM. *Treatise on the Art of Music*. London, 1784.

JUNKER, KARL LUDWIG. *Zwanzig Componisten: Eine Skizze*. Bern, 1776. Published anonymously as *Portfeuille für Musikliebhaber: Characteristik von 20 Componisten*. Leipzig, 1792.

———, ed. *Musikalischer Almanach auf das Jahr 1782*. Alethinopel [Leipzig], 1782.

KAMES, LORD. *See* Henry Home.

KANT, IMMANUEL. *Critique of Aesthetic Judgement*. Translated by James Creed Meredith. Oxford: Clarendon Press, 1911.

———. *Gesammelte Schriften*. Edited by Königlich Preussische Akademie der Wissenschaften. Berlin: G. Reimer, 1910.

KINDLEBEN, CHRISTIAN WILHELM. *Student-Lexikon*. Halle, 1781.

KOCH, HEINRICH CHRISTOPH, ed. *Journal der Tonkunst*. Braunschweig and Erfurt, 1795.

———. *Kurzgefaßtes Handwörterbuch der Musik*. Erfurt, 1807. Reprint. Hildesheim: George Olms, 1981.

———. *Musikalisches Lexikon*. Frankfurt am Main, 1802. Reprint. Hildesheim: George Olms, 1964.

———. *Versuch einer Anleitung zur Composition*, vol. 3. Leipzig, 1793. Reprint. Hildesheim: Georg Olms, 1969. Translated by Nancy Kovaleff Baker as *Introductory Essay on Composition*. New Haven: Yale University Press, 1983.

KOLLMANN, AUGUST F. *An Essay on Musical Harmony.* . . . London, 1796.

KÜTTNER, CHARLES GOTTLOB, and WILLIAM NICHOLSON. *New and Complete Dic-*

tionary of the German Language for Englishmen According to the German Diction-
ary of Mr. J. C. Adelung. 3 vols. Leipzig, 1805.

Literary Magazine and British Review. London, 1788–94.
LOCKE, JOHN. *An Essay Concerning Human Understanding.* London, 1690. Edited by
Alexander Campbell Fraser. New York: Dover, 1959.

MATTHESON, JOHANN. *Der vollkommene Capellmeister.* Hamburg, 1739. Translated
and edited by Ernest C. Harriss. Ann Arbor, Mich.: UMI Research Press, 1981.
MEIER, GEORG FRIEDRICH. *Gedanken von Scherzen.* 2d ed. 1754. Anonymously trans-
lated as *Thoughts on Jesting.* London, 1764. Edited by Joseph Jones. Austin: Univer-
sity of Texas Press, 1947.
Mercure de France. Paris, 1672+.
MICHAELIS, CHRISTIAN FRIEDRICH. *Über den Geist der Tonkunst mit Rücksicht auf
Kants Kritik den aesthetischen Urteilskraft.* 2 vols. Leipzig, 1795–1800.
———. "Über das Humoristische oder Launige in der musikalischen Komposition."
AMZ 9, no. 46 (12 August 1807): cols. 725–29.
Monthly Magazine and British Register. London, 1796+.
The Monthly Review. London, 1749–1789.
The Morning Chronicle. London, 1791+.
MORRIS, CORBYN. *An Essay towards Fixing the True Standards of Wit, Humour, Rail-
lery, Satire, and Ridicule.* London, 1744. Essays on Wit, no. 4. [Los Angeles]: Augus-
tan Reprint Society, 1947. 2d reprint. New York: Garland, 1970.
Musikalische Real-Zeitung für das Jahr 1788 [1789, 1790]. Berlin.

NÄGELI, HANS GEORG. *Vorlesungen über Musik mit Berücksichtigung der Dilettanten.*
Stuttgart and Tübingen, 1826. Reprint. Darmstadt: Wissenschaftliche Buchgesell-
schaft, 1983.
NICOLAI, FRIEDRICH. *Beschreibung einer Reise durch Deutschland und die Schweiz, im
Jahre 1781: Nebst Bemerkungen über Gelehrsamkeit, Industrie, Religion und Sitten.*
12 vols. Berlin and Stettin, 1783–96.
NOVALIS [Friedrich von Hardenberg]. *Vermischte Bemerkungen.* 1797. Selections
translated in *German Aesthetic and Literary Criticism: The Romantic Ironists and
Goethe,* edited by Kathleen M. Wheeler, 84–92. Cambridge: Cambridge University
Press, 1984.

PAULI, CHARLES. *Elémens de la danse.* Leipzig, 1756.
PETRI, JOHANN SAMUEL. *Anleitung zur praktischen Musik.* 2d ed. Leipzig, 1782.

QUANTZ, JOHANN JOACHIM. *Versuch einer Anweisung die Flöte traversiere zu spielen.*
Berlin, 1752. 2d ed. 1780. 3d ed. 1789. Translated by Edward R. Reilly as *On Playing
the Flute.* London: Faber & Faber, 1966.

RAMEAU, PIERRE. *Le maître à danser.* Paris, 1725.
REED, ISAAC, ed. *The Repository: A Select Collection of Fugitive Pieces of Wit and
Humour in Prose and Verse by the Most Eminent Writers.* 2 vols. London, 1777. 2d
ed. 1789.
REICHARDT, JOHANN FRIEDRICH. *Briefe eines aufmerksam Reisenden die Musik betref-
fend.* Frankfurt and Leipzig, 1774–76.
———. *Vertraute Briefe geschrieben auf einer Reise nach Wien und den österreichischen*

Staaten zu Ende des Jahres 1808 und zu Anfang 1809. 2 vols. Amsterdam: Im Kunst und Industrie-Comtoir, 1810.

———, ed. *Musikalischer Almanach für Deutschland.* Berlin, 1796.

———, ed. *Musikalisches Kunstmagazin.* Berlin, 1782, 1791.

———, ed. *Musikalisches Wochenblatt.* Berlin, 1791–92. Continued as *Musikalische Monathsschrift.* Berlin, 1792. Both titles reprinted as *Studien für Tonkünstler und Musikfreunde.* Berlin, 1793.

RICHARDSON, WILLIAM. *Essays on Shakespeare's Dramatic Character of Sir John Falstaff.* London, 1788.

ROBERTSON, THOMAS. *An Inquiry into the Fine Arts.* Vol. 1. *Of Music.* London, 1784. Reprint. New York: Garland, 1971.

ROUSSEAU, JEAN-JACQUES. *Dictionnaire de musique.* 2 vols. Geneva, 1767. 2d ed. Paris and Amsterdam, 1768. Reprint. Hildesheim: Georg Olms, 1969.

SCHILLER, FRIEDRICH VON. *On the Aesthetic Education of Man.* 1795. Translated by Reginald Snell. New York: Ungar, 1974.

———. *Naive and Sentimental Poetry.* 1795–96. Translated by Julius A. Elias. New York: Ungar, 1984.

[SCHÖNFELD, JOHANN F. VON.] "Haiden, Joseph." *Jahrbuch der Tonkunst von Wien und Prag* (Vienna, 1796): 20–23. Reprint. Munich: E. Katzbichler, 1976.

SCHUBART, CHRISTIAN FRIEDRICH DANIEL. *Ideen zu einer Aesthetik der Tonkunst* [1784–85]. Edited by Ludwig Schubart. Vienna, 1806.

SHAFTESBURY, ANTHONY ASHLEY COOPER, 3d Earl of. "*Sensus Communis,* An Essay on the Freedom of Wit and Humour" [1709]. In *Characteristics of Men, Manners, Opinions, Times.* London, 1711, rev. ed. 1714. Edited by John M. Robertson. Indianapolis: Bobbs Merrill, 1964.

SMITH, ADAM. *Essays on Philosophical Subjects.* London, 1795.

SMITH, REV. SYDNEY. "Lectures on Wit and Humor." In *Elementary Sketches of Moral Philosophy delivered at the Royal Institution, London, 1804–6.* Reprint in *Wit and Wisdom of the Rev. Sydney Smith,* edited by Evert A. Duyckinck. New York: Redfield, 1856.

SPAZIER, JOHANN GOTTLIEB KARL. "Über Menuetten in Sinfonien." *Musikalisches Wochenblatt* 2, no. 12 (1792): 91–92.

STEIN, K. [Keferstein, pseud.] "Versuch über das Komische in der Musik." *Caecelia* 15, no. 60 (1834): 221–66.

STEINBART, GOTTHILD SAMUEL. *Grundbegriffe zur Philosophie über den Geschmack.* Zullichau, 1785.

STENDHAL [Marie Henri Beyle]. *The Lives of Haydn, Mozart and Metastasio.* Translated by Richard N. Coe. London: Calder-Boyers, 1972.

STEWART, DUGALD. *Elements of the Philosophy of the Human Mind.* 2 vols. Edinburgh, 1792. 2d ed. Boston, 1814.

STOCKHAUSEN, JOHANN CHRISTOPH. *Critischer Entwurf einer auserlesenen Bibliothek für die Liebhaber der Philosophie und schönen Wissenschaft.* 4th ed. Berlin, 1771.

SULZER, JOHANN GEORG. *Allgemeine Theorie der schönen Künste.* 2 vols. Leipzig, 1771–74. Rev. ed. 4 vols. 1792–97. Reprint of the rev. ed., Hildesheim: Georg Olms, 1967–70.

SWIFT, JONATHAN. *Poems of Jonathan Swift.* Edited by Harold Williams. 3 vols. Oxford: Clarendon Press, 1937.

TAUBERT, GOTTFRIED. *Rechtschaffender Tanzmeister.* . . . Leipzig, 1717.

[THRALE,] HESTER LYNCH PIOZZI. *British Synonymy.* Dublin, 1794.

TOMLINSON, KELLOM. *The Art of Dancing Explained.* . . . London, 1735.

TRIEST, JOHANN KARL FRIEDRICH. "Bemerkungen über die Ausbildung der Tonkunst in Deutschland im achtzehnten Jahrhundert." *AMZ* 3, in consecutive installments from nos. 14 (1 January 1801) to 19 (4 February 1801) and 22 (25 February 1801) to 26 (25 March 1801).

TRUSLER, JOHN. *The Difference Between Words Esteemed Synonymous.* London, 1766. Rev. ed. 2 vols. London, 1783. Reprint. Menston, England: Scholar Press, 1970.

VOGLER, ABBÉ GEORG JOSEPH. *Betrachtungen der Mannheimer Tonschule.* 3 vols. Mannheim, 1778–79. Reprint. 4 vols. Hildesheim: Georg Olms, 1974.

WEBB, DANIEL. *Observations on the Correspondence between Poetry and Music.* London, 1769.

WEBER, FRIEDRICH AUGUST. "Über komische Charakteristik und Karrikatur in praktischen Musikwerken." *AMZ* 3, no. 9 (26 November 1800): cols. 137–43; no. 10 (3 December 1800): cols. 157–62.

WENDEBORN, GEBHARD FRIEDRICH AUGUST. *A View of England towards the Close of the Eighteenth Century.* 2 vols. London, 1791.

Selected Secondary Sources

ABERT, ANNA AMALIE. "Johann Adam Hiller." *NGD* 8, pp. 464–68.

ABERT, HERMANN. *W. A. Mozart. Neubearbeitete und erweiterte Ausgabe von Otto Jahns "Mozart."* 2 vols. Leipzig: Breitkopf & Härtel, 1923–24.

ABRAMS, M. H. *The Mirror and the Lamp: Romantic Theory and the Critical Tradition.* New York: Oxford University Press, 1953.

ADORNO, THEODOR W. *Introduction to the Sociology of Music.* Translated by E. B. Ashton. New York: Seabury Press, 1976.

AGAWU, V. KOFI. *Playing with Signs: A Semiotic Interpretation of Classic Music.* Princeton, N.J.: Princeton University Press, 1991.

AIKEN, HENRY DAVID. "The Aesthetic Relevance of Belief." *JAAC* 9 (1950): 301–15.

AIKEN-SNEATH, BETSY. *Comedy in Germany in the First Half of the Eighteenth Century.* Oxford: Clarendon Press, 1936.

ALLANBROOK, WYE JAMISON. *Rhythmic Gesture in Mozart: "Le Nozze di Figaro" and "Don Giovanni."* Chicago: University of Chicago Press, 1983.

ANGERMÜLLER, RUDOLF. "Haydns 'Der Zerstreute' in Salzburg (1776)." *H-St* 4, no. 2 (1978): 85–93.

BADURA-SKODA, EVA. "The Influence of the Viennese Popular Comedy on Haydn and Mozart." *PRMA* 100 (1974): 185–99.

———, ed. *Joseph Haydn: Bericht über den Internationalen Joseph Haydn Kongreß, Wien Hofburg, 5.–12. September 1982.* Munich: G. Henle, 1986.

BAKER, NANCY KOVALEFF. "Heinrich Koch's Description of the Symphony." *StM* 9 (1980): 303–16.

BALET, LEO and EBERHARD REBLING, eds. *Die Verbürgerlichung der deutschen Kunst, Literatur und Musik im 18. Jahrhundert.* Frankfurt: Ullstein Materialien, 1981.

BARTHA, DÉNES. "Thematic Profile and Character in the Quartet-Finales of Joseph Haydn," *StM* 11 (1969): 35–62.

——. "Volkstanz-Stilisierung in Joseph Haydns Finale-Themen." In *Festschrift für Walter Wiora zum 30. Dezember 1966*, edited by Ludwig Finscher and Christoph-Hellmut Mahling, 375–84. Kassel: Bärenreiter, 1967.

——, ed. *Joseph Haydn: Gesammelte Briefe und Aufzeichnungen. Unter Benützung der Quellensammlung von H. C. Robbins Landon.* Kassel: Bärenreiter, 1965.

BARTHA, DÉNES, and LÁSZLÓ SOMFAI. *Haydn als Opernkapellmeister.* Budapest: Verlag der ungarischen Akademie der Wissenschaften, 1960.

BATE, W. JACKSON. *Samuel Johnson.* New York: Harcourt Brace Jovanovich, 1977.

BATESON, GREGORY. "The Message 'This is Play.'" In *Conference on Group Processes: Transactions of the Second Conference, October 9, 10, 11, and 12, 1955, Princeton, N.J.*, ed. Bertram Schaffner, 145–242. New York: Josiah Macy, Jr., Foundation, 1955.

——. "The Position of Humor in Human Communication." In *Cybernetics. Circular Causal and Feedback Mechanisms in Biological and Social Systems: Transactions of the Ninth Conference on Cybernetics, 1952*, ed. Heinz von Foerster, 1–47. New York: Josiah Macy, Jr., Foundation, 1953.

BAUMAN, THOMAS, "Courts and Municipalities in North Germany." In *The Classical Era, from the 1740s to the End of the 18th Century*, ed. Neal Zaslaw, 240–67. Englewood Cliffs, N.J.: Prentice-Hall, 1989.

——. "The Music Reviews in the *Allgemeine deutsche Bibliothek*," *Acta musicologica* 49 (1977): 69–85.

BEARDSLEY, MONROE C. *Aesthetics from Classical Greece to the Present: A Short History.* Tuscaloosa: University of Alabama Press, 1982.

BEENK, EUGENE L. "Ländler Elements in the Symphonic Minuets of Joseph Haydn." Ph.D. diss., University of Iowa, 1969.

BERGSON, HENRI. *Le rire.* Translated as *Laughter*, in *Comedy*, edited by Wylie Sypher, 61–190. Baltimore: Johns Hopkins University Press, 1956.

BERLYNE, DANIEL E. "Humor and Its Kin." In *The Psychology of Humor*, edited by Jeffrey H. Goldstein and Paul E. McGhee, 43–60. New York: Academic Press, 1972.

——. "Laughter, Humor, and Play." In *The Handbook of Social Psychology*, vol. 3, *The Individual in a Social Context*, edited by Gardner Lindzey and Elliot Aronson, 795–852. 2d ed. Reading, Mass.: Addison-Wesley, 1969.

BLUME, FRIEDRICH. "Joseph Haydns künstlerische Persönlichkeit in seinen Streichquartetten." *JbMP* 38 (1931): 24–48. Reprint in *Syntagma musicologicum*, edited by Martin Ruhnke, 526–51. Kassel: Bärenreiter, 1963.

BONDS, MARK EVAN. "Haydn, Laurence Sterne, and the Origins of Musical Irony." *JAMS* 41 (1991): 57–91.

——. "Haydn's False Recapitulations and the Perception of Sonata Form in the Eighteenth Century." Ph.D. diss., Harvard University, 1988.

BOOTH, WAYNE C. "Metaphor as Rhetoric: The Problem of Evaluation." In *On Metaphor*, edited by Sheldon Sacks, 47–70. Chicago: University of Chicago Press, 1981.

BÖRNER, WOLFGANG. "'Was eine Sache nicht im ersten Moment enthüllt': Die Pariser Sinfonien von Joseph Haydn." *Musik und Gesellschaft* 32, no. 3 (1982): 135–40.

BORRIS, SIEGFRIED. "Das Lächeln der Melpomene: Betrachtungen über das Komische in der Musik." In *Festschrift für einen Verlager: Ludwig Strecker zum 90. Geburtstag*, edited by Carl Dahlhaus, 111–18. Mainz: B. Schott's Söhne, 1973.

BROWN, A. PETER. "Critical Years for Haydn's Instrumental Music: 1787–1790." *MQ* 62 (1976): 374–94.

——. "The Earliest English Biography of Haydn." *MQ* 59 (1973): 339–54.

——. *Joseph Haydn's Keyboard Music: Sources and Style.* Bloomington: Indiana University Press, 1986.

BROYLES, MICHAEL. "Organic Form and the Binary Repeat." *MQ* 66 (1980): 339–60.
BRUCE, I. M. "Calculated Unpredictability in Beethoven's Sonata-Designs." *Soundings* 1 (1970): 36–53.
BRUFORD, WALTER. *Germany in the Eighteenth Century: The Social Background of the Literary Revival.* Cambridge: Cambridge University Press, 1965.

CAMPIANU, EVA. "Die Tänze der Haydn-Zeit." In *JHK 1982*, 470–75
CAZAMIAN, LOUIS. *The Development of English Humor.* Durham, N.C.: Duke University Press, 1952.
CHAPMAN, ANTONY J. and Hugh C. Foot, eds. *It's a Funny Thing, Humour: International Conference on Humour and Laughter, 1976.* New York: Pergamon Press, 1977.
CHEW, GEOFFREY. "The Night-Watchman's Song Quoted by Haydn and Its Implications." *H-St* 3, no. 2 (1974): 106–24.
CHURGIN, BATHIA. "The Symphony as Described by J. A. P. Schulz (1774): A Commentary and Translation." *CM* 29 (1980): 7–16.
CLIFTON, THOMAS. *Music as Heard: A Study in Applied Phenomenology.* New Haven, Conn.: Yale University Press, 1983.
COHEN, TED. "Jokes." In *Pleasure, Preference and Value: Studies in Philosophical Aesthetics*, edited by Eva Schaper, 120–36. Cambridge: Cambridge University Press, 1987.
———. "Metaphor and the Cultivation of Intimacy." In *On Metaphor*, edited by Sheldon Sacks, 1–10. Chicago: University of Chicago Press, 1981.
COLE, MALCOLM S. "Rondos, Proper and Improper." *ML* 51 (1970): 388–99.
———. "The Vogue of the Instrumental Rondo in the Late Eighteenth Century." *JAMS* 22 (1969): 425–55.
CONE, EDWARD T. *The Composer's Voice.* Berkeley and Los Angeles: University of California Press, 1974.
———. *Musical Form and Musical Performance.* New York: Norton, 1968.
———. "The Uses of Convention: Stravinsky and His Models." *MQ* 48 (1962): 287–99. Reprint in *Music: A View from Delft*, edited by Robert P. Morgan, 281–92. Chicago: University of Chicago Press, 1989.
CORRIGAN, ROBERT W. "Comedy and the Comic Spirit." In *Comedy: Meaning and Form*, edited by Robert W. Corrigan, 1–11. Scranton, Pa.: Chandler, 1965.

DAHLHAUS, CARL. *Esthetics of Music.* Translated by William Austin. Cambridge: Cambridge University Press, 1982.
———. "Some Models of Unity in Musical Form." *JMT* 19 (1975): 2–30.
DAMROSCH, LEOPOLD, Jr. "Samuel Johnson and Reader-Response Criticism." *The Eighteenth Century: Theory and Interpretation* 21, no. 2 (Spring 1980): 91–108.
DAVERIO, JOHN. "Schumann's 'Im Legendenton' and Friedrich Schlegel's *Arabeske*." *19th-Century Music* 11 (1987): 150–63.
DEUTSCH, WALTER. "Volkslied und Geniemusik: Ein Beitrag zur Darstellung ihrer Beziehungen im Werke J. Haydns." *Jahrbuch des österreichischen Volksliedwerkes* 8 (1959): 1–9.
———. "'Volkstümliche' Wirkungen in der Musik Joseph Haydns." *Musikerziehung* 14 (1960): 88–92.
DOUGLAS, MARY. "Jokes." In *Implicit Meanings: Essays in Anthopology*, 90–114. London: Routledge & Kegan Paul, 1975.
DURANT, JOHN and JONATHAN MILLER, eds. *Laughing Matters: A Serious Look at Hu-*

mor: *Proceedings of the 1987 Meeting of the British Association for the Advancement of Science.* London: Longman Scientific & Technical and John Wiley & Sons, 1989.

EASTMAN, MAX. *Enjoyment of Laughter.* New York: Simon & Schuster, 1936.

EGGEBRECHT, HANS. "Der Begriff des Komischen in der Musikaesthetik des 18. Jahrhunderts." *Mf* 4 (1951): 144–52.

———, ed. *Handwörterbuch der musikalischen Terminologie.* Wiesbaden: Franz Steiner Verlag, 1972–.

EHRMANN, JACQUES, ed. *Game, Play, Literature.* Originally published as special issue, *Yale French Studies* 41 (1968). Reprint. Boston: Beacon Press, 1971.

ELLEDGE, SCOTT, ed. *Eighteenth-Century Critical Essays.* 2 vols. Ithaca, N.Y.: Cornell University Press, 1961.

ELSCHEK, OSKAR. "Problem of Variation in 18th-Century Slovak Folk Music Manuscripts." *StM* 7 (1965): 47–59.

EMPSON, WILLIAM. *The Structure of Complex Words.* London: Chatto & Windus, 1951.

ENGLISH, JAMES F. "The Laughing Reader: A New Direction for Studies of the Comic." *Genre* 19 (1986): 129–54.

EPSTEIN, DAVID. *Beyond Orpheus: Studies in Musical Structure.* Cambridge: MIT Press, 1979.

FABIAN, BERNHARD. "English Books and Their German Readers." In *The Widening Circle: Essays on the Circulation of Literature in 18th-Century Europe,* edited by Paul Korshin, 117–96. Philadelphia: University of Pennsylvania Press, 1976.

FARB, PETER. "Speaking Seriously about Humor." *Massachusetts Review* 22, no. 4 (Winter 1981): 760–76.

FEDER, GEORG. "Haydns Paukenschlag und andere Überraschungen." *ÖMz* 21 (1966): 5–8.

———. "Joseph Haydn als Mensch und Musiker." *ÖMz* 27 (1972): 57–68.

———. "Ein vergessener Haydn-Brief," *H-St* 1, no. 2 (1966): 114–16.

———. [Work-list]. In *The New Grove Haydn,* 122–208. New York: Norton, 1982.

FEDER, GEORG, HEINRICH HÜSCHEN, and ULRICH TANK, eds. *Joseph Haydn: Tradition und Rezeption: Bericht über die Jahrestagung der Gesellschaft für Musikforschung, Köln, 1982.* Regensburg: Gustav Bosse, 1985.

FELLERER, KARL G. "Zum Joseph-Haydn-Bild im frühen 19. Jahrhundert." In *Anthony van Hoboken: Festschrift zum 75. Geburtstag,* edited by Joseph Schmidt-Görg, 73–86. Mainz: B. Schott's Söhne, 1962.

FINSCHER, LUDWIG. *Studien zur Geschichte des Streichquartetts.* Vol. 1. *Die Entstehung des klassischen Streichquartetts: Von den Vorformen zur Grundlegung durch Joseph Haydn.* Saarbrücker Studien zur Musikwissenschaft, ed. Walter Wiora, no. 3. Kassel: Bärenreiter, 1974.

FISH, STANLEY. "Literature in the Reader: Affective Stylistics." In *Is There a Text in This Class? The Authority of Interpretive Communities,* 21–67. Cambridge: Harvard University Press, 1980.

FISHER, STEPHEN, C. "Haydn's Overtures and their Adaptations as Concert Orchestral Works." Ph.D. diss., University of Pennsylvania, 1985.

FLOTZINGER, RUDOLF, and GERNOT GRUBER. "Die Wiener Klassik und ihre Zeit." In *Musikgeschichte Österreichs* 2:152–53. Graz: Verlag Styria, 1979.

FREUD, SIGMUND. *Jokes and Their Relation to the Unconscious.* Translated and edited by James Strachey. New York: Norton, 1963.

FREUND, ELIZABETH. *The Return of the Reader: Reader-Response Criticism.* New York: Methuen, 1987.

GADAMER, HANS-GEORG. *The Relevance of the Beautiful and Other Essays.* Translated by Nicholas Walker. Edited by Robert Bernasconi. Cambridge: Cambridge University Press, 1987.

GEIRINGER, KARL. *Haydn: A Creative Life in Music.* New York: Norton, 1946. Rev. ed. Berkeley and Los Angeles: University of California Press, 1968.

GILBERT, HENRY F. "Humor in Music." *MQ* 12 (1926): 40–55.

GMEINER, JOSEF. *Menuet und Scherzo: Ein Beitrag zur Entwicklungsgeschichte und Soziologie des Tanzsatzes in der Wiener Klassik.* Tutzing: Hans Schneider, 1979.

GOLDBERG, M. A. "Wit and the Imagination in Eighteenth-Century Aesthetics," *JAAC* 16 (1957–58): 503–9.

GOLDSTEIN, JEFFREY H., and PAUL E. MCGHEE, eds. *Handbook of Humour Research.* 2 vols. New York: Springer-Verlag, 1983.

GOTWALS, VERNON. "The Earliest Biographies of Haydn." *MQ* 45 (1959): 439–59.

———. *Haydn: Two Contemporary Portraits.* Madison: The University of Wisconsin Press, 1968. *See above,* "Primary Sources," Dies and Griesinger.

GRANT, KERRY S. *Dr. Charles Burney as Critic and Historian of Music.* Ann Arbor, Mich.: UMI Press, 1983.

GRAVE, FLOYD K., and MARGARET G. GRAVE. *In Praise of Harmony: The Teachings of Abbé Georg Joseph Vogler.* Lincoln: University of Nebraska Press, 1987.

GREEN, ROBERT A. " 'Il Distratto' of Regnard and Haydn: a re-examination." *HYb* 11 (1980): 183–95.

GRUHN, WILFRIED. "Wie heiter ist die Kunst? Semiologische Aspekte musikalischer Komik." *ÖMz* 38 (1983): 677–88.

GÜLKE, PETER. "Nahezu ein Kant der Musik." *Musik-Konzepte* 41: *Joseph Haydn* (1985): 67–73.

HADOW, SIR WILLIAM HENRY. *A Croatian Composer: Notes toward the Study of Joseph Haydn.* London: Seeley, 1897. Reprint. Freeport, N.Y.: Books for Libraries, 1972.

HALM, AUGUST. "Humor und Musik." In *Von Grenzen und Ländern der Musik: Gesammelte Aufsätze.* Munich: Georg Muller, 1916.

HANDELMAN, DON. "Play and Ritual: Complementary Frames of Meta-Communication." In *It's a Funny Thing, Humour,* edited by Antony J. Chapman and Hugh C. Foote, 185–92. New York: Pergamon Press, 1977.

HANNING, BARBARA R. "Conversation and Musical Style in the Late Eighteenth-Century Parisian Salon." *ECS* 22 (1989): 512–28.

HARICH, JÁNOS. "Das Repertoire des Opernkapellmeisters Joseph Haydn in Eszterháza (1780–1790)." *HYb* 1, no. 1 (1962): 9–110.

HEARTZ, DANIEL. "Ditters, Gluck und der Artikel 'Von dem wienerischen Geschmack in der Musik." *Kongreßbericht, Gluck in Wien: Wien, 12–16 November 1987,* edited by Gerhard Croll and Monika Woitas, 78–80. Kassel: Bärenreiter, 1989.

HEDGES, STEPHEN A. "Dice Music in the Eighteenth Century." *ML* 59 (1978): 180–87.

HERSHKOWITZ, AARON. "The Essential Ambiguity of, and in, Humour." In *It's a Funny Thing, Humour,* edited by Antony J. Chapman and Hugh C. Foote, 139–42. New York: Pergamon Press, 1977.

HEUSS, ALFRED. "Der Humor im letzten Satz von Haydns Oxford-Symphonie." *Die Musik* 12 (1912): 270–86.

HILTON, WENDY. *Dance of the Court and Theater: The French Noble Style 1690–1725.* n.p. Princeton Book Co., 1981.

HOBOKEN, ANTHONY VAN. *Joseph Haydn: Thematisch-bibliographisches Werkverzeichnis.* 3 vols. Mainz: B. Schotts Söhne, 1957–78.

HOHENEMSER, RICHARD. "Über Komik und Humor in der Musik." *JbMP,* 1917 (1918): 65–83.

HOOKER, EDWARD NILES. "The Discussion of Taste, from 1750 to 1770, and the New Trends in Literary Criticism." *PMLA* 49 (1934): 577–92.

———. "Humour in the Age of Pope." *Huntington Library Quarterly* 11 (1947–48): 361–85.

HORÁNYI, MÁTYÁS. *The Magnificence of Eszterháza.* Translated by András Deák. London: Barrie and Rockliff, 1962.

HOSLER, BELLAMY. *Changing Aesthetic Views of Instrumental Music in 18th-Century Germany.* Ann Arbor, Mich.: UMI Research Press, 1981.

HÜBLER, KLAUS K. "'Zusetzen, wegschneiden, wagen': Anmerkungen zu einigen 'Versuchen' Joseph Haydns." *Musik-Konzepte* 41: *Joseph Haydn* (January 1985): 24–46.

HUIZINGA, JOHAN. *Homo ludens: A Study of the Play Element in Culture.* Boston: Beacon Press, 1955.

HUTCHINSON, PETER. *Games Authors Play.* London: Methuen, 1983.

IRVING, HOWARD. "Haydn and Laurence Sterne: Similarities in Eighteenth-Century Literary and Musical Wit." *CM* 40 (1985): 34–49.

ISER, WOLFGANG. *The Act of Reading: A Theory of Aesthetic Response.* Baltimore: Johns Hopkins University Press, 1978.

———. *The Implied Reader: Patterns of Communication in Prose Fiction from Bunyan to Beckett.* Baltimore: Johns Hopkins University Press, 1974.

JACOBSON, BERNARD. "Once More with Feeling: A Polemic on Repeats." *Musical Newsletter* 7 (1977): 3–7.

JAUSS, HANS ROBERT. *Aesthetic Experience and Literary Hermeneutics.* Translated by Michael Shaw. Theory and History of Literature, no. 3. Minneapolis: University of Minnesota Press, 1982.

———. *Toward an Aesthetic of Reception.* Translated by Timothy Bahti. Theory and History of Literature, no. 2. Minneapolis: University of Minnesota Press, 1982.

JONES, DAVID WYN. "Haydn's Music in London in the Period 1760–1790" [Part 1]. *HYb* 14 (1983): 144–72.

KASSLER, MICHAEL. "On the Name of Haydn's 'Surprise' Symphony." *ML* 52 (1971): 106.

KEITH-SPIEGEL, PATRICIA. "Early Conceptions of Humor: Varieties and Issues." In *The Psychology of Humour,* edited by Jeffrey H. Goldstein and Paul E. McGhee, 4–39. New York: Academic Press, 1972.

KERMAN, JOSEPH. "Theories of Late Eighteenth-Century Music." In *Studies in Eighteenth-Century British Art and Aesthetics,* edited by Ralph Cohen, 217–44. Berkeley and Los Angeles: University of California Press, 1985.

KIRKENDALE, WARREN. *Fugue and Fugato in Rococo and Classical Chamber Music.* Rev. ed. Translated by the author and Margaret Bent. Durham, N.C.: Duke University Press, 1979.

KIRKPATRICK, RALPH. *Domenico Scarlatti.* Rev. ed. Princeton, N.J.: Princeton University Press, 1983.

KLIMA, SLAVA, GARRY BOWERS, and KERRY GRANT, eds. *Memoirs of Dr. Charles Burney, 1726–1769.* Lincoln: University of Nebraska Press, 1988.

KOESTLER, ARTHUR. *The Act of Creation: A Study of the Conscious and Unconscious in Science and Art.* New York: Dell, 1964.

KORSHIN, PAUL J. "Types of Literary Patronage." *ECS* 7 (1974): 453–73.

———, ed. *The Widening Circle: Essays on the Circulation of Literature in 18th-Century Europe.* Philadelphia: University of Pennsylvania Press, 1976.

KRAMER, JONATHAN D. *The Time of Music: New Meanings, New Temporalities, New Listening Strategies.* New York: Schirmer Books, 1988.

KRONES, HARTMUT. "Das 'hohe Komische' bei Joseph Haydn." *ÖMz* 38 (1983): 2–8.

KUCABA, JOHN. "Beethoven as Buffoon." *MR* 41 (1980): 103–20.

KUNZE, STEFAN. "Mozarts *Don Giovanni* und die Tanzszene im ersten Finale." *Analecta musica* 18 (1974): 172–77.

LAAF, ERNST. "Der musikalische Humor in Beethovens achter Symphonie." *AfMw* 19–20 (1962–63): 213–29.

LANDON, H. C. ROBBINS. *Haydn: Chronicle and Works.* 5 vols. Bloomington: Indiana University Press, 1976–80.

———. *The Symphonies of Joseph Haydn.* New York: Macmillan, 1956. *Supplement.* London: Barrie & Rockliff, 1961.

———, ed. *The Collected Correspondence and London Notebooks of Joseph Haydn.* London: Barrie and Rockliff; Fair Lawn, N.J.: Essential Books, 1959.

———, ed. *Joseph Haydn. Critical Edition of the Complete Symphonies.* 12 vols. Rev. ed. Vienna: Universal Edition, 1981.

LANGER, SUZANNE. *Feeling and Form.* New York: Scribner, 1953.

LANHAM, RICHARD A. *The Motives of Eloquence: Literary Rhetoric in the Renaissance.* New Haven, Conn.: Yale University Press, 1976.

———. *Tristram Shandy: The Games of Pleasure.* Berkeley and Los Angeles: University of California Press, 1973.

LARSEN, JENS PETER. *Die Haydn-Überlieferung.* Copenhagen: Einer Munksgaard, 1939. Reprint with foreword by the author. Munich: Kraus International, 1980.

———. *Drei Haydn Kataloge in Faksimile mit Einleitung und ergänzenden Themenverzeichnissen.* Copenhagen: Einar Munksgaard, 1941. Reprint. *Three Haydn Catalogues.* New York: Pendragon Press, 1979.

———. *Handel, Haydn, and the Viennese Classical Style.* Ann Arbor, Mich.: UMI Research Press, 1988.

———. "Some Observations on the Development and Characteristics of Vienna Classical Instrumental Music," *StM* 9 (1967): 115–39.

LARSEN, JENS PETER, and GEORG FEDER (work-list). *The New Grove Haydn.* New York: Norton, 1983.

LARSEN, JENS PETER, HOWARD SERWER, and JAMES WEBSTER, eds. *Haydn Studies. Proceedings of the International Haydn Conference, Washington, D.C., 1975.* New York: Norton, 1981.

LAURENCIE, LIONEL DE LA. "L'apparition des oeuvres d'Haydn à Paris." *Revue de musicologie* 16 (1932): 191–205.

LAUSBERG, HEINRICH. *Elemente der literarischen Rhetorik.* Rev. ed. Munich: Max Hueber, 1963.

LE HURAY, PETER and JAMES DAY. *Music and Aesthetics in the Eighteenth and Early-Nineteenth Centuries.* Cambridge: Cambridge University Press, 1981.

LEVY, JANET M. "Gesture, Form and Syntax in Haydn's Music," In *HS 1975*, 355–62.

———. "*Quatuor concertant* in Paris in the Latter Half of the Eighteenth Century." Ph.D. diss., Stanford University, 1971.

———. "Texture as a Sign in Classic and Early Romantic Music." *JAMS* 35 (1982): 482–531.

LEWIS, C. S. *Studies in Words.* Cambridge: Cambridge University Press, 1960.

LEWIS, PAUL. *Comic Effects: Interdisciplinary Approaches to Humor in Literature.* Albany: State University of New York Press, 1989.

LIPPS, THEODOR. *Komik und Humor.* 2d ed. Leipzig: Leopold Voss, 1922.

LISSA, ZOFIA. "Über das Komische in der Musik." In *Aufsätze zur Musikaesthetik*, 91–136. Berlin: Henschel, 1969.

LITTLE, MEREDITH ELLIS. "Minuet." *NGD*, 12:353–58.

LOFTIS, JOHN. *Comedy and Society from Congreve to Fielding.* Stanford Studies in Language and Literature, no. 19. Stanford, Calif.: Stanford University Press, 1959.

LOVEJOY, ARTHUR O. *The Great Chain of Being: A Study of the History of an Idea.* Cambridge: Harvard University Press, 1936.

LOWINSKY, EDWARD. "Taste, Style, and Ideology in Eighteenth-Century Music." In *Aspects of the Eighteenth Century*, edited by Earl R. Wasserman, 163–205. Baltimore: Johns Hopkins University Press, 1969.

LÜDEKE, R. "Joseph Haydn: Meistershaft und Popularität." In *Der Komponist und sein Adressat*, edited by Siegfried Bimberg, 107–12. Halle: Wissenschaftliche-Beiträge der Martin-Luther-Universität, 1976.

MACDONALD, HUGH. "To Repeat or Not to Repeat?" *PRMA* 111 (1984/85): 121–38.

MAHR, JUSTUS. "Tanzmusik auf Don Giovannis Schloss: Anmerkungen zum Ballfinale des ersten 'Don Giovanni'-Aktes." *Neue Zeitschrift für Musik* 127, no. 12 (1966): 473–78.

MALLOCH, WILLIAM. "Carl Czerny's Metronome Marks for Haydn and Mozart Symphonies." *EM* 16 (1988): 72–81.

———. "Toward a 'New' (Old) Minuet," *Opus* 1 (1985): 14–21.

MARKS, PAUL F. "Aesthetics of Music in the Philosophy of *Sturm und Drang*: Gerstenberg, Hamann and Herder," *MR* 35 (1974): 247–59.

MARTIN, ROBERT BERNARD. *The Triumph of Wit: A Study of Victorian Comic Theory.* Oxford: Clarendon Press, 1974.

MEYER, EVE. "The Viennese Divertimento." *MR* 29 (1968): 165–71.

MEYER, LEONARD B. *Emotion and Meaning in Music.* Chicago: University of Chicago Press, 1960.

———. *Explaining Music: Essays and Explorations.* Chicago: University of Chicago Press, 1973.

———. *Music, the Arts, and Ideas.* Chicago: University of Chicago Press, 1967.

———. *Style and Music: Theory, History, and Ideology.* Philadelphia: University of Pennsylvania Press, 1989.

MILBURN, D. JUDSON. *The Age of Wit, 1650–1750.* New York: Macmillan, 1966.

MILLAR, SUSANNA. *The Psychology of Play.* Baltimore: Penguin Books, 1969.

MILNER, G. B. "Homo Ridens: Towards a Semiotic Theory of Humour and Laughter," *Semiotica* 5 (1972): 1–30.

MISCH, LUDWIG. "Das Komische in der Musik." In *Neue Beethoven-Studien und andere Themen*, 211–22. Munich: G. Henle, 1967.

MOE, ORIN, Jr. "The Implied Model in Classical Music." *CM* 23 (1977): 46–55.
———. "The Significance of Haydn's Opus 33." In *HS 1975*, 445–50.
MONRO, D. H. *Argument of Laughter.* Melbourne, Australia: Melbourne University Press, 1951.
MÖRNER, STELLAN. *Joseph Haydn, musikens Humorist.* Stockholm: Lindfors, 1945.
MORREALL, JOHN. *Taking Laughter Seriously.* Albany: State University of New York Press, 1983.
———, ed. *The Philosophy of Laughter and Humor.* Albany: State University of New York Press, 1987.
MORROW, MARY SUE. *Concert Life in Haydn's Vienna.* Stuyvesant, N.Y.: Pendragon Press, 1989.
Mozart en France. Exhibition Catalogue. Paris: Bibliothèque Nationale, 1956.
MRAZ, GERDA, ed. *Joseph Haydn und seine Zeit.* Jahrbuch für österreichische Kulturgeschichte 2. Eisenstadt: Institut für österreichische Kulturgeschichte, 1972.

NEUBAUER, JOHN. *The Emancipation of Music from Language: Departure from Mimesis in Eighteenth-Century Aesthetics.* New Haven, Conn.: Yale University Press, 1986.
NEUMANN, FREDERICK. "How Fast Should Classical Minuets Be Played?" *Historical Performance* 4 (1991): 3–13.
NEWCOMB, ANTHONY. "Schumann and Late Eighteenth-Century Narrative Strategies." *19th-Century Music* 11 (1987): 164–74.
———. "Sound and Feeling." *Critical Inquiry* 10 (1984): 614–43.

O'BIERNE, THOMAS H. "940, 369, 969, 152: Dice-Music Trios." *MT* 109 (1968): 911–13.
OSSBERGER, HAROLD. "Musikalischer Humor an Beispielen der Klaviermusik." *ÖMz* 38 (1983): 696–701.

PANDI, MARIANNE and FRANZ SCHMIDT. "Musik zur Zeit Haydns und Beethovens in der Preßburger Zeitung." *HYb* 8 (1971): 165–293.
PAUL, STEPHEN E. "Comedy, Wit, and Humor in Haydn's Instrumental Music." In *HS 1975*, 450–56.
———. "Wit and Humour in the Operas of Haydn." In *JHK 1982*, 386–402.
———. "Wit, Comedy, and Humour in the Instrumental Music of Franz Joseph Haydn." Ph.D. diss., Cambridge University, 1980.
PENKERT, ANTON. "Die musikalische Formung von Witz und Humor." In *Kongreß für Aesthetik und allgemeine Kunstwissenschaft, Berlin 7.-9. Oktober 1913*, 482–89. Stuttgart: F. Enke, 1914.
PERRY-CAMP, JANE. "A Laugh a Minuet: Humor in Late Eighteenth-Century Music." *College Music Symposium* 19 (1970): 19–29.
PETERMANN, KURT. "Die deutschsprachigen Tanzlehrbücher des 18. und 19. Jahrhunderts als Quelle für den Volkstanz." In *Festschrift für Karl Horak*, edited by Manfred Schneider, 35–54. Innsbruck: Thaurdruck-Giesriegl, 1980.
PLUMB, J. H. "The Public, Literature, and the Arts in the Eighteenth Century." In *The Triumph of Culture: Eighteenth-Century Perspectives*, edited by Paul Fritz and David Williams. Toronto: A. M. Hakkert, 1972. Reprint in *The Emergence of Leisure*, edited by Michael R. Marrus, 11–27. New York: Harper Torchbooks, 1974.
POHL, CARL F. *Joseph Haydn.* Vol. 1. Berlin, 1875. Reprint. Leipzig, 1878. Vol. 2. Leip-

zig, 1882. Vol. 3 completed by Hugo Botstiber. Leipzig, 1927. Reprint. Vaduz, Liechtenstein: Sändig, 1970–84.

———. *Mozart und Haydn in London.* 2 vols. Vienna: Carl Garold's Sohn, 1867. Reprint. New York: Da Capo Press, 1971.

PRICE, LAWRENCE MARSDEN. *The Reception of English Literature in Germany in the 18th Century.* Berkeley and Los Angeles: University of California Press, 1932.

PRICE, MARJORIE B., and LAWRENCE MARSDEN Price. *Publications of English Literature in Germany in the 18th Century.* University of California Publications in Modern Philology, vol. 17. Berkeley and Los Angeles: University of California Press, 1934.

RATNER, LEONARD G. "*Ars combinatoria:* Chance and Choice in Eighteenth-century Music." In *Studies in 18th-Century Music: A Tribute to Karl Geiringer on his Seventieth Birthday,* edited by H. C. Robbins Landon and Roger E. Chapman, 343–63. New York: Oxford University Press, 1970.

———. *Classic Music: Expression, Form, and Style.* New York: Schirmer Books, 1980.

RAVIZZA, VICTOR. "Möglichkeiten des Komischen in der Musik. Der Letzte Satz des Streichquintetts in F dur, op. 88 von Johannes Brahms." *AfMw* 31 (1974): 137–50.

RICOEUR, PAUL. "The Metaphorical Process as Cognition, Imagination, and Feeling." *Critical Inquiry* 5 (1978). Reprint in *On Metaphor,* edited by Sheldon Sacks, 141–57. Chicago: University of Chicago Press, 1981.

ROBINSON, FRED MILLER. "Festivity and Invention in Comedy." *Massachusetts Review* 22 (1981): 595–99.

ROSEN, CHARLES. *The Classical Style: Haydn, Mozart, Beethoven.* New York: Viking Press, 1971.

———. *Sonata Forms.* New York: Norton, 1980.

ROUTLEDGE, JOYCE S. "The Delayed Reflex: Journalism in Josephinian Vienna." *Studies in Eighteenth-Century Culture* 9 (1979): 79–92.

RUDOLF, MAX. "Inner Repeats in the Da Capo of Classical Minuets and Scherzos." *Journal of the Conductor's Guild* 3 (1982): 145–50.

RUSSELL, TILDEN A. "Minuet, Scherzando, and Scherzo: The Dance Movement in Transition, 1781–1825." Ph.D. diss., University of North Carolina at Chapel Hill, 1983.

———. "'Über das Komische in der Musik': The Schütze-Stein Controversy." *JM* 4 (1985/86): 70–90.

SACHS, CURT. *World History of the Dance.* Translated by Bessie Schönberg. New York: Norton, 1937.

SADIE, STANLEY J. "Concert Life in Eighteenth-Century England." *PRMA* 85 (1958–59): 17–30.

———. *The New Grove Mozart.* New York: Norton, 1984.

———, ed. *The New Grove Dictionary of Music and Musicians.* 20 vols. London: Macmillan, 1980.

SANDBERGER, ADOLF. "Zur Einbürgerung der Kunst Joseph Haydns in Deutschland." *Neues Beethoven-Jahrbuch* 6 (Braunschweig, 1935): 5–25.

———. "Zur Geschichte des Haydnschen Streichquartetts." *Altbayerische Monatshefte* (1900): 1–24. Reprint in *Ausgewählte Aufsätze zur Musikgeschichte,* 224–65. Munich: Drei Masken, 1921. Reprint. Hildesheim: Georg Olms, 1973.

SCHERING, ARNOLD. "Bemerkungen zu J. Haydns Programmsinfonien." *JbMP* 46

(1939): 9–27. Reprint in *Vom musikalischen Kunstwerk*, edited by Friedrich Blume, 246–77. Leipzig: Koehler & Amelang, 1949.

———. "Künstler, Kenner und Liebhaber der Musik im Zeitalter Haydns und Goethes." *JbMP* 38 (1931): 9–23. Reprint in *Von grossen Meistern der Musik*, 90–123. Leipzig: Koehler & Amelang, 1940.

SCHLEUNING, PETER. *Das 18. Jahrhundert: Der Bürger erhebt sich*. Reinbek bei Hamburg: Rowohlt Taschenbuch Verlag, 1984.

SCHMALFELDT, JANET. "Cadential Processes: The Evaded Cadence and the 'One More Time' Technique." *Journal of Musicological Research* 12, nos. 1–2 (1992): 1–51.

SCHMIDT-HIDDING, WOLFGANG, ed. *Europäische Schlüßelwörter*. Vol. 1. *Humor und Witz*. Munich: Max Hueber, 1963.

SCHMITT-THOMAS, REINHOLD. *Die Entwicklung der deutschen Konzertkritik im Spiegel der Leipziger Allgemeinen Musikalischen Zeitung (1798–1848)*. Kultur im Zeitbild, vol. 1. Frankfurt am Main: Kettenhof Verlag, 1969.

SCHMITZ, EUGEN. *Unverwelkter Volksliedstil: J. A. P. Schulz und seine "Lieder im Volkston."* Leipzig: Breitkopf & Härtel, 1956.

SCHOLZ, GOTTFRIED. "Zu Haydns Menuetten." In *JHK 1982*, 465–70.

SCHROEDER, DAVID P. "Audience Reception and Haydn's London Symphonies." *IRASM* 16 (1985): 57–72.

———. *Haydn and the Enlightenment: The Late Symphonies and their Audience*. Oxford: Clarendon Press, 1990.

SCHUELLER, HERBERT. "The Pleasures of Music: Speculation in British Music Criticism, 1750–1800." *JAAC* 8 (1950): 155–71.

———. "The Use and Decorum of Music as Described in British Literature, 1700–1780." *JHI* 13 (1952): 73–93.

SCHWARTING, HEINO. "Ungewöhnliche Repriseneintritte in Haydns späterer Instrumentalmusik." *AfMw* 17 (1960): 168–82.

SHKLOVSKY, VICTOR. "Art as Technique." In *Russian Formalist Criticism: Four Essays*, translated by Lee T. Lemon and Marion Reis, 3–24. Regents Critics Series. Lincoln: University of Nebraska Press, 1965.

SISMAN, ELAINE R. "Haydn's Theater Symphonies." *JAMS* 43 (1990): 292–352.

———. "Haydn's Variations." Ph.D. diss., Princeton University, 1978.

SOMFAI, LÁSZLÓ. "Haydn's London String Quartets," In *HS 1975*, 389–91.

———. "'Learned Style' in Two Late String Quartet Movements of Haydn." *StM* 28 (1986): 325–49.

———. "Vom Barock zur Klassik: Umgestaltung der Proportionen und des Gleichgewichts in zyklischen Werken Joseph Haydns." In *Joseph Haydn und seine Zeit*, edited by Gerda Mraz, et al. *Jahrbuch für österreichische Kulturgeschichte* 2 (Eisenstadt, 1972): 64–72; tables 160–64.

SONDHEIMER, ROBERT. *Haydn: A Historical and Psychological Study Based on his Quartets*. London: Bernoulli, 1951.

SPARIOSU, MIHAI. *Literature, Mimesis and Play: Essays in Literary Theory*. Tübingen: Gunter Narr Verlag, 1982.

STEBLIN, RITA. *A History of Key Characteristics in the Eighteenth and Nineteenth Centuries*. Ann Arbor, Mich.: UMI Research Press, 1983.

STEINBECK, WOLFRAM. *Das Menuett in der Instrumentalmusik Joseph Haydns*. Freiburger Schriften zur Musikwissenschaft, no. 4. Munich: Musikverlag Emil Katzbichler, 1973.

———. "'Ein wahres Spiel mit musikalischen Formen': Zum Scherzo Ludwig van Beethovens." *AfMw* 38 (1981): 194–226.

STEWART, SUSAN. *Nonsense: Aspects of Intertextuality in Folklore and Literature.* Baltimore: Johns Hopkins University Press, 1979.

STROMMER, ROSWITHA. "Die Rezeption der englischen Literatur im Lebensumkreis und zur Zeit Joseph Haydns." In *Joseph Haydn und die Literatur seiner Zeit,* edited by Herbert Zeman, 123–55. Jahrbuch für österreichische Kulturgeschichte 6. Eisenstadt: Institute für österreichische Kulturgeschichte, 1976.

STRUNK, W. OLIVER. "Haydn." In *From Bach to Stravinsky: The History of Music by Its Foremost Critics,* edited by David Ewen, 77–87. New York: Norton, 1933. Reprint in *Essays on Music in the Western World,* 114–25. New York: Norton, 1974.

SULEIMAN, SUSAN, and INGRE CROSSMAN, eds. *The Reader in the Text: Essays on Audience and Interpretation.* Princeton, N.J.: Princeton University Press, 1980.

SWABEY, MARIE. *Comic Laughter: A Philosophical Essay.* New Haven, Conn.: Yale University Press, 1961.

SZABOLSCI, BENCE. "Folk Music—Art Music—History of Music." *StM* 7 (1965): 171–79.

———. "Joseph Haydn und die ungarische Musik." *Beiträge zur Musikwissenschaft* 1 (1959): 62–73. Reprint in *Bericht über die Internationale Konferenz zum Andenken Joseph Haydns, Budapest, 17.–22. September 1959,* edited by Bence Szabolcsi and Dénes Bartha, 159–75. Budapest: Akadémiai Kiadó, 1961.

TAVE, STUART M. *The Amiable Humorist: A Study in the Comic Theory and Criticism of the Eighteenth and Early Nineteenth Centuries.* Chicago: University of Chicago Press, 1960.

TEMPERLEY, NICHOLAS. "Tempo and Repeats in the Early Nineteenth Century." *ML* 47 (1966): 323–38.

THOMAS, GÜNTHER. "Haydns Tanzmusik—zeitgebunden oder persönlich geprägt?" *Musica* 36, no. 2 (1982): 140–47.

———. "Studien zu Haydns Tanzmusik." *H-St* 3 (1973): 5–28.

TODD, R. LARRY. "Joseph Haydn and the *Sturm und Drang*: A Revaluation." *MR* 41 (1980): 172–96.

TOMPKINS, JOYCE MARJORIE SANXTER. *The Popular Novel in England, 1770–1800.* Westport, Conn.: Greenwood Press, 1976.

TOMPKINS, JANE P., ed. *Reader-Response Criticism.* Baltimore: Johns Hopkins University Press, 1980.

TOVEY, DONALD FRANCIS. *Essays in Musical Analysis.* Vol. 1. *Symphonies.* 3d ed. London: Oxford University Press, 1938.

———. "Haydn, Franz Joseph, 1732–1809." In *Cobbett's Cyclopedic Survey of Chamber Music,* edited by Walter W. Cobbett. 2 vols. 2d ed. London: Oxford University Press, 1963.

TYSON, ALAN. "Notes on the Genesis of Mozart's 'Ein musikalischer Spass', KV 522." In *Festschrift Rudolf Elvers zum 60. Geburtstag,* edited by Ernst Herttrich and Hans Schneider, 505–18. Tutzing: Hans Schneider Verlag, 1985. Reprint in Tyson, *Mozart: Studies of the Autograph Scores,* 234–45. Cambridge: Harvard University Press, 1987.

VEIDL, THEODOR. *Der musikalische Humor bei Beethoven.* Leipzig: Breitkopf & Härtel, 1929.

WAIN, JOHN, ed. *Johnson as Critic.* London: Routledge & Kegan Paul, 1973.

WALLACE, ROBIN. *Beethoven's Critics: Aesthetic Dilemmas and Resolutions During the Composer's Lifetime.* Cambridge: Cambridge University Press, 1986.

WASSERMAN, EARL R., ed. *Aspects of the Eighteenth Century.* Baltimore: Johns Hopkins University Press, 1965.

WATES, ROYE D. "Karl Ludwig Junker (1748–1797), Sentimental Music Critic." Ph.D. diss., Yale University, 1965.

WEBER, WILLIAM. "Mass Culture and the Reshaping of European Musical Taste, 1770–1870." *IRASM* 8 (1977): 5–22.

———. "The Muddle of the Middle Classes." *19th-Century Music* 3 (1979): 175–85.

WEBSTER, JAMES. "The Chronology of Haydn's String Quartets." *MQ* 61 (1975): 17–46.

———. "Prospects for Haydn Biography After Landon." *MQ* 68 (1982): 476–95.

———. "Towards a History of Viennese Chamber Music in the Early Classical Period." *JAMS* 27 (1974): 212–47.

WELLEK, ALBERT. *Witz, Lyrik, Sprache.* Bern and Munich: A. Francke Verlag, 1970.

WHEELER, KATHLEEN M., ed. *German Aesthetic and Literary Criticism: The Romantic Ironists and Goethe.* Cambridge: Cambridge University Press, 1984.

WHEELOCK, GRETCHEN A. "Engaging Strategies in Haydn's Opus 33 String Quartets." *ECS* 25, no. 1 (Fall, 1991): 1–30.

———. "Marriage à la Mode: Haydn's Instrumental Works 'Englished' for Voice and Piano." *JM* 8 (1990): 356–96.

———. "What's Going On When the Music 'Stops'? Measured and Unmeasured Rests in Haydn's Piano Sonatas." In *Proceedings of the Westfield Center for Early Keyboard Studies Conference on Haydn's Piano Sonatas*, edited by Elaine Sisman (forthcoming).

———. "Wit, Humor, and the Instrumental Music of Joseph Haydn." Ph.D. diss., Yale University, 1979.

WILLEY, BASIL. *The Eighteenth-Century Background: Studies on the Idea of Nature in the Thought of the Period.* London: Chatto and Windon, 1940. Reprint. Boston: Beacon Press, 1961.

WINKLER, KLAUS. "Alter und neuer Musikstil im Streit zwischen den Berlinern und Wienern zur Zeit der Frühklassik." *Mf* 33 (1980): 37–45.

WOLLENBERG, SUSAN. "A New Look at C. P. E. Bach's Musical Jokes." In *C. P. E. Bach Studies*, edited by Stephen L. Clark, 295–314. Oxford: Clarendon Press, 1988.

WYNN, SHIRLEY. "The Minuet." In *Institute of Court Dances of the Rennaissance and Baroque Periods*, edited by Juana de Laban, 41–56. New York: Dance Notation Bureau, 1972.

YOUNGREN, WILLIAM. "Haydn Recovered." *The Hudson Review* 27 (1974): 69–81.

ZASLAW, NEAL. "Mozart, Haydn, and the *Sinfonia da chiesa.*" *JM* 1 (1982): 95–124.

———. *Mozart's Symphonies: Context, Performance Practice, Reception.* Oxford: Oxford University Press, 1989.

———, ed. *The Classical Era, from the 1740s to the End of the 18th Century.* Englewood Cliffs, N.J.: Prentice-Hall, 1989.

ZEMAN, HERBERT. "Joseph Haydns Begegnungen mit der Literatur seiner Zeit—zur Einleitung." In *Joseph Haydn und die Literatur seiner Zeit*, edited by Herbert Zeman, 7–23. Jahrbuch für österreichische Kulturgeschichte 6. Eisenstadt: Institut für österreichische Kulturgeschichte, 1976.

———, ed. *Joseph Haydn und die Literatur seiner Zeit.* Jahrbuch für österreichische Kulturgeschichte 6. Eisenstadt: Institut für österreichische Kulturgeschichte, 1976.

Index

In general, entries for such concepts as *Comic, Decorum, Humor, Laughter, Style, Wit,* and the like, refer the reader to eighteenth-century sources rather than to my own use of these terms in discussing specific pieces of music.

I